FICTIONS
OF ART HISTORY

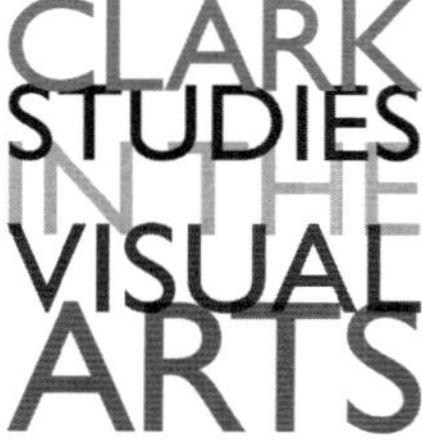
CLARK
STUDIES
IN THE
VISUAL
ARTS

FICTIONS
OF ART HISTORY

Edited by Mark Ledbury

Sterling and Francine Clark Art Institute
Williamstown, Massachusetts

Distributed by Yale University Press, New Haven and London

This publication was conceived by the Research and Academic Program at the Sterling and Francine Clark Art Institute. A related conference, also titled "Fictions of Art History," was held 29–30 October 2010 at the Clark. For information on programs and publications at the Clark, visit *www.clarkart.edu.*

Produced by the Sterling and Francine Clark Art Institute
225 South Street, Williamstown, Massachusetts 01267

Anne Roecklein, *Managing Editor*
Dan Cohen, *Special Projects Editor*
Sarah Hammond, *Publications Associate*
Julie Walsh and Hannah Rose Van Wely, *Program Assistants*

Designed by David Edge
Layout by Carol S. Cates
Copyedited by Audrey Walen
Proofread by June Cuffner
Printed by Excelsior Printing, North Adams, Massachusetts
Distributed by Yale University Press, New Haven and London
www.yalebooks.com/art

Printed and bound in the United States of America
10 9 8 7 6 5 4 3 2 1

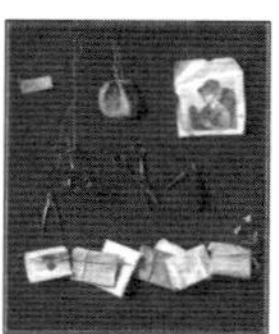

Title page and divider page illustration: Louis-Léopold Boilly (French, 1761–1845), *Various Objects*, c. 1785. Oil on canvas, 28 1/2 x 23 3/4 in. (72.4 x 60.3 cm). Sterling and Francine Clark Art Institute, Williamstown, Massachusetts

Library of Congress Cataloging-in-Publication Data

Fictions of art history / edited by Mark Ledbury.
pages cm—(Clark studies in the visual arts)
"A related conference, also titled 'Fictions of Art History,' was held 29–30 October 2010 at the Clark."
ISBN 978-1-935998-10-5 (clark pbk. : alk. paper)—ISBN 978-0-300-19192-9 (yale pbk. : alk. paper)
1. Art—Historiography—Congresses. 2. Art in literature—Congresses. 3. Fiction—History and criticism—Congresses. I. Ledbury, Mark (Andrew Mark), editor of compilation. II. Fictions of Art History (Conference) (2010 : Sterling and Francine Clark Art Institute)
N7480.F53 2013
700.72'2—dc23

2012051140

Contents

Part Three: Artists, Stories, Objects

Introduction: Compelling Fictions

Michael Hatt and Mark Ledbury

This volume has its origins in the 2010 Clark Conference, "Fictions of Art History," which brought together artists, art historians, and creative writers over a period of two days. We set out to explore the extent to which the discipline of art history, the writing of fiction, and the making and viewing of art might be commingled. This collection of texts by leading art historians, critics, poets, and novelists reflects the complexity of the entanglements and the excitement of the encounter. That questions of art history and fiction are current is clear not only from the engagements reflected in these essays but also in simultaneous publications, most notably the recent volume of *Art History* dedicated to the relationship between art history and creative writing published shortly after our conference, among other thoughtful and provocative texts.[1]

The texts gathered here, mostly oriented to the Western tradition and focused on writing rather than art making cannot represent the spectrum of strategic fiction and knowing pseudo-art history that has been at the heart of so much challenging global artistic practice over the last ten years. This fascinating and powerful trend is outside the scope of the present book. But, within the parameters of our stated aims to explore art history's relationship with fiction, the wealth of ideas and the diversity of tone in the essays that follow are indicative of the experimental spirit of the conference and the sense that our discipline needs to embrace, rather than repel, the spate of forms and genres in which art writing is engaged.

It would almost be remiss to begin a volume such as this without a reminder of the definition of one of our key terms: *fiction*. The *Oxford English Dictionary* reminds us that fiction's first definitions were to do with crafting, making: "the act of fashioning or imitating," to be precise.[2] More than this, the word's etymology and early use emphasize its links not just with fabric but with the notion of cunning artifice in visual art, as opposed to nature—with Shaftesbury's *Characteristicks* and its reference to:

> [T]he completely imitative and illusive art of Painting, whose character it is to employ in her works the united force of different colors; and

> who, surpassing by so many degrees, and in so many privileges, all other human fiction, or imitative art, aspires in a directer manner towards deceit, and a command over our very sense.[3]

We note William Cowper's less flattering allusion to the visual arts in his contrast between the beauty of nature and the "unscented fictions of the loom . . . th'Inferiour wonders of an artist's hand."[4]

Histories of art, then, are accounts of fictions, tales of crafted simulations of the real, or, at the very least, of beauties already at one remove from and in some senses opposite to the wonders of nature. But what sort of accounts? This is the question to which this volume returns frequently. As the very diversity of voices and topics that follow demonstrates, there has never precisely been a "standard" of art-historical writing. It is not a fixed or agreed-upon genre or collection of genres, and the astonishing variety of ways of responding to the multiple fictions of art is unsurprisingly, therefore, enmeshed with a complex weave of available modes of writing, from the lyric poem to detective fiction.

Histories and Fictions

One framing and sometimes inhibiting debate that no volume such as this can fully escape is of course created by the tensions in historical writing. Discussions of fiction and history tend to generate two kinds of responses: those which assert a very clear distinction between the two, maintaining that history is the very opposite of fiction; and those which embrace the connection, proposing that history simply cannot be extricated from fiction.[5] We know that there is a distinction to be made between fact and fiction. But we also know that fiction can reveal fact, and that the interpretation of facts involves fictionalizing. No matter how we try to conceptualize the difference—true and false, objective and subjective, the real and the invented—the kissing cousins of fact and fiction refuse to be prized apart. Our gathering aimed to move beyond the caricature of fact versus fiction, but, of course, truth-claim and fictionality still feature prominently in the essays in this volume. Ralph Lieberman's careful and revealing analysis of the photograph as a "document" of works of art beautifully demonstrates how the fictions of art history are visual as well as verbal; novelist Joanna Scott's meditation on fiction and the mask concludes with the beautiful and yet troubling statement about fiction:

> Through the supple movement of its prose, it gives new meaning to old words, making our well-worn language startling and strange. It leaves

> behind the haunting impression of trompe l'esprit rather than certain knowledge. And, to its lasting credit, it's close to useless as a means of conveying information, since no matter what it says, it can't be trusted.

Untrustworthy but deeply illuminating, then, fiction is also, as Thomas Crow and Alexander Nemerov argue, potentially rich in its insights into works of art. Many of the essays in this volume consider the place and value of fiction in the writing of art history, and address the fictions that circulate in the wider world, the expanded field of art history that, dare we say, now must include the complex realm of historical fiction and the many spaces outside academia where art history is made, from museums to microblogs, from television to artists' collectives, from Google art project to volumes of verse. Contributors to this volume argue that art history as an academic discipline finds it difficult to talk about its relationship with other forms of art-historical work (and play), but many of them try to do just that, reflecting their desire to think beyond their familiar territory and keep fiction and artwork in a delicate and complex balance.

Fictions of Artists

We begin, somewhat inevitably, with the artist. From its very beginnings the discipline of art history has argued about the status of the artist: Is the artist the origin of meaning and agent of historical change or just the vehicle for metaphysical or economic or historical forces? This debate has intensified in the past thirty years with such developments as the rise of visual studies, which built on the antihumanism of much Cold War-era theory and the pronouncement of the death of the author. Despite everything, art history continues to love its artists. The compelling, and even hypnotic, pull of the artist as center of explanation makes our discipline the heir and the sibling of genres such as the saint's life, popular biography, gossip columns, and the docusoap. For all our institutional critique of exhibition practice, brilliant and complex studies of identity, explorations of the meta-art histories of Picasso, Vermeer, or Rembrandt, or whomever, even the most radical of our accounts seem to rely on a heroic narrative that we cannot shake out of our heads. A narrative that endows artists with some form of specialness, a heroism of resistance, subversion, or plain old transcendence and superhuman power in a way that connects our modes of writing, more closely than we might admit, to genres as diverse as compendia of the miracles of the saints, poems of national heroism, or even the superpowered pantheon of Marvel comics. In this volume, Marianna Torgovnick teases out one such recent example of the superhuman, saintly framing of the artist in her reactions to the recent Marina Abramović retrospective.

Television, of course (whose role in molding the modern shape of art history is yet to be fully explored), has brought these generic overlaps into sharp focus. In the UK, there was once a simple map: the comfortingly antagonistic authorized versions of Kenneth Clark and John Berger and the gloriously and unashamedly academic twilight zone of the Open University; now we have a visually and intellectually sophisticated spectrum of engagements with art history, often conducted by highly qualified, academically minted art historians, a near-nightly multichannel challenge to the prosaic PowerPoints of the lecture room. One example among many: Simon Schama's *Power of Art* was a bold televisual mix of reconstructions of artists' brawls, loves, and creative bursts, beautiful and privileged filming of artwork (in close-ups and impressive kinetic panoramas that were made possible by the resources that guarantee the media industry privileged access), and Schama's wonderful scripts with their fusion of Kenneth Clark and Jeremy Clarkson.[6] Can a book-based art history speak as seductively, as powerfully, of the *Power of Art*? But of course, for every Simon Schama or Robert Hughes, there are many instances where it is easy to tell art history from televisual fodder. To cite a concrete example: in 2010 BBC Television broadcast a series about the Pre-Raphaelite Brotherhood titled *Desperate Romantics.* This was a remake of a series about the Pre-Raphaelite Brotherhood from the early 1970s called *The Love School*. The titles distinguish a lot. *The Love School* had a distinct neo-hippy ethos, with Janey Morris and Fanny Cornforth swishing around in what looked like Laura Ashley frocks while Rossetti took drugs. *Desperate Romantics* was altogether tougher, more interested in sex than vague sentiment, the screen frequently taken up with naked bodies. Moreover, the Pre-Raphaelite boys themselves strutted like Bruce Willis to the sound of David Bowie's "Heroes."[7] Art historians might sneer—and many did. Much had been done in the decades since the 1970s in sophisticated and serious art history to give new meaning, context, and vitality to the Pre-Raphaelite Brotherhood in scholarship—and the TV series left much to be desired. However, even such visual pap is telling—and parallels scholarly thought, however crudely or parodically. We might easily trace how the scholarly literature on Dante Gabriel Rossetti could and did generate its own set of motivated fictions about the artist, decade by decade: in the 1970s, sensitive outsider; in the 1980s, sexist bastard; and, more recently, sensual proto-modernist. The titles might not be viable—although there is a book about Rodin called *Triumphant Satyr*—but there is, nonetheless, a connection to be examined.[8]

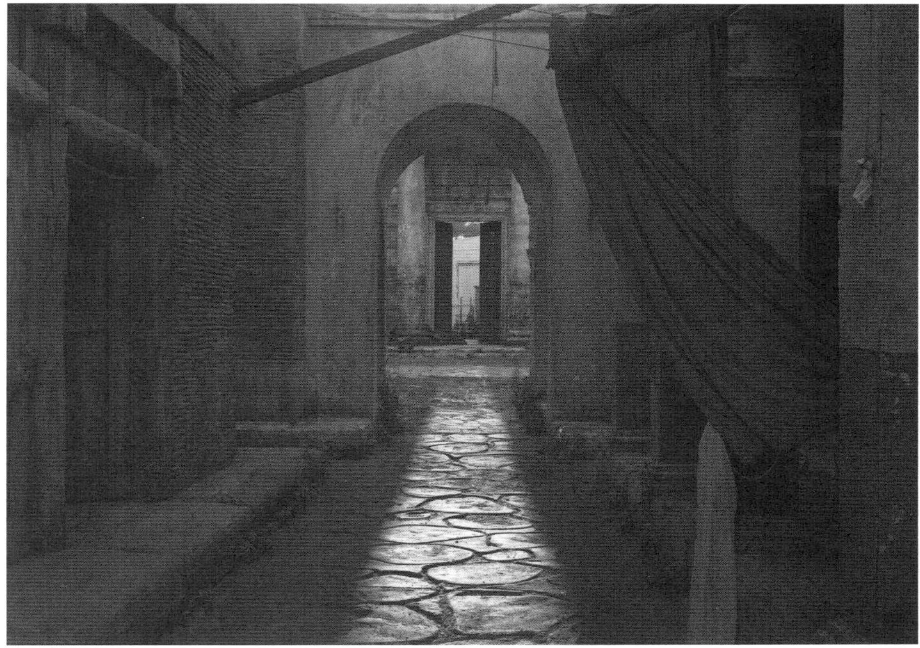

Fig. 1. Gregory Crewdson (American, b. 1962), *Untitled* (17), 2009. Pigmented inkjet print, 28 1/2 × 35 1/4 in. (72.4 × 89.5 cm). © Gregory Crewdson. Courtesy Gagosian Gallery, New York

These televisual "Lives of the Pre-Raphaelites" owe much, of course, to Vasari's model of artists' lives and their debt to ancient "secret histories." As one of our contributors, Paul Barolsky, has made it his lifetime's work to demonstrate, and Cole Swenson reiterates in her beautifully subtle investigation of the ekphrastic operations of the famous story of Giotto's "O," Vasari is a deep well from which art history continues to drink—and Vasari, let us not forget, was an artist as well as a storyteller. Artists have always been heavily engaged with creating and reinterpreting art-historical narrative. Contemporary artists, many of whom now are credentialed with PhDs, and others of whom have always been informal historians of their art and the art of others, argue vociferously that they must write their own art histories, their own narratives of their art and lives, to avoid becoming characters in someone's fiction. Something of the complexities of one art's story of another was presented at the conference through Gregory Crewdson's haunting photographic essays on Cinecitta as ancient ruin (fig. 1).[9] One might also cite the complex, and increasingly convoluted engagement of, say, Eve Sussman and the Rufus Corporation with art-historical narrative, from *Las Meninas* through David's *Intervention of the Sabine Women* to Malevich's *White on White* as an example of the kind of complex and fertile reframing fictions of contemporary art.

Fictions of the Spectator

Fictions of art history are also at the very heart, wittingly or unwittingly, of debates about spectatorship. While the spectator has frequently been posited as an alternative to the artist and attendant fictions, the spectator is more often than not a proxy, the figure who can recognize and report the same stories of resistance and subversion and special cultural understanding. Or, alternatively, the spectator is cast as the figure who recognizes what artists do not know about their own work and so assumes those heroic qualities him- or herself. Fictions of viewing have transformed the discipline, and the historical spectator can serve as an emblem of the historian's heroic endeavors in discovering and unveiling meaning, value, or power.

The figure of the detective features in more than one essay in this volume, and with good reason. It is not simply that detection is an appropriate metaphor for art-historical endeavor, for finding clues and traces and interpreting evidence, but that the metaphor of the detective constitutes such a self-fashioning for the historian.[10] This too has its own historical dimension. R. G. Collingwood, in *The Idea of History*, described changing historiographical trends in the early twentieth century as a shift from the methods of Sherlock Holmes to those of Hercule Poirot.[11] Gloria Kury's essay in this volume, a witty and adventurous exploration of the fictional art historian at work, is a meditation on the art historian as detective and hero.

Where fictions of viewing have been particularly significant is in the bid to address the history of experience. The historical experience of artworks is, of course, exactly what evades the archive. We might argue that all discussions of reception and spectatorship, all accounts of the power of the artwork, are indebted to fiction, since the data used is always mediated. What was it like for a member of the Burgundian court to view a tapestry? What happened when working-class visitors to the Crystal Palace studied *The Greek Slave*? Any answer relies on fictions; indeed, novels, stories, and poems constitute a rich source for research here. Proust or Browning, or even, as Paul Barolsky provocatively argues, Raymond Chandler, may get us closer to the historical texture of viewing, as well as to finding ways of describing visual experience and its embeddedness in history. But while fictions may help us speculate about experience in the past, they require us to identify the limits of what we might do in the interests of historical plausibility. Many are the scrupulous "documentary" accounts in our field that lurch into entirely unjustifiable speculation about how someone "must have felt" or "must have understood" when it comes to discussing the impact, effect, or resonance of the artwork.

Objects and Fictions

The art object itself has a complicated relationship to both history and fiction. Art objects, novels, and poems create fictions, generate fictions, use history and fiction, and acquire their own factual and fictional histories. If artists and viewers are characters in the art-historical plot, this can also be true of the work of art. As Mark Ledbury's essay speculates, and as Michael Ann Holly has in the past eloquently argued, when we have objects, images, or material remnants without stories or with scant stories, we feel the compulsion to create narratives in order to give them back their sense, or their dignity.[12] We are dealing not just with the past but with an object in the present that "needs" a past. Whether we are concerned with provenance or context or iconography, these methods are, at heart, devices for generating stories. That process might be more or less difficult; easier if one works on Victorian painting than if one works in some areas of classical antiquity or with the artifacts of oral cultures (although Caroline Vout demonstrates what can be done in her essay in this volume). Marina Warner explores the animation of objects in great fictional and documentary enterprises across different cultural traditions as a way into a profound discussion of what is at stake when we represent, describe, and animate the object. She reminds us at the outset of Hofmannsthal's beautiful articulation of a motivating fantasy of art history in his *Lord Chandos Letter*:

> These mute and sometimes inanimate beings rise up before me with such a plenitude, such a presence of love that my joyful eye finds nothing dead anywhere . . . mute things speak to me.[13]

That several contributors discuss portraiture is significant in this context: as Maria Loh argues, artworks can serve as a fetish, as "a magic portal that enables the connoisseur or historian to commune with or otherwise revisit the past as it was." And as Caroline Vout eloquently proves, "if portraits are the opposite of fiction, they are also the opposite of fact. They weather, but do not age; body forth individuals that assume the physical attributes of others." In these two contributions, and elsewhere, the portrait serves as particular provocation to meditation on fictions of identity and on the fundamental work of identification that has so long been considered a ground bass of all art-historical activity.

Grand Fictions

In many of the contributions to this volume, it will not be hard to sense some frustration with something that is variously called "orthodox" or "academic" art history. And, of course, in this, our contributors are reaping the whirlwind of dissatisfaction with the grand narratives we use to turn art into history. It is certainly true that we love big narratives: nothing is so compelling and yet so unsettling as "Antiquity," "Renaissance," "modernism," "absorption," etc, and art historians are in a constant struggle to create and subvert these same narratives. Of course, partly this is a matter of the rhythms and pulses of a discipline: at certain moments, in response to skepticism about the big story, art history has moved away from the *longue durée* to deal with a single object, with volumes dedicated to sets of case studies or recognition of fragmented and multiple narratives, and we may be in one of those moments now. Yet the thirst for explanatory sweep and broad and convincing understanding of historical change remains abiding for our discipline. How are we to negotiate this? What is the relationship between the big story and the little story? Is there a path between the Scylla of pompous and authoritarian generality and the Charybdis of tedious, self-regarding over-specificity? Is the creative text (novel, poem, or whatever) part of the solution to that dilemma, somehow allowing a passage from specificity to generality in a nuanced way? Certainly several of our contributors hint that this may be the case. Thomas Crow's contrast of the subtlety of novelist Gordon Burn's multivocal approach to the YBAs with prevailing art-critical cliché argues this forcefully. As he puts it, "Burn puts these two conventional voices—sensationalist lowbrow versus didactic highbrow—into a game of equivalency and a test of relative vividness."

Certainly, for some of our contributors, art history needs to attend to the grain of its writing—and here, of course, fiction is pertinent to the surface of our writing as well as the deep structures. Anecdote and metaphor; the rhythm of prose and the density of jargon; the intrusive use of the first person or the bizarre censoring of the word "I" by some journals and presses: these are more than stylistic tics and traits. They are points where the relationship between fiction and history is most carefully balanced or most carelessly disavowed.

Fiction Finding Things Out

We opened with the bare bones of dictionary definition: let us close with one of the most influential and resonant critical definitions of fiction, one which, explicitly or not, informs many of our contributions. In *The Sense of an Ending*, Frank Kermode sketches the difference between myth and fiction:

> Myth operates within the diagrams of ritual, which presupposes total and adequate explanations of things as they are and were; it is a sequence of radically unchangeable gestures. Fictions are for finding things out, and they change as the needs of sense-making change. Myths are the agents of stability, fictions the agents of change. Myths call for absolute, fictions for conditional assent. Myths make sense in terms of a lost order of time . . . fictions, if successful, make sense of the here and now.[14]

The idea of fiction as a form of inquiry that is open to change and of fiction as something to which one assents seems very helpful. This suggests why art history should engage with fiction rather than resist it, or, to put it more strongly, why art history should own up to its fictions. It also suggests, though, that in finding things out, fiction needs history, indeed, needs art history. As Alexander Nemerov so beautifully argues in his essay, the contrary forces of scholarly gravity and airborne levity—meaning, as he puts it, those "moments of ungrounded abandon—these moments of inspiration," which "create powerful, believable insights into the past, unattainable in any other way"—create a necessary and productive force field, one that animates this volume, and, we hope, energizes our discipline.

This volume has its origins in a conference at the Clark in 2010 titled "Fictions of Art History," that was proposed to the Clark as a topic back in 2009 by Professor Michael Hatt of the University of Warwick, whose voice as intellectual champion and convivial co-organizer this introduction seeks to preserve. What follows is firmly based on the introduction to the conference that we cowrote and copresented; it is also the space to acknowledge Michael's fundamental place in the project. ML

1. *Art History* 34, no. 2 (April 2011), special issue on Art History and Creative Writing; Jaś Elsner, "Art History as Ekphrasis," *Art History* 33, no. 1 (2010): 10–27.

2. "Fiction, n.": *Oxford English Dictionary*, n.d., http://www.oed.com/view/Entry/69828?rskey=aHWiAt&result=1&isAdvanced=false#eid.

3. Anthony Ashley Cooper Shaftesbury (Earl of), *Characteristics of Men, Manners, Opinions, Times: With a Collection of Letters. By the Right Honorable Antony Earl of Shaftesbury* (printed [by J. J. Tourneisen] for J. J. Tourneisen; and J. L. Legrand, 1790), 318.

4. William Cowper, *The Task, and Other Poems* (George M'Dowell and Son, 1831), 18, 415.

5. Much of this debate famously circulated around Hayden White and responses to him. See Hayden V. White, *The Content of the Form: Narrative Discourse and Historical Representation* (Baltimore: Johns Hopkins University Press, 1987); Robert Doran and Hayden V. White, *The Fiction of Narrative: Essays on History, Literature, and Theory, 1957–2007* (Baltimore: Johns Hopkins University Press, 2010); Kuisma Korhonen, *Tropes for the Past: Hayden White and the History/Literature Debate* (Amsterdam and New York: Rodopi, 2006), http://public.eblib.com/EBLPublic/PublicView.do?ptiID=556379; Beverley Southgate, "History and Metahistory: Marwick Versus White," *Journal of Contemporary History* 31, no. 1 (January 1, 1996): 209–14.

6. Simon Schama et al., *Simon Schama's Power of Art* (London; Burbank, Calif.: BBC Video: 2/entertain; Distributed in the USA and Canada by Warner Bros. Video, 2007).

7. Rafe Spall et al., *Desperate Romantics* (United States: BBC Worldwide Americas, 2010).

8. Denys Sutton, *Triumphant Satyr: The World of Auguste Rodin* (New York: Hawthorn Books, 1967); Michaela Giebelhausen and T. J. Barringer, *Writing the Pre-Raphaelites: Text, Context, Subtext* (Farnham, UK; Burlington, Vt.: Ashgate, 2009); Ellen Harding, *Re-framing the Pre-Raphaelites: Historical and Theoretical Essays* (Aldershot, UK; Brookfield, Vt.: Scolar Press; Ashgate, 1996).

9. Gregory Crewdson and A. O. Scott, *Sanctuary* (New York and London: Abrams, 2010).

10. Carlo Ginzburg, "Morelli, Freud, and Sherlock Holmes: Clues and Scientific Method," *History Workshop Journal* 9, no. 1 (1980): 5–36.

11. Robin George Collingwood, *The Idea of History* (Oxford, UK: Oxford University Press, 1956), esp. 281.

12. Michael Ann Holly, "The Melancholy Art," *The Art Bulletin* 89, no. 1 (March 1, 2007): 7–17.

13. Hugo von Hofmannsthal, *The Lord Chandos Letter and Other Writings* (New York: New York Review of Books, 2005), 125–26.

14. Frank Kermode, *The Sense of an Ending: Studies in the Theory of Fiction with a New Epilogue* (Oxford, UK: Oxford University Press, 2000), 39.

PART ONE

ENTANGLEMENTS

Weightless History: Faulkner, Bourke-White, and Eisenstaedt

Alexander Nemerov

Gravity is the scholar's element—the weight of the past, the weight of bibliographic sources, the weight of an academic discipline. But I will explore another metaphor for what the scholar does while researching and writing: the scholar floats, even flies, free and somehow above it all. Rather, I should say that the scholar should or might be so free, or that there might be at least *moments* when such floating or flying happens (you see how quickly I qualify), and that these moments of ungrounded abandon—these moments of inspiration—create powerful, believable insights into the past, unattainable in any other way.

Scholarship, however, being so grounded, unfortunately offers few examples of this floating and flying. So I turn instead to fiction and photography to explain what I have in mind, in particular to the novels of William Faulkner and the photographs of Margaret Bourke-White, Alfred Eisenstaedt, and their *Life* magazine colleague Walter Sanders. My aim is to pursue the links between elevation and inspiration in their work. I also hope to tell a story about America in the 1930s and '40s in a way that will require me to leave the ground—to be quite groundless in my claims—if that past is to be heard.

Faulkner's elevations come in different forms. I will give three, the first from *Absalom, Absalom!*, published in 1936. In that novel, the monomaniacal Thomas Sutpen conscripts a French architect to build a mansion in the Mississippi woods in 1833. The architect, desperate and stuck there against his will, a virtual prisoner in Sutpen's back-country world, one day escapes. He walks into the woods and then, to elude the dogs and search party he knows will come after him, uses a sapling pole to haul himself into a tree, lifting the sapling pole up after him. "Calculat[ing] stress and distance and trajectory," he vaults himself from that tree to the next. The gap between the two trees is wide enough "that a flying squirrel could not have crossed and traveled," but the architect proceeds "from tree to tree for almost half a mile before he put foot on the ground again." When the search party finds the sapling pole on the ground, the dogs smell not only the architect but his "exultation" itself—his pleasure at having invented a way to elude them.[1]

The exultation of escape and the forced labor of building the house: in the plot these are contrasts, but as expressions of the architect's creativity they are the same. "The architect," Faulkner writes, "had used architecture, physics, to elude them as a man always falls back upon what he knows best in a crisis."[2] As a principle of his craft and as the finest expression of that craft, he escapes it: he takes leave of it, in a leap of inspiration, using his skills to do so.

This inspiration, born of desperation—this "exultation"—is one and the same thing with writing in *Absalom, Absalom!* The architect's lift matches an old letter on Quentin Compson's desk in his freshman dormitory room at Harvard in 1909. The letter is before Quentin as he tells his roommate Shreve the story of Sutpen and the French architect on a bitterly cold night in Cambridge seventy-six years after the architect's escape. Faulkner notes how "one half" of this letter "slanted upward from the transverse crease without support, as if it had learned half the secret of levitation." Earlier Faulkner describes the letter as "open, three quarters open," so that its "bulk had raised half itself by the leverage of the old crease in weightless and paradoxical levitation."[3]

Faulkner embraces this principle of weightless and paradoxical levitation in his writing, which is deservedly famous for its extraordinary invention. Even when his metaphors are grounded—for example, Gail Hightower's wheel of thought churning ever more slowly in the sand of his dying moments in *Light in August* (1932)—they come out of nowhere.[4] Moreover, these inventive passages, like the ones concerning the architect in *Absalom, Absalom!*, have a way of making the reader believe in the story—of securing the reader's belief, once and for all—as if Faulkner's work consistently explored the unlikely kinship between extravagant imaginative flights and persuasiveness. When I read *Absalom, Absalom!*, I noted my incredulity at the architect's invention and then, almost simultaneously, my belief: my feeling of having been secured by means of this improbable invention into the plausible and truthful world Faulkner had created, as if only by imaginatively risking the reader's doubt had the story attained its full measure of persuasiveness. Accordingly, levitation and storytelling—the architect's vaulting, the writer's invention, and the levitating page—combine in these passages to form a grand imaginative flight whose hallmark is a truthfulness as solemn and grave as that of Quentin Compson, the historian who relies on the levitating letter to describe the past.

My second example of elevation in Faulkner's work comes from his novel *The Wild Palms*, published in 1939. In one of that novel's two parallel stories, a convict is taken from prison as part of a work gang to help with evacuation, rescue, and public works during a great flood in 1927. Gazing out at the flood water, the convict tells the warden he knows how to handle a small boat, and the warden sends him out to help rescue stranded people. In fact, the convict does not know much about paddling boats, and no sooner is he out alone on the water than the skiff starts to spin and drift, pulled beyond his control (at one point he inadvertently rescues a pregnant woman perched in a tree his boat runs into), so that he floats away and ends up escaping by accident—without meaning to and without even wanting to. Not long after—and this is the scene of elevation that concerns me—the convict hears a loud sound and, turning as he paddles to look back, he sees an enormous wave. This wave, "curled, crested with its straw-like flotsam of trees and debris and dead beasts," soon "began to rear above his head in its thunderous climax." With the pregnant woman on board, the convict turns to face front and paddles like mad, altering his course (though he does not know why) to make the skiff follow a deer he sees swimming in front of him "as the wave boiled down." A scene of levitation follows:

> The skiff rose bodily . . . on a welter of tossing trees and houses and bridges and fences, he still paddling even while the paddle found no purchase save air and still paddled even as he and the deer shot forward side by side at arm's length, he watching the deer now, watching the deer begin to rise out of the water bodily until it was actually running along upon the surface, rising still, soaring clear of the water altogether, vanishing upward in a dying crescendo of splashing and snapping branches, its damp scut flashing upward, the entire animal vanishing upward as smoke vanishes.[5]

The description of the deer running on water and then ascending out of sight is a kinetic altarpiece, a vision of transcendence, of apotheosis, a miracle out of nowhere, gone in sacrificial smoke. As a set piece, the description also asserts the religious power of fiction itself, its power to make us believe in the unbelievable, to see it with our own eyes, and to be most persuasive when it summons its energies to take leave of the world, to give us an image we never dreamed of, let alone ever thought could be true. Once, when I read this quotation out loud, a person in the audience afterward told me that Faulkner must have experienced this event himself to describe it so truly. It is much more likely, of course, that Faulkner invented it, and the audience member's belief that the passage could only be a journalistic report of a real event acknowledges the truth of invention.

The elevated state is timeless for Faulkner, as in my third example, from *Pylon*, published in 1935. It is not surprising that airplanes would be another form of elevation for Faulkner, who flew during World War I and remained fascinated by flying for some years afterward. It is not, however, the novel's racing pilots and airplanes that concern me—not their peregrinations around the pylons at the New Valois Airport—but rather the peculiarly aerial, light, and ungrounded figure of the novel's main character, the reporter (the writer, we could call him) who covers the air show.

This reporter, as Faulkner describes him, is without weight. Tall and incredibly thin, he appears "made of air" and "intact of his own weightlessness like a dandelion burr moving where there is no wind." When the reporter hears his name repeatedly announced on the loudspeaker at the airport, that name, which we never learn in the novel, floats in loudspeaker sound that makes it seem "as though he had to be summoned not out of the living world of population but evoked peremptory and repetitive out of the air itself." Otherwordly, nameless, the reporter filters through Mardi Gras crowds "like a phantom." He passes between people "like a playing card," "without alteration or diminution of bulk," and when he moves he does so "apparently without contact with earth like one of those apocryphal nighttime batcreatures . . . which are seen only in midswoop."[6]

This reporter—this writer—is serious without gravity. He is like the New Valois Airport, which, when we first see it, hazy in the morning air, "seemed to float lightly like the apocryphal turreted and battlemented cities in the colored Sunday sections, where beneath silless and floorless arches people with yellow and blue flesh pass and repass: myriad, purposeless, and free from gravity." Not everything in *Pylon* is as weightless as the apocryphal funnies. Newspapers have their weight. A stack of them sits beneath an inverted watch in the newspaper building's elevator—an allegory of the accumulated weight of the everyday. Aviators and airplanes also have their gravity. Shumann, the tragic pilot of the story, crashes into a lake and is permanently entombed, trapped forever among the deliberately sunken junk automobiles and other heavy trash such as pavement and "fallen walls" dumped there previously to keep the lake's sluggish muddy bottom from silting up. Even the reporter has his weight, since on an earlier flight he accompanies Shumann and lies down in the fuselage to adjust the plane's "weight distribution."[7] But, fundamentally, the reporter is weightless.

This makes him, for Faulkner, "beyond all mere restrictions of flesh and time." The reporter, "possessing no intrinsic weight or bulk himself," can be "everywhere," as Faulkner writes, everywhere and nowhere, and be thus apart from the "calculable doings of calculable people."[8] Scholars produce weighty works—or so we are supposed to—but the writer, Faulkner says, makes something without weight, summoning visions out of thin air. The writer, then, is no calculable being, like a scholar, but a magician, a sorcerer, a batwing funnyman, whose final act of magic—or is it the first?—is to make himself float amid the mirages he makes us believe are really there.

Margaret Bourke-White is at first an odd match with Faulkner; her medium was steel and his was dust. But her work is also about elevation and inspiration. A photograph taken by her assistant Oscar Graubner in the early 1930s shows Bourke-White standing in one of the Chrysler Building gargoyles outside her studio window on the sixty-first floor of the then-new building (fig. 1). Graubner's photograph establishes Bourke-White's airborne credentials once and for all. She had always been fascinated by great heights. As a young girl, she had drawn a picture of herself on the moon with an accompanying verse ("A comet took me up to the moon / And it left me far too soon . . ."),[9] and at the Terminal Tower in Cleveland in the late 1920s, her dramatic photographs from the new building's sky-high ramparts helped make her reputation as America's canniest and slickest celebrator of industrial modernity. Working for Henry Luce's newly created *Fortune* magazine and other clients, Bourke-White came to New York and established her studio eight hundred feet up in the Chrysler Building.

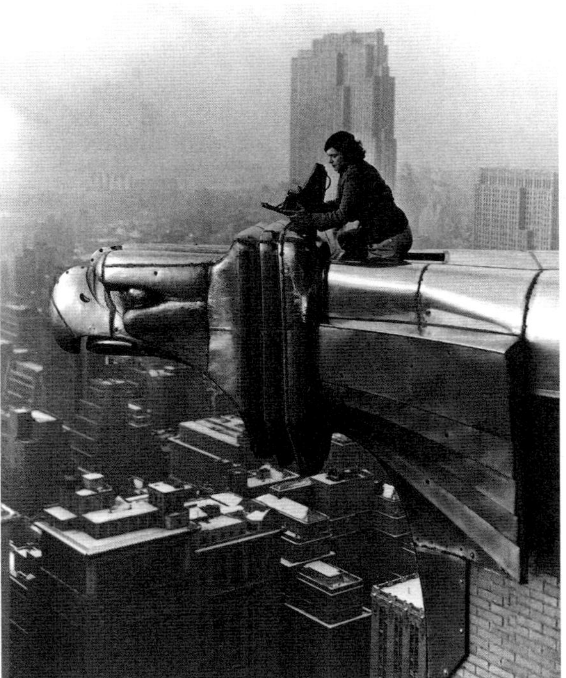

Fig. 1. Oscar Graubner, *Bourke-White on the Chrysler Building*, c. 1931–34. Oscar Graubner / Time & Life Pictures / Getty Images

What was Bourke-White's lightness? Her genius was not necessarily her risk-taking and fearlessness, which were impressive, but arguably only part of her celebrity, elements in a slick and self-created packaging no less shiny and vainglorious than the industrial implements and architecture she was so skilled at portraying. Her special and weightless gift was instead the quality of being *carried away* by what she photographed. By this I mean two things: that the world in her photographs seems to escape her grasp; and that, in so escaping, the world carried her away, producing the quality of her having been inspired and even ravished by what she saw.

At first this will make no sense. In Graubner's photograph, Bourke-White appears to be immersed in the view in her camera. She had precise standards about the images she made, and she knew just what she wanted. She insisted, for example, that her negatives be printed to the edges so that there could be no question that the finished photographs reflected exactly her fastidious compositions.[10] "The major control is the photographer's point of view," she wrote in 1936, describing the careful design of her images.[11] Once she became sought after as a commercial photographer in New York, her control of the image intensified as she squared her vision with her clients' demands, "adopting the advertiser's point of view."[12] So, where is the state of being carried away?

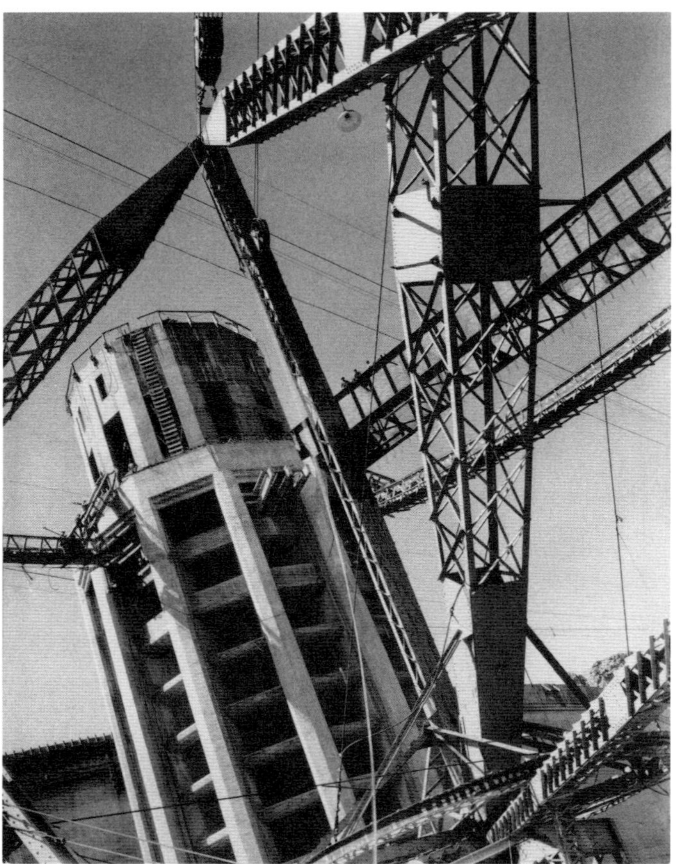

Fig. 2. Margaret Bourke-White (American, 1904–1971), *Boulder Dam Construction*, 1935. Gelatin silver print, 13 1/8 x 10 1/8 in. (33 x 26 cm). Margaret Bourke-White Papers, Special Collections Research Center, Syracuse University Library. Photo © Estate of Margaret Bourke-White / Licensed by VAGA, New York, NY

It is partly to be found in the centrifugal quality of her photographs. The girders and hoists in *Boulder Dam Construction* of 1935 go this way and that, extending beyond the frame in every direction (fig. 2). The Chrysler Building tower,

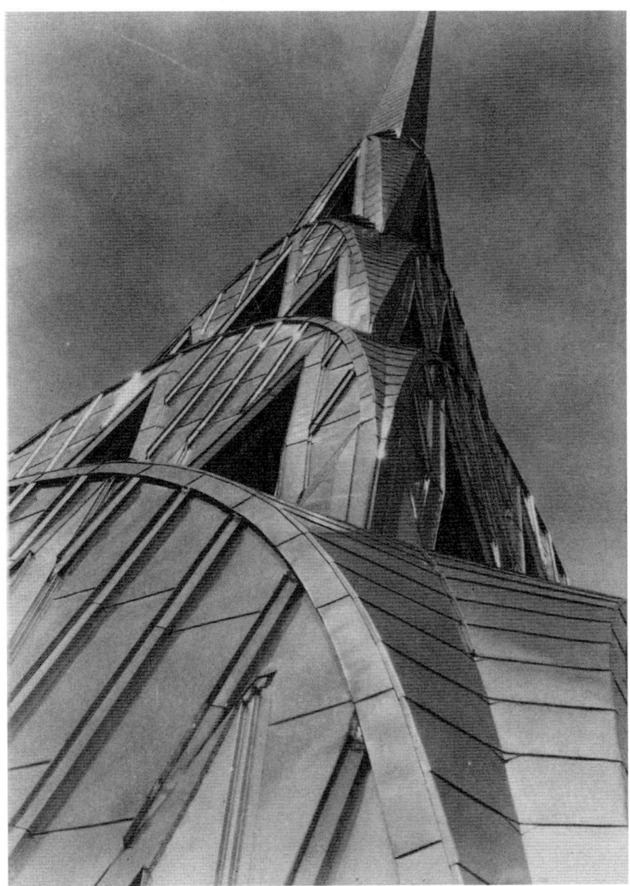

Fig. 3. Margaret Bourke-White, *Chrysler Building: Tower*, 1931. Gelatin silver print, 5 1/2 x 3 3/4 in. (14 cm x 9.5 cm). The Metropolitan Museum of Art, New York, Ford Motor Company Collection. Gift of Ford Motor Company and John C. Waddell, 1987 (1987.1100.338). Photo © Estate of Margaret Bourke-White/Licensed by VAGA, New York, NY

in a photograph of 1931, angles away like a jack-in-the-box (fig. 3). The mass production of objects, such as those in the *Five-Gallon Water Bottles* of 1932 and the *Pails* of 1934 (fig. 4), appears to go on nearly without limits, indicating the plenitude of American manufacture, but also crossing the line into some alternate, more magical, and finally crazier world akin to that of the Sorcerer's Apprentice in Walt Disney's *Fantasia* (1940).

Then there are the surfaces of Bourke-White's objects, notably the glamorous shine of silver, but really of all her things. "Everything in her pictures looked like it was made out of some kind of polished synthetic, even the skins of people," said the longtime Museum of Modern Art photography curator John Szarkowski.[13] Szarkowski's criticism notwithstanding, Bourke-White's avoidance of naturalism showcases a bizarre energy, a halo glow whose virtue is its fakery. Like the phrases that the 1940s film critics Manny Farber and James Agee devised to describe the overproduced falsity of Hollywood movies—their "lacquered shadow" and "chromium-and-glucose" details—Bourke-White's surfaces have the exuberance of a pure concoction, a linguistic coinage.[14] She could bend her shadows like rubber around a pipe and she could pour you a vial of light as thick as concrete. If you wanted that concrete to resemble the slickness of the magazine page on which it would appear, she could blend the two together until the pulp and the pulp mill

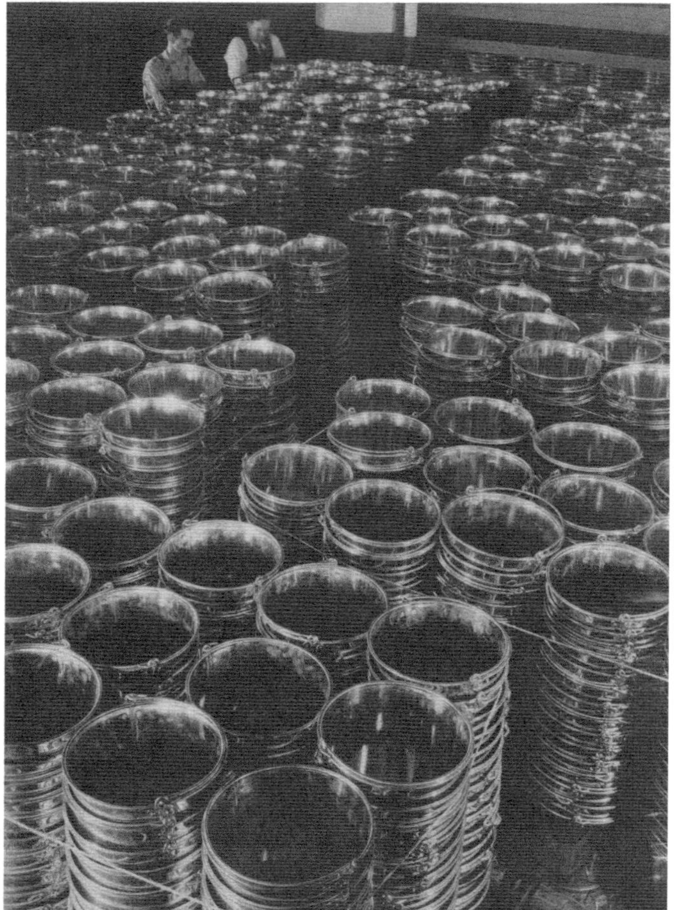

Fig. 4. Margaret Bourke-White, *Montgomery Ward: Pails*, 1934. Gelatin silver print, 13 1/4 × 9 5/16 in. (33.7 × 23.6 cm). Margaret Bourke-White Papers, Special Collections Research Center, Syracuse University Library. © Margaret Bourke-White/Time & Life Pictures/Getty Images

were one and the same. Rather than regard these improbable qualities as failures of naturalism, we might as easily note that Bourke-White invented a visual style whose crazed virtue was that it did not correspond to real life.

No doubt this otherworldly look was what her various employers wanted. They paid her to make modern fantasies. "In photographing the Douglas [airplane], we wish to make very sure we get a metallic, silvery finish of the ship and not a dull grey," one of them specified to her in 1935.[15] No doubt the centrifugal excitement and infinite production of modern industry were what they wanted, too. But Bourke-White's photographs are more than ephemeral documents of a desperately self-celebrating moment of American capitalism. The reason? She knew that the image must court the moment when the world leaves the control even of the photographer paid to depict it. Only then would the fantasy be persuasive. Only when her subject had become truly unbelievable would it engender faith and belief. She realized that she had to make a car not a car for the advertiser to be satisfied: "This car was not an automobile in the ordinary sense; it was a winged chariot which floated smoothly off into space."[16] Bourke-White tried to capture the moment when the world escaped her.

Consider *Wind Tunnel Construction, Fort Peck Dam, Montana* one of the images she made for the first issue of *Life* magazine on February 23, 1936, documenting a WPA project about the new dam in Montana (fig. 5). The cylindrical pipes and circular hubs establish a feel of rotation, the centrifugal quality Bourke-White so often favored. To convey the power of the dam and the excitement of the magazine in its first issue, she strove for a feeling of outflung excess, of spin and swirl, giving the sense of a radiating and dizzying energy beyond her control. The opening of Yeats's "Second Coming" (1920) is not out of place here—"Turning and turning in the widening gyre / The falcon cannot hear the falconer; / Things fall apart; the center cannot hold; / Mere anarchy is loosed upon the world"—even if the anarchy of an out-of-control globe runs counter to Bourke-White's editorial purpose. She shows powers anarchically let loose into a free spin, a wild and untrammeled arc, free from the encumbrance of calculation or even the finicky devising of the image itself. It was this wheeling lightness that she sought; a falcon beyond the range of her falconer.

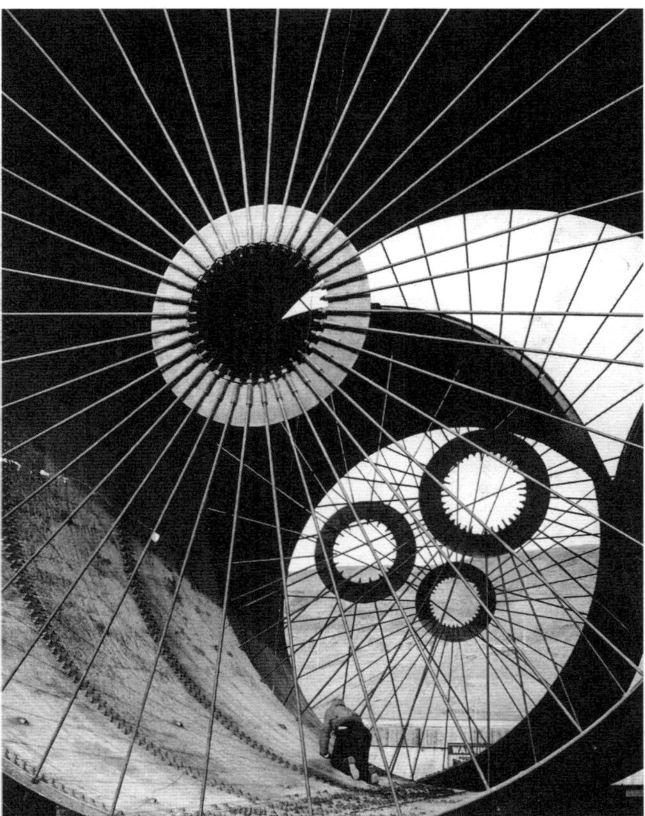

Fig. 5. Margaret Bourke-White, *Wind Tunnel Construction, Fort Peck Dam, Montana*, 1936. Gelatin silver print, 13 x 10 in. (33 x 25.4 cm). Margaret Bourke-White / Time & Life Pictures / Getty Images

Moreover, it was not enough for the world to be simply over there, away from her, a distanced spectacle fleeing and exceeding her grasp. It had to be inside her. In the early 1920s Bourke-White took a course at the New York City school of the great pictorialist photographer Clarence White (no relation), a major influence on her subsequent photography.[17] The circles in *Fort Peck Dam, Montana*, for example, relate to White's recurrent use of circles in his own work, such as *Drops of Rain* of 1903 (fig. 6). At stake here is not so much Bourke-White's skill at adapting the poetic beauty of pictorialist photography to industrial subjects but a capacity she learned from Clarence White to internalize the world, to let it germinate inside her.

White's circles have a way of emphasizing childhood and pregnancy. The child in *Drops of Rain* holds a womb-like crystal ball, one of many such images of bellies and germination in White's photography. Similarly, the work of his students often concerns childhood and nurturing—see, for example, the little girl in Ema Spencer's *Kitten's Party* who pours milk into bowls for a play party (fig. 7). The creativity of the child and the actual creation of the child are more than sentimental themes; they suggest the art photographer's insistence that photography itself is a generative, creative medium, not a mechanical one. The photographer internalizes the world, with the result that the photograph is impregnated with a vision and a sensibility.

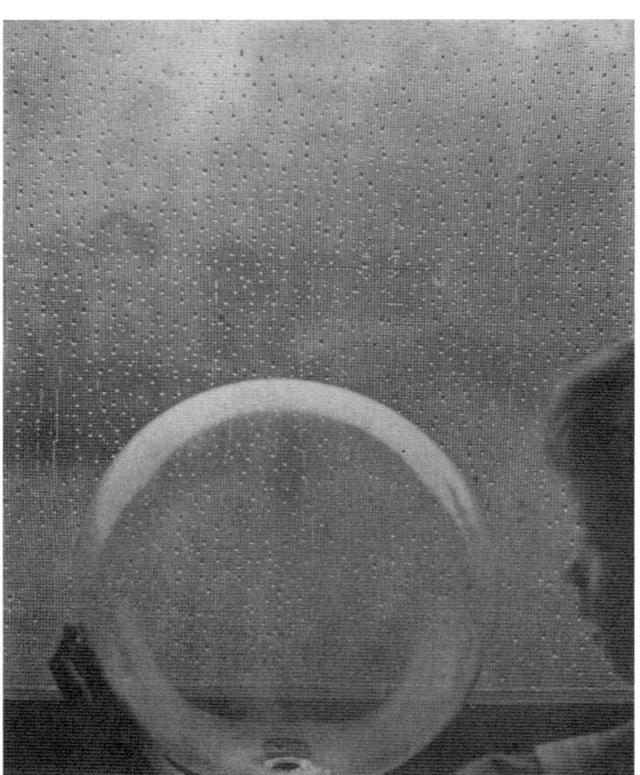

Fig. 6. Clarence White (American, 1871–1925), *Drops of Rain*, 1903. Platinum print, 7 5/8 x 6 in. (19.4 x 15.2 cm). The Museum of Modern Art, New York. Gift of Mrs. Mervyn Palmer, 567.1967

Bourke-White's *Fort Peck Dam, Montana* is equally about internalizing a subject. When she compiled notes in 1937 for a lecture to be given to "embryonic photographers," her choice of phrase hearkened to this quality in pictorialist photography and in her own work. When she noted in 1936 that "sleeping babes" were a staple of art photography before being replaced by "rhythmic gear wheels and gleaming pistons," she invited an analogy between the two.[18] When Museum of Modern Art curator Thomas Mabry wrote

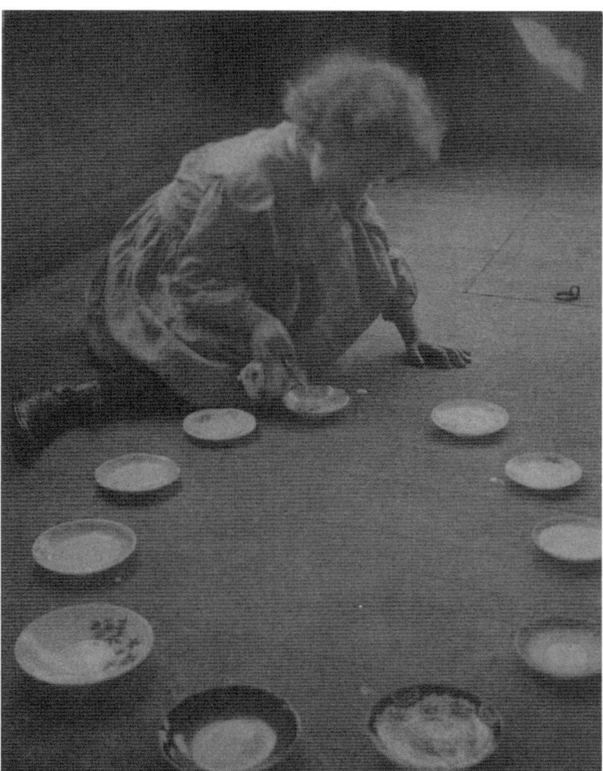

Fig. 7. Ema Spencer (American, 1857–1941), *Kitten's Party (Child Study)*, c. 1899. Platinum print, 6 7/8 × 5 1/4 in. (17.5 × 13.3 cm). Library of Congress Prints and Photographs Division, Washington, D.C.

to Lincoln Kirstein in 1938 that Bourke-White's photographs were "just as bad to me as any kind of *Herald Tribune* beautiful baby contest photography," he, too, inadvertently named this germinating quality in her work.[19] Bourke-White put it succinctly, describing her choice not to have a family but to focus on her career instead: "If I didn't have the photographs, I'd have children, but the photographs are my children."[20]

The germinating of the image indicates more than the simple internalization of the world; that is too general a description. It suggests instead the state of being abducted or ravished, a state that has horrific real-world connotations, but that has long been sought by artists and poets who desire nothing less than to be carried away or inspired by their subjects. Then they are breathed into by an outside spirit, and the world they see is not so much a cheap and muted reflection but an image blown in glass. "Make me such a vessel of your worth as you require for granting your beloved laurel," Dante writes at the start of the *Paradiso*, invoking Apollo. "Enter into my breast and breathe there as when you drew Marsyas from the sheath of his limbs" (*Paradiso*, 1.13–15, 19–20). Flay me, take me out of myself, fill me with your spirit, and I will make the world. When she stood in the Chrysler gargoyle for Graubner's photograph, Bourke-White wanted to chronicle her own abduction, to capture what captivated her: an Olympian bird taking her away like Jupiter did Ganymede, eight hundred feet above the city streets, where she was free, borne aloft in artistic ecstasy, inspired by what she saw.

The most famous photograph by Alfred Eisenstaedt, Bourke-White's good friend, is also about being carried away—or so it seems at first (fig. 8). *V-J Day, Times Square* first appeared in *Life* magazine on August 27, 1945. The moment it shows is exuberant: V-J Day, near the time of the loudspeaker announcement at 7 P.M. proclaiming the end of World War II. A sailor kisses a nurse, and Eisenstaedt, who had been out looking for photographs that night, had seen it coming: the sailor had been kissing women young and old as he moved down the street; the photographer, already well-versed in showing wartime kisses, saw the nurse approaching, knew the sailor would want to kiss her, and positioned himself and his camera accordingly to make a picture of what he would see: a yin and yang of joy, release, and abandon.

But the picture is not so exuberant, after all. The sailor's act is violent as he steals his unsolicited kiss. His right hand clenches the woman's waist and his left hand curls into a near-fist as he takes his pleasure. Eisenstaedt also grasps the situation. Knowing what he wanted, he shows the sailor and the nurse locked in more than their own embrace. They are stuck in the squeeze of the historical moment Eisenstaedt made it his business to portray. That squeeze has grown more vise-like since, for the photograph has become so tightly bound to national mythology that it has become closed to anything but the understandably jubilant note Eisenstaedt wanted to strike. The picture is not, therefore, an inspiration, neither on the part of the photographer nor the sailor. They both seize the moment, calculating what can be done. No wonder Eisenstaedt so breathlessly champions the crude sailor, that Davy Crockett of the spit-swappers. If any photograph could be said *not* to float or fly or inspire flights, it would be this one.

The photograph's larger meanings enforce its atmosphere of closure and violence. Between 7 P.M. on V-J Day and 7 A.M. the following morning, 890 people were treated for injuries in New York, 130 of them requiring hospitalization, 50 people were arrested for felonies, 78 automobiles were stolen, and 377 fire alarms were sounded (only 102 of them false). In Los Angeles, "impromptu pedestrian parades and motor cavalcades whirled along" on Hollywood Boulevard, "hindered only by hurled whiskey bottles, amorous drunks, and collisions." In San Francisco, the revels turned into a riot as drunken servicemen "defaced statues, overturned street cars, ripped down bond booths, [and] attacked girls," the chaos resulting in more than one thousand casualties.[21] The advent of peace was dangerous; the sailor's aggressive advance indicates the larger-scale mayhem of that day.

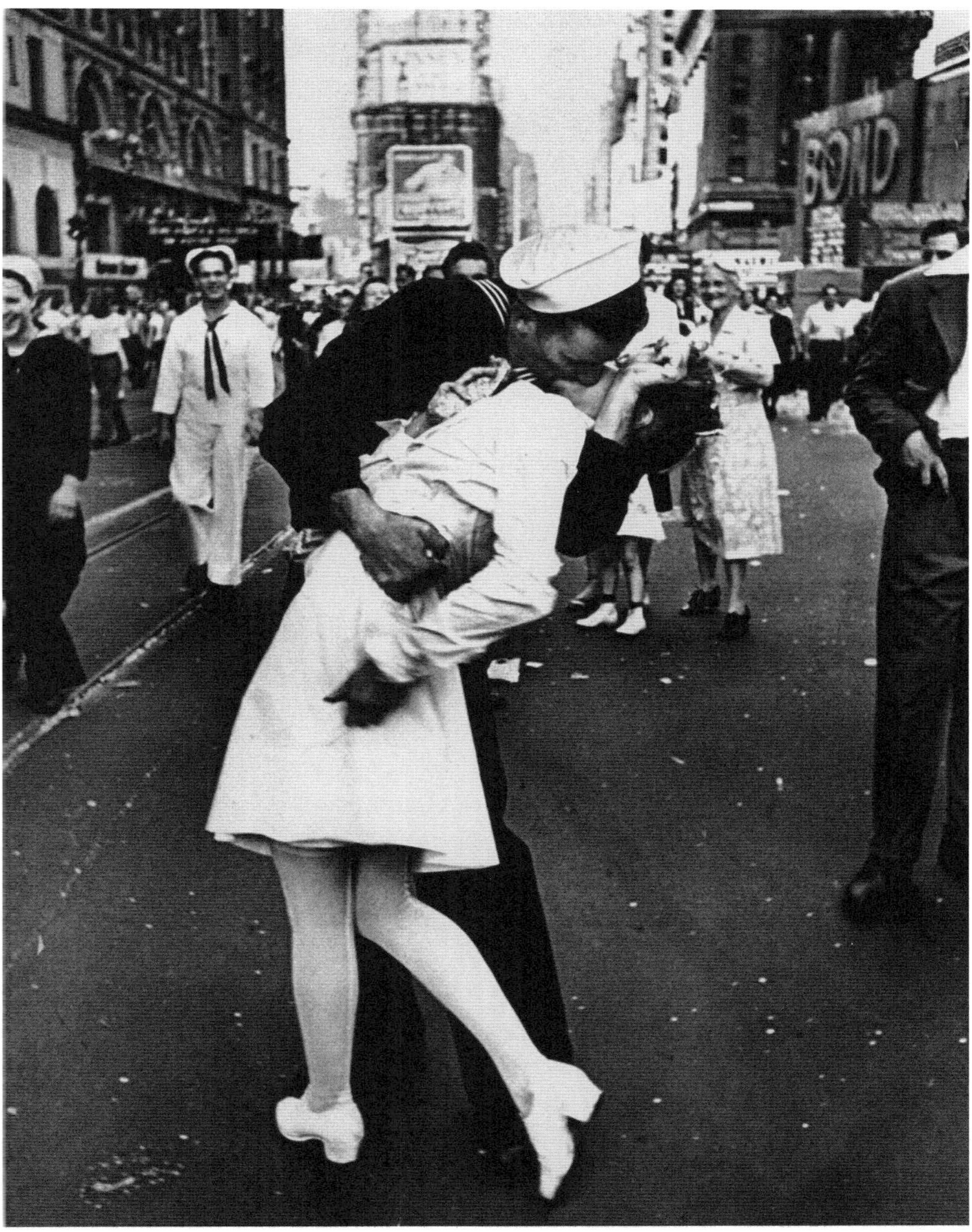

Fig. 8. Alfred Eisenstaedt (American, 1898–1995), *V-J Day, Times Square, New York City*. Gelatin silver print. Alfred Eisenstaedt/ Time & Life Pictures/Getty Images

V-J Day, Times Square intimates a far greater violence and finality—that of the atomic bombs that ended the war, the first dropped on Hiroshima on August 6 and the second on Nagasaki on August 9. "The metropolis exploded its emotions . . . with atomic force," wrote Alexander Fineberg in the *New York Times*, describing the peace celebration. "The victory roar that greeted the announcement [of peace] beat upon the eardrums until it numbed the senses. For twenty minutes wave after wave of that joyous roar surged forth."[22] The two people in Eisenstaedt's photograph celebrate because of the bomb. The triple-decker headline news of the mystery super-weapon would have been fresh in their minds. And they clasp in a way that anticipates and maybe even inaugurates the link between sexuality and atomic destruction—the dropping of the bomb at Bikini Atoll on July 1, 1946, for example, that led to the naming of the new two-piece swimsuit introduced that year, or the sexualized imagery of atomic destruction in Stanley Kubrick's 1964 film *Dr. Strangelove*. Eisenstaedt's photograph was no intentional depiction of the bomb, of course, but rather some inchoate and displaced early response to the new weapon, unrecognizable as such to the photographer and his viewers. Unintentional as they are, these connotations emphasize the grip of a picture that seems to intuit all its possible meanings, gathering them in a relentless grasp of the historical moment.

But there is one connotation—a floating, flying one—that *V-J Day, Times Square* cannot anticipate. It is one that disrupts the closure of Eisenstaedt's photograph in historical terms even as it speaks to the weightless act of scholarship that would discern it. The photograph by Walter Sanders on the cover of the August 27, 1945, issue of *Life* shows the ballet swimmer Belita Jepson-Turner performing her maneuvers in the Town House pool in Los Angeles (fig. 9). Sanders's image has nothing to do with the Times Square kiss contained in the same issue. Or does it?

Sanders's photograph is itself a V-J Day image. Belita Jepson-Turner's grace is an image of peace, of peacefulness, appropriate for a magazine cover less than two weeks after the war's end. It is also no less topical an image of destruction. Jepson-Turner descends like a bomb, like the new weapon dropped over Hiroshima on August 6 from the belly of the Enola Gay, a B-29 with a woman's name whose pin-up art (had that plane featured any) might have resembled Jepson-Turner's bomber pin-up pose in *Life*. The relation between Sanders's photograph and Eisenstaedt's comes across visually as well. The two women share not only comparable arcs and swoons and eroticism but an identical scale on

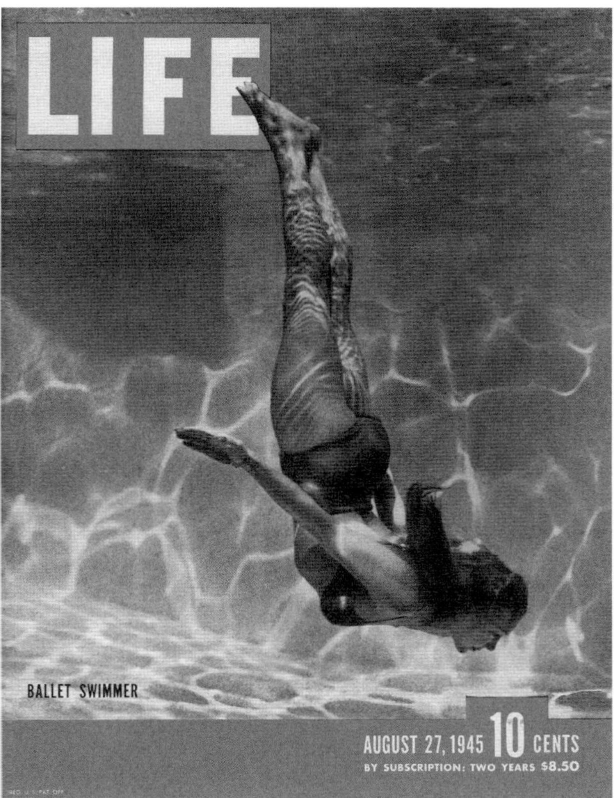

Fig. 9. Walter Sanders, *Ballet Swimmer Belita Jepson-Turner Performing in the Los Angeles Town House Pool* on the cover of *Life* magazine, August 27, 1945. Walter Sanders / Time & Life Pictures / Getty Images

the page: Jepson-Turner is ten inches long from her toes to her nose and the nurse, whose name was Edith Shain, is nine and a half inches from her left shoe-tip to her forehead. Sanders and Eisenstaedt, both German émigrés (Sanders emigrated in 1933, Eisenstaedt in 1935),[23] both show a kind of American forgetting: the war still in the air, American leisure proceeds in shows of scheduled spontaneity and filtered lust.

I doubt anyone saw or bothered with any of these relations at the time the issue came out, or since. They are without weight. If we were to make anything of them at all, perhaps it would be to say that together the two pictures show the house style of *Life* magazine—a certain dependable visual code, heavily calculated, calling for erotic figures, most often women, and imaged at a size sufficient to fill the fourteen-inch vertical and ten and a quarter-inch horizontal dimensions of a *Life* page. According to this house code, the women would be caught in the precision of their gambols, pure but with a little filth, a little confetti in the chlorine, in just the right antiseptic inoculations, delivered to the reader in premeasured dosages.

Yet that is too sociological an explanation. Sanders's photograph not only relates to Eisenstaedt's, it offers an alternative. Belita Jepson-Turner is free and alone, almost as though she were Edith Shain, except now minus the sailor, released from that picture and its lockdown of calculations. Jepson-Turner is also a weightless alternative to the V-J Day photograph's definition of history. This is because the swimmer is suspended, caught in an ongoing moment. Neither sinking nor swimming, cut off from life and in her own world, she floats in an element outside of time. Yes, she may be compassed by calendar and cost—she seems to note the date and price of that week's issue, putting her face right where this information is, as though the magazine's price, 10 cents, were a dime that had floated to the bottom of the pool—but she maintains the quality of being beyond it all, outside history, outside human concerns. No matter how compromised her vulgar water-slick of magazine might seem, why should we scorn the tawdry form some otherworldly vision might take when pulp may be its only way to appear?

Jepson-Turner herself left a strong historical trace on the world—starting with her participation in the figure-skating competition at the 1936 Olympics at age twelve—although history of this kind is not what Sanders's photograph literally shows. An unlikely vision of transcendence, Jepson-Turner is not frozen in her moment but suspended in it, as in the title of the film noir in which she would star in 1946, *Suspense.* Time with her is paused, the dilating wash of a moment simultaneously draining and filling, held in the sieve of the photograph and the act of scholarship that would make a point not to grasp it.

The photograph teaches us that the historical moment has much in common with an aesthetic moment. Time in an aesthetic moment is "racked into a dread armistice," to use Thomas De Quincey's unsurpassed description:

> We must be made sensible that the world of ordinary life is suddenly arrested—laid asleep—tranced—racked into a dread armistice; time must be annihilated; relation to things without abolished; and all must pass self-withdrawn into a deep syncope and suspension of earthly passion.[24]

The historian too might seek a past in which all things are suspended, left floating, in some eternity of slow-motion becoming, rather than try to find a clarified sharpness of rugged and lascivious outlines, an opportunistic hold, or an ever-clasped significance. The suspended moment is curved, but chaste. It floats like an angel, arms bent back as though they were wings, more a suspension of earthly passion than a big fat kiss. The grotesque embrace of the historical moment is the opportunity of a day, maybe of a lifetime, but it is not the same thing as inspiration.

Let Belita Jepson-Turner be our muse of history—a figure for the inspiration, coming from nowhere, that might guide us. The history, to be sure, is apocryphal, to use that word so important to Faulkner. It is outside the canon of scripture, it is spurious, false, and of questionable authenticity. It is occult and comic, too. The stories she inspires are legends without validation. Her element—no surprise—is the mirage, the water as weightless as air, where the halos, such as they are, seem tricks of the sun, the image, or both. Yet she is the guiding angel of that domain, where all is unreal, not quite true, in that shimmering swim of discipline: the fictional space of a land that never was, where we have nothing to show for our efforts except that we have been touched, and changed, by what is not there.

1. William Faulkner, *Absalom, Absalom!* (New York: Vintage, 1990), 193, 196–97.

2. Ibid., 193.

3. Ibid., 192–93, 176.

4. William Faulkner, *Light in August* (New York: Vintage, 1990), 491–92.

5. William Faulkner, *The Wild Palms* (New York: Vintage, 1995), 147–48.

6. William Faulkner, *Pylon* (New York: Vintage, 1987), 17, 172, 226, 56, 76.

7. Ibid., 14, 241–42, 223.

8. Ibid., 174.

9. Margaret Bourke-White, untitled poem and drawing, Margaret Bourke-White Papers, Box 1, Special Collections, Syracuse University Library, Syracuse, New York.

10. Vicki Goldberg, *Margaret Bourke-White: A Biography* (New York: Harper and Row, 1986), 185.

11. Margaret Bourke-White, "Photographing This World," *The Nation* (February 19, 1936): 217.

12. Ibid., 218.

13. John Szarkowski, quoted in Goldberg, *Margaret Bourke-White: A Biography*, 185.

14. Manny Farber, "The Heroes of the Mary Ann," *The New Republic* (February 22, 1943), reprinted in *Farber on Film: The Complete Film Writings of Manny Farber*, ed. Robert Polito (New York: Library of America, 2009), 55; James Agee, Untitled, *The Nation* (November 25, 1944), reprinted in *Agee on Film: Criticism and Comment on the Movies* (New York: Modern Library, 2000), 112.

15. "Memorandum on Schedule Eastern Airways," Margaret Bourke-White Papers, Box 15, Special Collections, Syracuse University.

16. Bourke-White, "Photographing This World," 218.

17. See Bonnie Yochelson and Kathleen A. Erwin, *Pictorialism into Modernism: The Clarence H. White School of Photography*, ed. Marianne Fulton (New York: Rizzoli, 1996), for an excellent account of the debt of modernist advertising photography to pictorialism.

18. Bourke-White, "Advice to Embryonic Photographers" (July 1937), in Bourke-White, "Photographing This World," 217.

19. Thomas Mabry, quoted in James R. Mellow, *Walker Evans* (New York: Basic Books, 1999), 368–69.

20. Bourke-White, quoted in Goldberg, *Margaret Bourke-White: A Biography*, 223–24.

21. "V-J Day Revelry Erupts Again with Times Square Its Focus," *New York Times*, August 16, 1945, 1, 6.

22. Alexander Fineberg, "All City Lets Go! Hundreds of Thousands Roar Joy After Victory Flash Is Received; Times Square Is Jammed, Police Estimate Crowd at 2,000,000—Din Overwhelming," *New York Times*, August 16, 1945, 1.

23. For Eisenstaedt, see *Eisenstaedt on Eisenstaedt: A Self-Portrait* (London: BBC, 1985); and *Eisenstaedt: Remembrances*, ed. Doris C. O'Neil (Boston: Little, Brown, 1990); for Sanders's background, see "The Road Back to Berlin: A *Life* photographer returns to a home and friends shattered by war," *Life* (November 11, 1946): 30–33.

24. Thomas De Quincey, "On the Knocking on the Gate in *Macbeth*," in *Shakespeare: Macbeth, A Casebook*, ed. John Wain (London: Macmillan, 1968), 90.

A Novelist among Artists: Gordon Burn and "Young British Art"

Thomas Crow

All art criticism and art scholarship consist in some form of paraphrase, that is, the creation of some more or less useful substitute in words for the object or the phenomenon under scrutiny; what the paraphrase sacrifices in nuance goes toward the instrumental value of the verbal surrogate in contexts other than immediate perceptual encounter. A general corollary to this proposition would be that critics tend to perform this function in the first instance, the filtered results of which then become the received verbal object on which art historians base their efforts at explanation.

A problem arises when the same agent who generated the initial paraphrase, exercising the freedom proper to the critic's task, then performs the later moment of historical processing, which attempts to legislate a definitive understanding. With the large-scale entry into the university of specialists in the critical judgment of contemporary art, works of art favored by competing forms of paraphrase tend not to be accorded much if any place in the curriculum. While this pattern is not exclusive to any one national discourse, it has become especially entrenched in the American academy. As the language of history aligns itself with one strand of criticism, whatever its partial validity, art making beyond its purview ceases to belong to history, even when demonstrably present and active in shaping the behavior of the art world.

A recent and salient instance of this phenomenon can be found in the mid-1990s eruption on the international scene of the so-called YBAs (Young British Artists), whose brand identity had been fostered by the sponsorship of collector Charles Saatchi, adman among admen, who created great cause for academic suspicion at the outset. Critical dismissals on both sides of the Atlantic have denied these artists—among them Tracey Emin, Sarah Lucas, Marcus Harvey, Jake and Dinos Chapman, Marc Quinn, Gavin Turk, and preeminently Damien Hirst—any standing in received histories of "serious" contemporary art: instead, their success must be seen to arise from the workings of the market, the media machine, the corruption of fame, that is, anything but the art itself. Hirst's prominence, in the words of American critic and historian Hal Foster, can only be credited to "an entire career strung together by shock and scandal and a body of work whose medium is a compound of media and market events."[1] Should that dismissive back of the hand appear insufficient, British acolytes of the American critical-historical hybrid have been ready to step in. As one put it, YBA art, chiefly Hirst's, represents "a diluted variant of 1980s appropriation art, anglicized and ontologized into aura-laden tableaux that dealt, not with the seriality or sign-value of the commodity but with timeless universals of the 'human condition.'"[2]

Most of the current corruption of descriptive and evaluative language in the study of art is on display in that statement; whatever cannot be paraphrased in such terms as seriality and commodity sign-value defaults to a discredited universal humanism. Rather than an attempt at fresh apprehension, one encounters the epistemological artifacts of a closed rhetorical loop. Putative aspiration toward "timeless universals" represents no more than a postmodern term of abuse, one, moreover, contradicted by the adjective "anglicized" earlier in the passage. The overarching charge of derivativeness, moreover, misfires in that it assumes an authority in the American models that time and use have not eroded. Hirst's sculptural containers and mode of presentation may well appear to be "a diluted variant of 1980s appropriation art," but they are only diluted to the degree that these prototypes—along with their austere predecessors in Minimalism—came to him rendered by repetition as ordinary and interchangeable as any other item susceptible to Pop appropriation: they had effectively become de-sacralized commodities in themselves.

How, then, would one go about paraphrasing YBA art if the established language of art interpretation ties itself in knots when the subject arises? One exemplary candidate takes the form of a journalist's report on a car wreckers yard in Brixton, South London, where the fetid and physically punishing work that went into the first wave of Hirst's bisected animals in formaldehyde took place. Here is how the account begins:

> Oh, it was brutal. It was a breakers yard in London SW9 that did exactly what it said it did on the board by the gate: it broke things; bent and totally totalled them. Mostly these were cars connected to some insurance fiddle, stripped and crushed and cubed. They also did re-spray jobs on stolen cars ("hot motors"). And that wasn't the half of it. They dealt drugs in the Breakers at night, hooded figures in the dark; and some nights had all-night, yard-style parties. Booma-booma-booma.

> Gerry, the guy who ran it, was a biker, and other bikers from his gang or chapter or whatever would zoom over and hang out. Gerry's clothes were black with sump oil; they were slick and ebonised. His nails were black, and his eyelids and scalp. . . . Gerry had a sidekick called Chico. Chico wore a greasy mac and bred puppies and was dubbed by the tabloids The Most Evil Man in Britain. He ran a puppy farm in Brixton Breakers, right in among the totalled Toyotas and hot motors. Feral dogs. Now and again, he'd throw them a bootful of raw chicken. Oh, man. Sometimes the feral dogs would escape from their compound and set about people—chase and bare their teeth at the artists. People using the alley down the right side of the yard were particularly susceptible. This was the way to the studios. It was a rat-run, pitted and cratered. The craters were full of oil and ooze. The rats came to feed on the heaps of crap dumped at the top of the alley by the fly-tippers. Heels of bread and stiletto shoes and burst mattresses. Rats the size of cats. It was bleak and cold and weird. With all this going for it, naturally it was going to attract some of the best artists and finest sensibilities of their generation.[3]

Apart from the last sentence of aesthetic affirmation, this passage comes couched in the breathless argot of the tabloid newspapers—the tone of which would count for serious-minded readers as no more than a symptom of the pandering, sensationalistic character of the art for which this scene is set. Among the critical detractors of YBA art, there has been a strong streak of suspicion that it has simply attracted too wide an audience to be taken seriously. The same younger British critic quoted above laments "the commerce between art and popular culture," claiming that "this broader audience is probably consuming . . . the spectacle itself, and the populist element in the art that provides the kinds of pleasures and sensations available elsewhere in the culture."[4]

The piece appeared, however, not in any mass-market tabloid but in the sophisticated, left-leaning *Guardian* broadsheet. Titled "Off the Scrapheap," its author was the late Gordon Burn, who first made his name with a 1984 non-fiction account of the so-called Yorkshire Ripper of the 1970s, Peter Sutcliffe. Such a subject might seem akin to the gothic squalor of the Brixton Breakers yard, but Burn's book, *Somebody's Husband, Somebody's Son*, could stand in the subtlety and restraint of its prose as the English counterpart to Truman Capote's *In Cold Blood*, which founded the genre of the non-fiction novel with a parallel fixation on shocking crimes. The amped-up style of the *Guardian* article asks to be taken as a deliberate choice, one chosen to say something about the art that could not be conveyed by addressing it directly.

For a clue to what that might be, one could turn to a passage that cites a specific work of art, though not one by Hirst. Daniel Coombs, another of the artists working at the Breakers yard, tells Burn:

> The strangeness of the place drew us together more. It made us all take quite a hard attitude to our work. It made us want to do something quite brutal. Everybody who produced beautiful work there was influenced by the surroundings. Marcus definitely. He was just starting the Myra piece when I moved in, and I remember being impressed by this giant canvas laid out on scaffolding.[5]

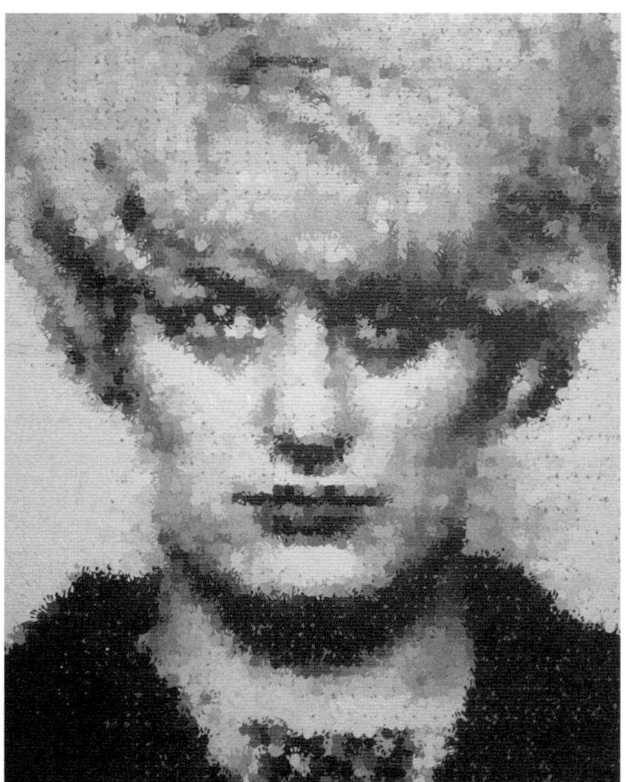

Fig. 1. Marcus Harvey (English, b. 1963), *Myra*, 1995. Acrylic on canvas, 156 × 126 in. (396.2 × 320 cm). Private collection. Courtesy of White Cube/DACS, London/Artists Rights Society (ARS), New York

In 1991, four years before Marcus Harvey started work on his immense portrait of the early 1960s serial murderer Myra Hindley (fig. 1), Burn published his first novel, *Alma Cogan* (fig. 2). The titular character is based on the British easy-listening cabaret and television star of the 1950s to early 1960s who was first marketed as "the girl with the giggle in her voice" (fig. 3). Cogan died prematurely, in 1966, after having made something of a transition to patroness of the new UK pop (one story is that Paul McCartney first wrote "Yesterday" at her piano). Burn's Alma, however, does not die: he imagines her in

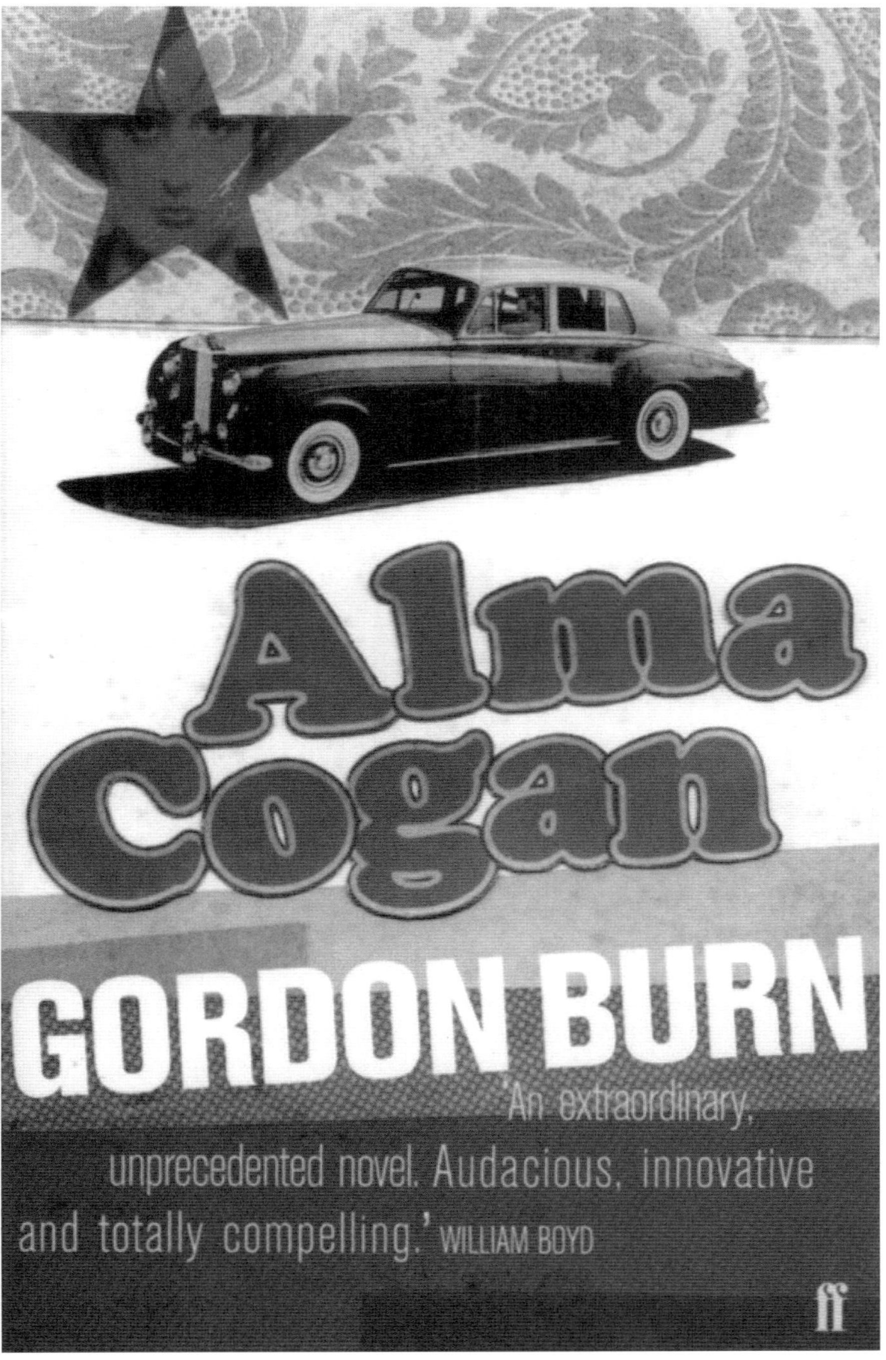

Fig. 2. Gordon Burn, *Alma Cogan* (London: Faber and Faber, 1991)

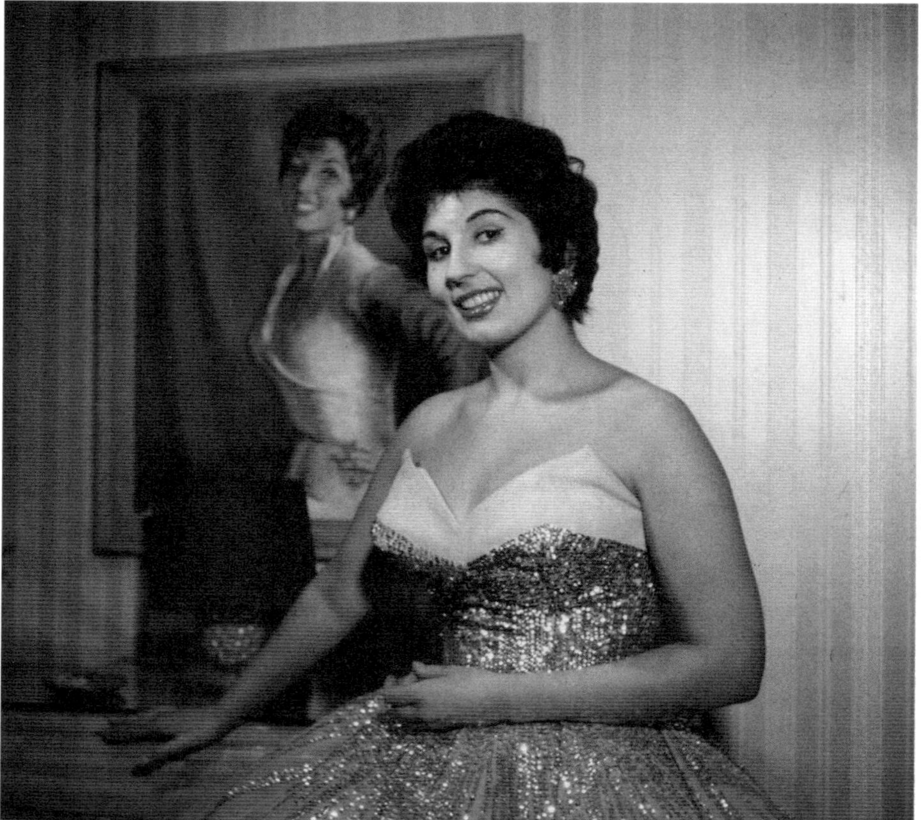

Fig. 3. *Alma Cogan*, c. 1950s. Paul Popper / Popperfoto / Getty Images

obscure, semi-rural retreat, where she becomes a spectator of her own posthumous fame and witness to the insidious expansion of pop celebrity as a snare for everyday consciousness (there is no better novel on this subject). The novel gradually incorporates the story of Hindley and her lover Ian Brady, the "Moors Murderers," who buried their multiple young victims on a bleak hillside in the South Pennines. Myra joins Cogan as a parallel 1960s female celebrity, likewise pushed out of sight, whose disembodied presence gradually takes over the narrative via her unavoidable media surrogates.

Hindley's most vivid appearances in the novel come in the shape of the same endlessly reproduced photograph that Harvey later magnified in his painting. In one scene, the imaginary Alma spots the image on a 1980s tabloid spread:

> SHAMEFUL, CYNICAL, AND CRUEL it says in letters as black as death across the front page. She asks herself, "Is it possible to discern evil, as so many have supposed, in the cavernous upturned eyes, the pasty planes, the heavy bones, the holed hedge of bleached blond fringe, the fondant of deep shadow, like a choke collar, under Hindley's chin? Is this the look—frontal, insolent, the unintimidated direct address to the camera—of *ein richtiger Teufelsbraten*, a true devil's dish?"[6]

In the British imagination, menace goes no higher than that. It had been a regular drama in the popular press to excoriate Hindley's villainy anew at each of the regular intervals that she applied for early release from prison, nor did this ritual excoriation cease at her death in 2002—whereas Brady, still living, has seemed barely to register in public consciousness. Invariably, the same grainy 1960s mug shot of Hindley, with dead eyes and blonde bouffant, appears next to the outraged headlines (fig. 4).

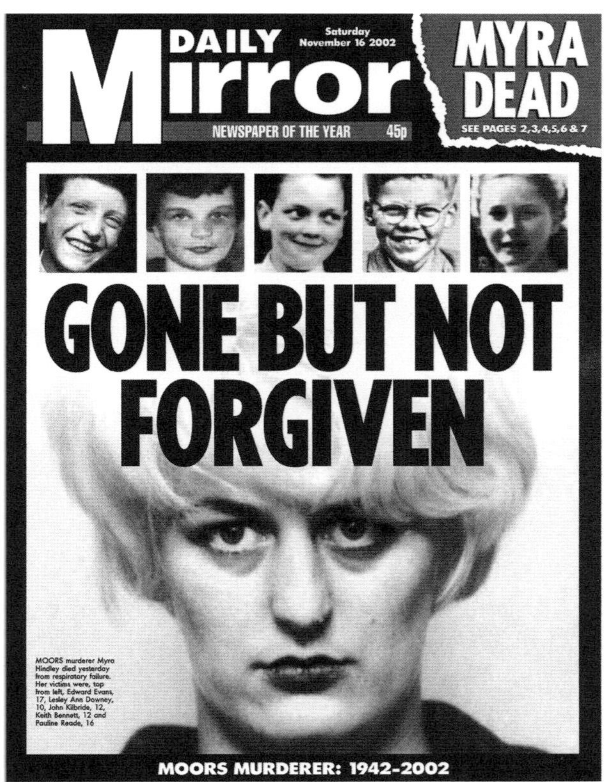

DAILY Mirror
Saturday November 16 2002
NEWSPAPER OF THE YEAR 45p
MYRA DEAD
SEE PAGES 2,3,4,5,6 & 7

GONE BUT NOT FORGIVEN

MOORS murderer Myra Hindley died yesterday from respiratory failure. Her victims were, top from left, Edward Evans, 17, Lesley Ann Downey, 10, John Kilbride, 12, Keith Bennett, 12 and Pauline Reade, 16

MOORS MURDERER: 1942-2002

Fig. 4. Front page of London's *Daily Mirror*, November 16, 2002, reporting on the death of convicted murderer Myra Hindley. Daily Mirror/Mirrorpix

Burn recognized that Hindley makes for an endlessly horrifying story (of genuine remembered terror) that the nation needs repeatedly to tell itself. There have been others before and since, but none possesses this kind of indelible icon as its sign and imprint. In that light (or lack of it), the first impression of Pop tabloid quotation in Harvey's painting—a hand-painted translation of Warhol's lo-fi, monochrome celebrity portraits—dissolves into another realm, still popular to be sure, but belonging to rooted folkloric, even mythic, traditions.

Such undercurrents—the stuff of shared fantasy and myth—are never far from the surface in the British popular media. A compact country with a truly national press, both in print and broadcast forms, Britain tends to propagate, share, and reinforce a limited set of elemental dramas. The story of the Moors Murders constitutes the pastoral in its darkest form: lonely wastelands, lost children, predatory witch; this is territory also occupied by Hirst. The grazing animals that he sliced and arrayed in formaldehyde make for a literally pastoral repertoire that is readily visible in living form on the close-cropped hillsides of the English countryside (fig. 5). One small metaphorical step from the pastoralism of dairymen and shepherds lie the homilies of every imagined village vicar, reliant on New Testament parables of flocks and lost sheep. But the violence done to that idyll lies on the less frequently illustrated reverse side of the animal vitrine, with organs and skeleton served up to the spectator. The most iconic of Hirst's productions, his 1991 *Physical Impossibility of Death in the Mind of Someone Living,*

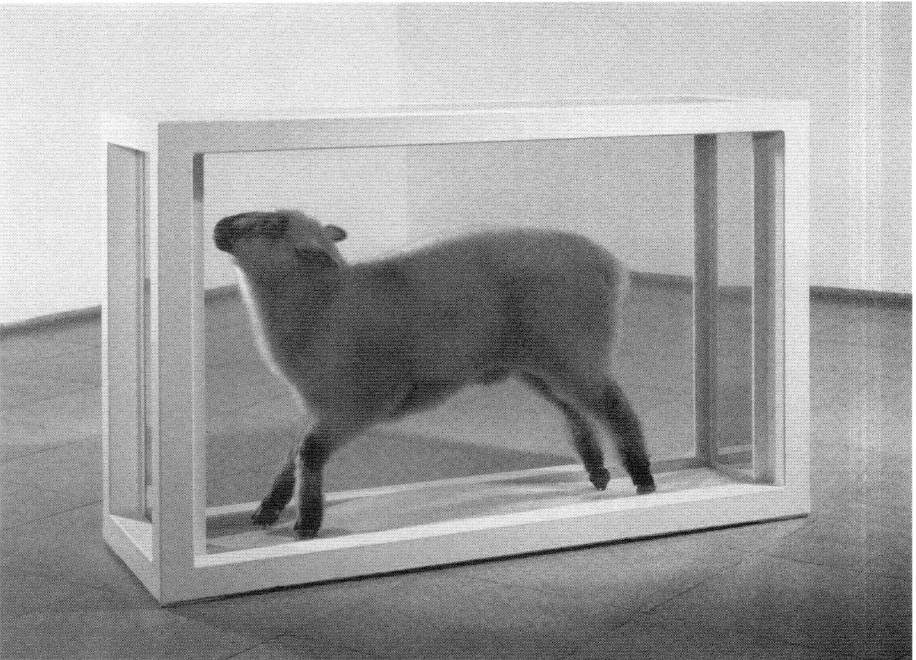

Fig. 5. Damien Hirst (English, b. 1965), *Away from the Flock*, 1994. Glass, painted steel, silicone, acrylic, plastic, lamb, and formaldehyde solution, 37 13/16 x 58 11/16 x 20 1/16 in. (96 x 149 x 51 cm). Edition 3 of 3 (plus 1 AP), Tate, London. ARTIST ROOMS. Acquired jointly with the National Galleries of Scotland through The d'Offay Donation with assistance from the National Heritage Memorial Fund and the Art Fund 2008. Photographed by Prudence Cuming Associates.

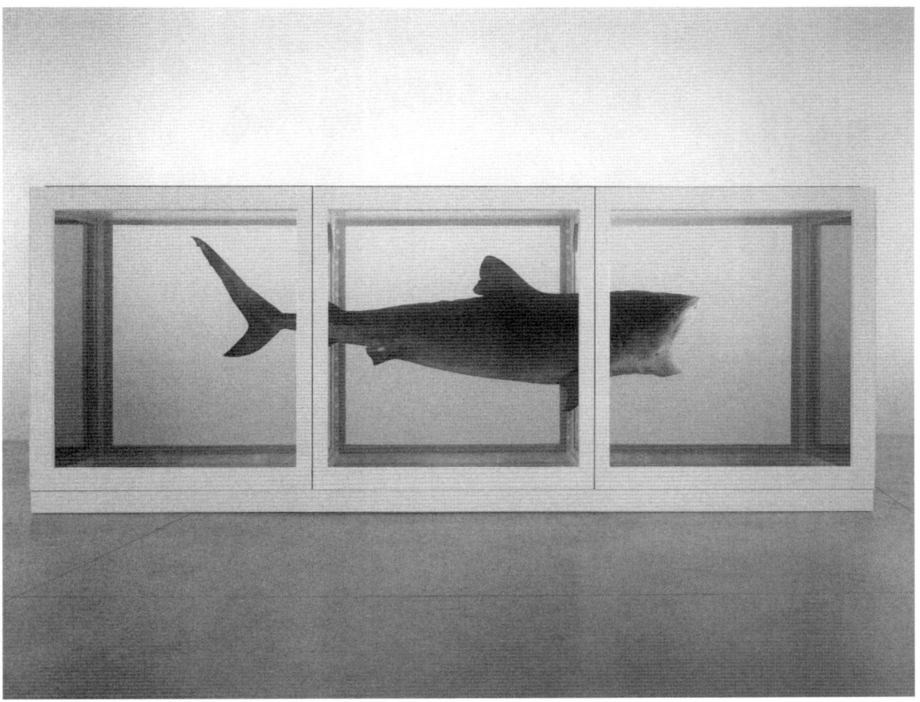

Fig. 6. Damien Hirst, *The Physical Impossibility of Death in the Mind of Someone Living*, 1991. Glass, painted steel, silicone, monofilament, shark, and formaldehyde solution, $85\frac{7}{16} \times 213\frac{3}{8} \times 70\frac{7}{8}$ in. (217 x 542 x 180 cm). Private collection. Photographed by Prudence Cuming Associates. © 2013 Damien Hirst and Science Ltd. All rights reserved / DACS, London / ARS, NY

provides the toothy maw of the predator (fig. 6). For its full effect, the isolation and vulnerability of the lamb requires a menace: the wolf in traditional European folklore (sin and the devil in the Christian allegory). Hirst's signature shark embodies the principle of predatory, soul-stealing monstrosity at a higher level of intensity and in a thrillingly exotic guise.

The visage of *Myra* presents the witch-like counterpart to the toothy maw of the shark. But Harvey took one step further by combining villainy and innocence in one monumental whole: he composed her colossal likeness, as is notoriously well known, out of the mock-indexical presence of her victims in the shape of tiny, life-sized handprints. This modular technique not only generates a synthesis of the witch with her prey (enlarging her menace through the simple contrast of scale), it also acts as a kind of homage to the photo-based portraits of American painter Chuck Close (fig. 7). Those works, begun in the later 1960s, channeled the scale and serial logic of American Minimalism into a form of figuration that answered,

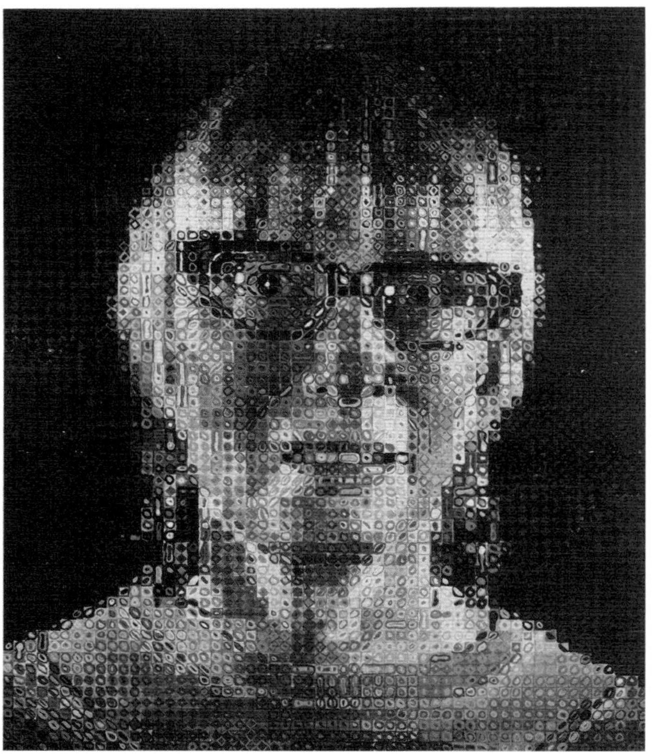

Fig. 7. Chuck Close (American, b. 1940), *Janet*, 1992. Oil on canvas, 100 x 84 in. (254 x 213.36 cm). George B. and Jenny R. Matthews Fund, 1992. Albright-Knox Art Gallery, Buffalo, NY. © Chuck Close, courtesy Pace Gallery

by means of the discipline of its underlying grid, a reigning demand for expressive coolness and neutrality. Harvey, by rendering Close's neutralized spots of paint into the emotional index of the handprint, takes that abstracting procedure from Close as itself a found object, one no more elevated than the tabloid mug shot and just as open to manipulation according to the requirements of the subject matter and occasion.

In a semi-comic vein, Burn used the *Guardian* article to create a parallel metaphor of menace—the dark underside of the village pastoral—complete with animals (of course) and a demonic pair of threatening outsiders, one with a suspiciously foreign name and the other turned entirely black as the visible mark of his villainy. Yet there can be no doubt concerning Burn's command of the various idioms of the art world. One need only turn to the bravura passage in *Alma Cogan* where the 1980s Alma anonymously visits the Tate Gallery hoping to see her own (actual) portrait by Peter Blake, made after a photograph back in the early 1960s. After much bewilderment, she finally is led to the storage rack where it hangs and is handed the curatorial file, the contents of which Burn creates with the finest ear for the absurdities of bureaucratized aesthetics.[7]

In his re-creation of the Brixton Breakers, Burn's own myth-making by analogy captures a dimension of this art—both Harvey's and Hirst's—occluded by an obdurate blind spot when more conventional modes of interpretation are brought to bear upon it. His chosen style inhabits a different world from the measured prose of approved art-critical discourse. Burn's conclusion confirms the parable form of the exercise in the way his chief villain exits the scene, while providing a final nudge to the reader's apprehension that the whole of the piece represents an exercise in stylized misdirection:

> The end, when it came last summer, came quickly. A fire spread through the breakers yard, and a week later, Gerry, the gaffer, was found dead in the alley among the rubble. The forklift he had been using to shift the burned-out cars had flipped over and crushed him. As a spectacle in a place that had seen the production of so much (museum quality) art whose theme was catastrophilia, it must have seemed grotesquely appropriate (catastrophilia: the longing for something terrible, for something that is terribly high, sad, or far, terribly mean, dangerous, or lovely, as long as it's terrible).
>
> "It was all very odd and very tragic," Dan Coombs says. "It was just like the last . . . it was like the finally horrific thing that could have happened."[8]

The intrusive definition of the neologism "catastrophilia," perfectly self-evident in its meaning, strikes a dissonant note of pedantry in the manner of a critic or Saatchi-like impresario hopefully trailing a new brand name for an art movement. Burn puts these two conventional voices—sensationalist lowbrow versus didactic highbrow—into a game of equivalency and a test of relative vividness.

As Hirst's regular interlocutor in a series of interviews conducted over the 1990s, Burn knew how to play the reasonable middle ground.[9] He also knew his subject's frankly disabused self-assessments as well as anyone could. But no standard idiom could capture the way in which Hirst's celebrity—with the aura it cast over his perceived cohort—had become less the by-product of his art than one of its central instruments.

One cannot bend the media without having achieved some power within it. The American artist assumes the mass media cannot be moved, so adopts a defensively superior attitude toward the whole popular realm—a stance dutifully mirrored in high-minded criticism and art history. Hirst and his British generation collectively acted on the contrary assumption that the mass media can indeed be moved by means of fine art, provided that the legacy procedures and processes of the latter be realistically regarded as so much expedient packaging, while freshly

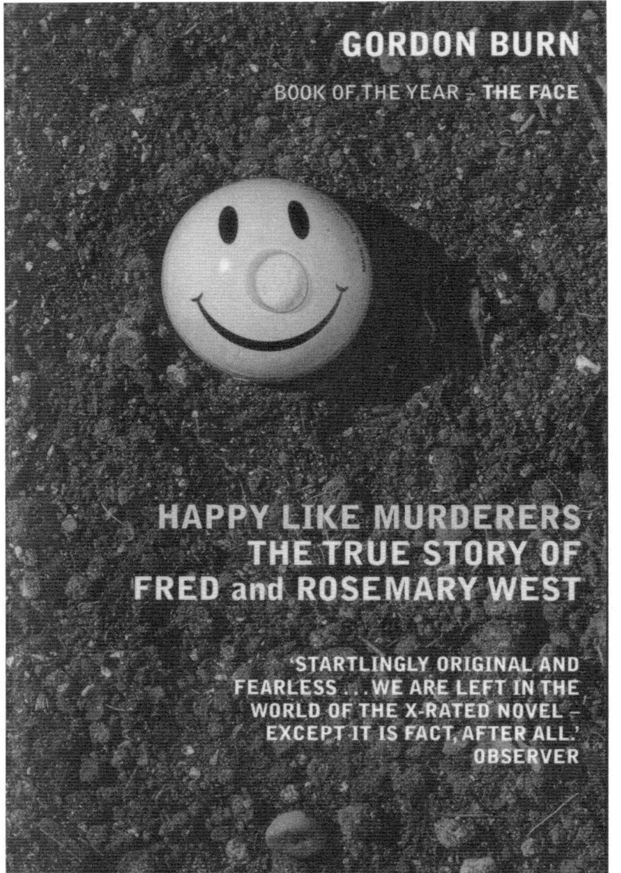

Fig. 8. Gordon Burn, *Happy Like Murderers* (London: Faber and Faber, 1998). Cover image by Damien Hirst, art directed by Hugh Allan, photographed by Mike Parsons

resonant and memorable forms of work were found for them to perform. Hirst possessed the temperament and nightlife stamina required for the gossip side of fame, but such attainments would have counted for little if he had he not found his way to tapping deeper repositories of the national collective consciousness—a path that demanded its own share of brutal, hazmat-heavy labors.

The retiring Harvey found this expedition toward the heart of darkness in the country's collective psyche a battering experience, as families of the victims joined in an outcry against what concern-trolls in the British media encouraged them to regard as exploitation of their pain: the decorum of his formal model offered little protection when operating so close to the national nerve.[10] Hirst's bestial allegories, by contrast, proved sufficiently generalized to evoke similar emotions without calling to mind the appallingly specific memories on which those responses are founded. Nothing less, tabloid antics or no, would have gained him the fame that has since been integral to his project.

This kind of bloodless description of the process, however, inevitably falls short in the explanatory stakes; its decorum as reasonable argument fails to channel the atavistic power of the social-psychological phenomenon in question. By the time he composed "Off the Scrapheap," in 2000, Burn had plumbed these depths not only in his account of the Yorkshire Ripper but in a further 1998 volume, similarly restrained in tone and diction, devoted to the Gloucester serial sex killers Fred and Rosemary West, *Happy Like Murderers* (fig. 8).[11] He had thus peered deeply not only into the appalling raw facts in each case but equally into their translation by the raucous voices of a salacious media cult. *Alma Cogan* had balanced both registers in a work of art, the resources of which he had at hand in creating the deceptively weightless Brixton Breakers miniature. Its aim would never be one of explaining the art or forming a judgment on its merits; its purpose was to reveal it with an indirect light in a way that no other stylistic genre could accomplish.

1. Hal Foster, "The Medium Is the Market," *London Review of Books*, October 9, 2008, 23.

2. Robert Garnett, "Britpopism and the Populist Gesture," in Duncan McQuorquodale, Naomi Siderfin, and Julian Stallabrass, eds., *Occupational Hazard: Critical Writing on Recent British Art* (London: Black Dog, 1998), 15.

3. Gordon Burn, "Off the Scrapheap," *The Guardian*, April 13, 2000.

4. Garnett, "Britpopism," 14

5. Burn, "Scrapheap."

6. Burn, *Alma Cogan* (London: Faber and Faber, 1994), 93–94.

7. Ibid., 137–51.

8. Burn, "Scrapheap."

9. Collected in Damien Hirst and Gordon Burn, *On the Way to Work* (London: Faber and Faber, 2000).

10. Burn had in a smaller way been subjected to parallel complaints by the family of Alma Cogan for having, in their eyes, hijacked and darkened the wholesome public memory of the singer; see Michael Thornton, "John Lennon's Secret Lover," *The Daily Mail*, November 7, 2006.

11. Burn, *Happy Like Murderers* (London: Faber and Faber, 1998); the original cover design, showing a yellow plastic happy-face ball resting in the dirt, is by Hirst with designer Hugh Allen. The company of other YBA artists helped Burn in the harrowing immersion the book entailed: he includes Harvey, Sarah Lucas, and Angus Fairhurst among his acknowledgments of "friendship and encouragement."

Philip Marlowe Meets the Art Historian

Paul Barolsky

I will put my cards on the table at the outset. I am an unabashed "hedonist." It matters to me not a whit that Bishop Butler dealt a deathblow to hedonism as a viable philosophy over seven hundred years into the last millennium. Not only a hedonist, I am also an amateur and a dilettante, an aesthete and an impressionist. What matters to me when it comes to art is aesthetic pleasure or delight. Art is a manifestation of play, which is not to say it is lacking in seriousness. What is more serious than a child at play?

I am not inclined to dwell on art history as a discipline, on the modes of understanding art, on viewing practices, rhetorical strategies, etcetera, although I fully recognize that to others these things matter. Art history is, strictly speaking, the story of art. But, too often, academic art history is not a good story, by which I mean it is not a story well told, with vivacity and delight, and written for the reader's pleasure as well as instruction. Much so-called art history is scarcely a story at all.

The story of art is not, in fact, a single story but a vast multitude of stories. The more that these many stories are absorbed into a single account, the more abstract, and therefore elusive, the overall story becomes. Although there is a famous textbook entitled *The Story of Art*, a book with such a title would not be written today. "*The* story of art" is a misleading phrase; it fails to convey the richness of the ever-expanding variety of stories of art that have been told or might yet be told. The history of art is a range of stories about art that takes many forms in various genres, some fictional. Such stories may be written in prose, poetry, or prose poetry; take form in orations, epitaphs, anecdotes, and letters; and appear in travel books, biographies, novels, technical manuals, theoretical treatises, and other forms, as well as in academic art history.

Art history depends on facts. Facts are often said to stand in opposition to fiction, but fiction also depends on facts. Otherwise, fiction would be meaningless: you cannot write fiction without facts. There is, nonetheless, a fundamental difference between the intentions of the modern art historian and those of the author of historical fiction. The historian must adhere as strictly as possible to the facts, even when these facts are bizarre, outrageous, and even unbelievable, whereas the author of fiction has license to embellish the facts, if he chooses, although he must always maintain a sense of verisimilitude.

At the same time, however, there are fundamental ways in which history and fiction are similar. Both are written in pursuit of truth, yet both are fictive, in the root sense of the Latin word *fingere*, meaning "to shape" or "to mold." When we stop to think about history and fiction, we realize that much modern academic art history, in its zealous efforts to separate fact from fiction, is a historical aberration. From the Greeks to the Romans, from the Romans to Vasari, and up to today, history has been mingled with legends, fables, fabrications, and myths. Facts combined with fictions have been a matter of course throughout the history of writing about art.

In any event, far too much academic art history, despite the best of intentions, is very badly written, artless, ponderous, and even lugubrious, giving little pleasure and serving to alienate readers from the art that it might otherwise illuminate. I take exception to the claim that art historians aspire to write beautifully. The evidence demonstrates that most art historians appear to be indifferent to the form of their writing, to their literary style or absence of style. Writing about art should convey a vivid sense of the work of art, so it necessarily must be artful and give the reader pleasure, not just information and ideas. The artfulness of verbal interpretation can bring us into close rapport with the wordless art that it illuminates. So much academic writing nowadays is so focused on context, however, that too often it fails to describe the work of art itself.

Description is necessarily a form of interpretation. There is a deep, well-known tradition of description that can be traced back to Homer's account of the shield of Achilles and that extends to the writings of Philostratus and later Vasari and Winckelmann. It has the technical name *ekphrasis.* All art historians know this tradition, but few practice it today. It has been said that this is so because we have photographs of works of art, but these photographs are mute, and what they represent still needs to be noticed and described in words. Moreover, the photograph is never a neutral or objective datum, but is itself an interpretation.

Art historians today resist description because they fear that it will be excessively subjective or too obvious. Also, it is incredibly difficult to do. They often escape to theory. We need to be reminded of the etymology of the word "theory," which comes from the Greek *theōria* and means "how one sees something."

A theory is a point of view. What we see needs to be described; we cannot take it for granted.

The pursuit of a theory of art, justifiably rooted in a philosophical approach, too often descends into the realm of radical pomposity. This often occurs to such a degree that the double-talk in contemporary academe reads like self-parody or farce. Let us consider a few examples of such babble in the spirit of fun. The first is a specimen from a book of terms used by art historians that was assembled, at least in part, for student use:

> The modern individual or subject is interpellated into its own position in the social order as a composer of its own life, in all of its facets. Ordinary habitation in the modern world is above all an occasion for the dramaturgy of the self, as this may be reflected ("represented") in a subject's relationships to the objects (from pitchers to paintings) with which it surrounds itself—which it may have "collected"—and with which it carries out the routines of daily life.

Is this, I ask you, a model for students or anyone to follow in writing about art? Talk about corrupting the youth!

Or, consider this bit of nonsense: "The central premise of the category 'Renaissance' suffers from *metalepsis*, or chronological reversal, meaning that the object of study seems to justify its presence on the basis of a preexisting historical context, whereas 'Renaissance' is the construction of a context based on the historian's prior understanding of history's significance." To which one can only reply: Duh!

How about, also just for fun, this further example of art-historical gibberish: "To articulate a narrative account of the history of art is to authorize a relational experience that is, ultimately, strategically situational." Finally, my favorite bit of pomposity from an art historian who, lecturing on art and sex, recently referred to having sex as "inter-corporeal relationality." (I wonder what *that* feels like.) Such "writing" is "born," I believe, of the fear that art history is not sufficiently profound. It is probably easier to use unnecessarily technical words with abandon than it is to write clear, vivid, and evocative descriptions of works of art.

In comparison with these examples of absurdity, here is a wonderfully vivid and engaging account of the main hall of an ostentatious house:

> The main hallway of the Sternwood place was two stories high. Over the entrance doors, which would have let in a troop of Indian elephants, there was a broad stained-glass panel showing a knight in dark armor rescuing a lady who was tied to a tree and didn't have any clothes on but some very long and convenient hair. The knight had pushed the visor of his helmet back to be sociable, and he was fiddling with the knots on the rope that tied the lady to the tree and not getting anywhere. I stood there and thought that if I lived in the house, I would sooner or later have to climb up there and help him. He didn't seem to be really trying.
>
> There were French doors at the back of the hall, beyond them a wide sweep of emerald grass to a white garage, in front of which a slim dark young chauffeur in shiny black leggings was dusting a maroon Packard convertible. Beyond the garage were some decorative trees trimmed as carefully as poodle dogs. Beyond them a greenhouse with a domed roof. Then more trees and beyond everything the solid, uneven, comfortable line of the foothills.
>
> On the east side of the hall a free staircase, tile-paved, rose to a gallery with a wrought-iron railing and another piece of stained-glass romance. Large hard chairs with rounded red plush seats were backed into the vacant spaces of the wall round about. They didn't look as if anybody had ever sat in them. In the middle of the west wall there was a big empty fireplace with a brass screen in four hinged panels, and over the fireplace a marble mantel with cupids at the corners. Above the mantel there was a large oil portrait, and above the portrait two bullet-torn or moth-eaten cavalry pennants crossed in a glass frame. The portrait was a stiffly posed job of an officer in full regimentals of about the time of the Mexican war. The officer had a neat black imperial, black mustachios, hot hard coal-black eyes, and the general look of a man it would pay to get along with. I thought this might be General Sternwood's grandfather. It could hardly be the General himself, even though I had heard he was pretty far gone in years to have a couple of daughters still in the dangerous twenties.

This is Philip Marlowe's description of General Sternwood's house at the beginning of Raymond Chandler's *The Big Sleep.* It is all there: architecture, landscape gardening, topiary art, stained glass, metalwork, painting, sculpture, and furniture—not to mention art criticism. No matter that Marlowe is a character in a novel, no matter that he is the subject of fiction, no matter that the world he describes is imaginary. His account has verisimilitude, and Chandler's prose is superb—lively, precise, lucid, spare, witty; attentive to scale, color, materials, psychology, class consciousness, social aspirations, and much more; and, above all, attentive to the art of storytelling. We can learn a thing or two about writing from Chandler, even we art historians who, too often plumbing the depths of our discipline, forget to describe what we see on the surfaces of art.

Authors of fiction often illuminate the meaning of art. Not trained formally in art history or its methods, the novelist often surpasses the art historian in describing, and thus interpreting, what he sees—he is more the art historian than the art historian. Although many scholars have supposed Bronzino's *An Allegory with Venus and Cupid* to be a Counter-Reformation exposé of luxury, the painting is more plausibly an amusingly coy and shameless celebration of sexuality (fig. 1). In his novel, *What's Bred in the Bone,* Robertson Davies captures the sensual fun of the picture when he says facetiously that Venus is "naked as a jaybird," indeed "astonishingly naked." This joking captures the tone of a picture that is scarcely moralizing. The novelist continues by observing that the

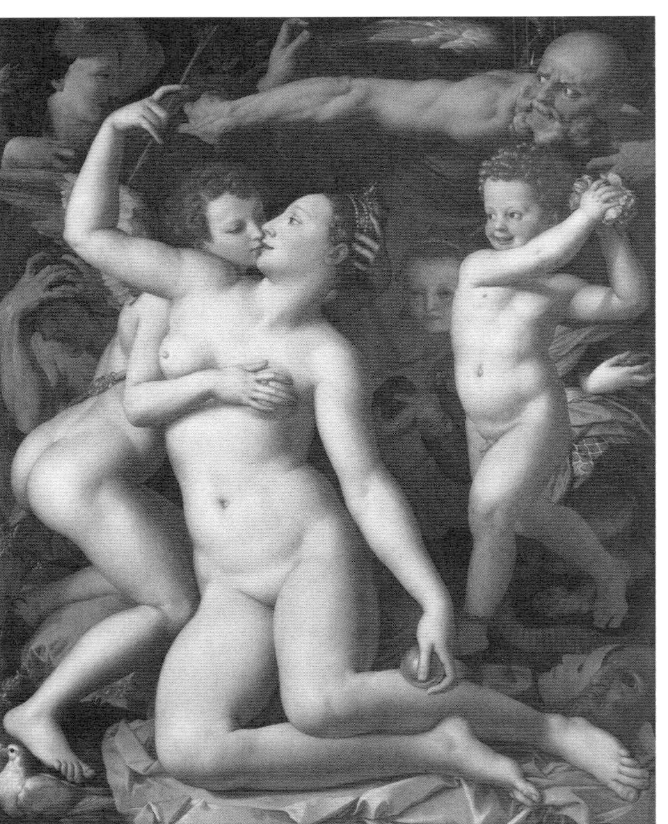

Fig. 1. Agnolo Bronzino (Italian, 1503–1572), *An Allegory with Venus and Cupid,* c.1540–50. Oil on wood, 51 1/2 × 45 3/4 in. (146.1 × 116.2 cm). National Gallery, London

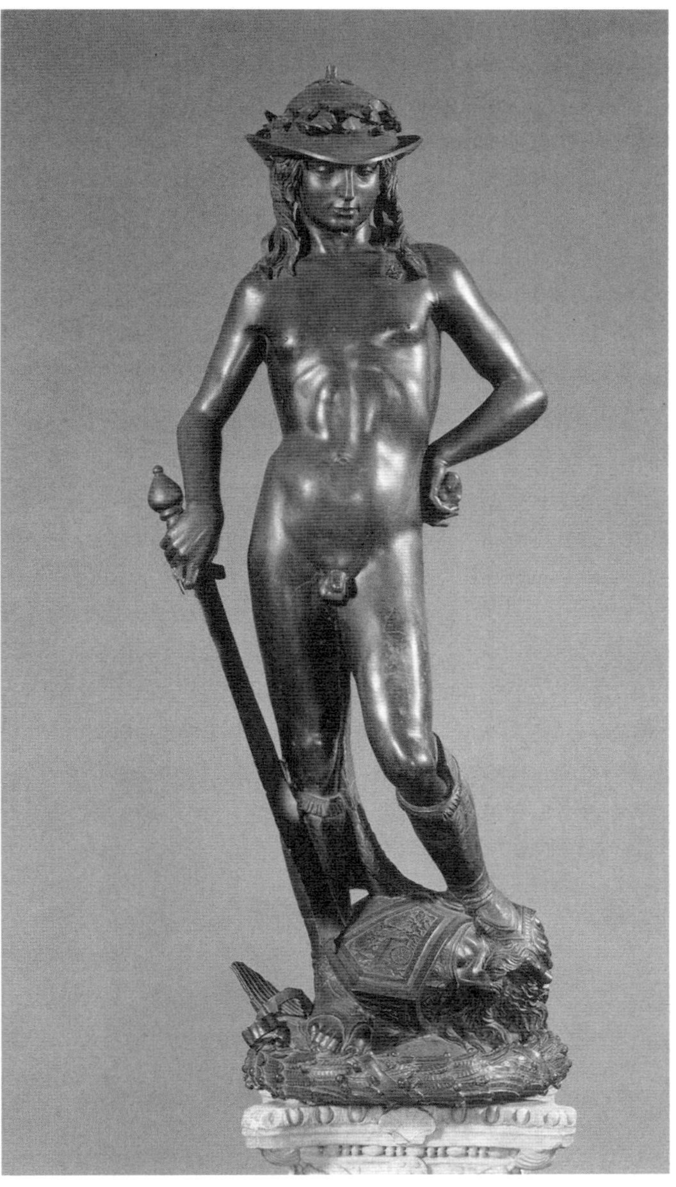

Fig. 2. Donatello (Italian, c. 1386–1466), *David*, 1428–32. Bronze, 62 ¼ in. (158 cm). Museo Nazionale del Bargello, Florence

kiss, which the picture represents, "meant more than good morning or something like that." If Venus and Cupid are really mother and son, Davies says, "it's a pretty queer situation." The author of fiction captures the bizarre playfulness of a painting that is rendered humorless in so many iconographical commentaries.

Or consider an observation of Richard Howard in a long poem, "The Giant on Giant-Killing," which is about Donatello's *David* (fig. 2). By now it is commonplace to observe the sensuous role of the feather of Goliath's helmet that rises to stroke the boy victor's inner thigh (fig. 3). Nice. How many art historians notice, however, a similar detail below—a detail that the poet sees and drolly describes in the voice of Goliath (fig. 4)? With amused pleasure Goliath asks us to "Notice the way my moustache turns over his triumphant toe (a kind of caress, and not the only one)." Ultimately, as Howard's Goliath proclaims, "the triumph is mine."

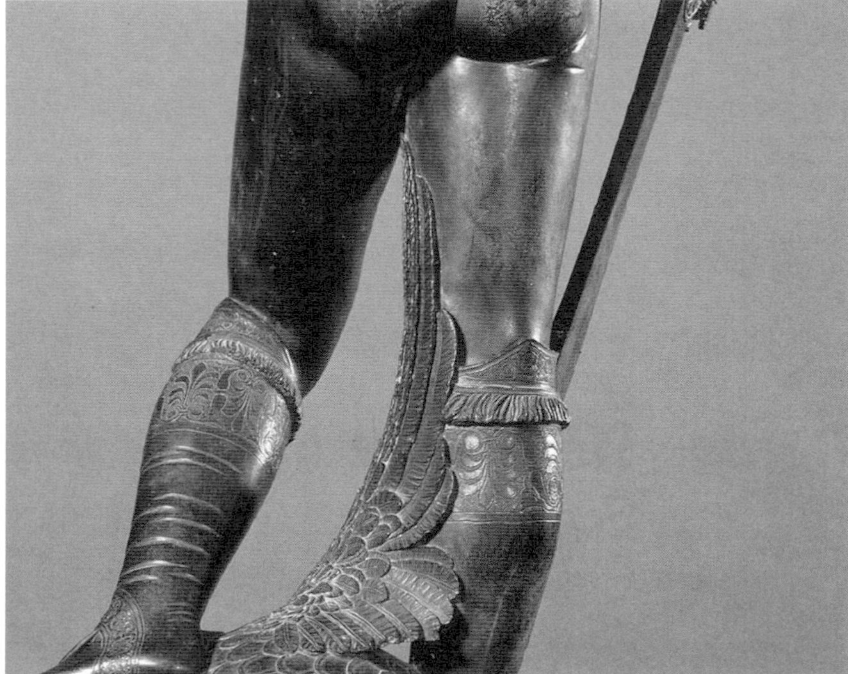

Fig. 3. Donatello, detail of *David*, back view, 1428–32

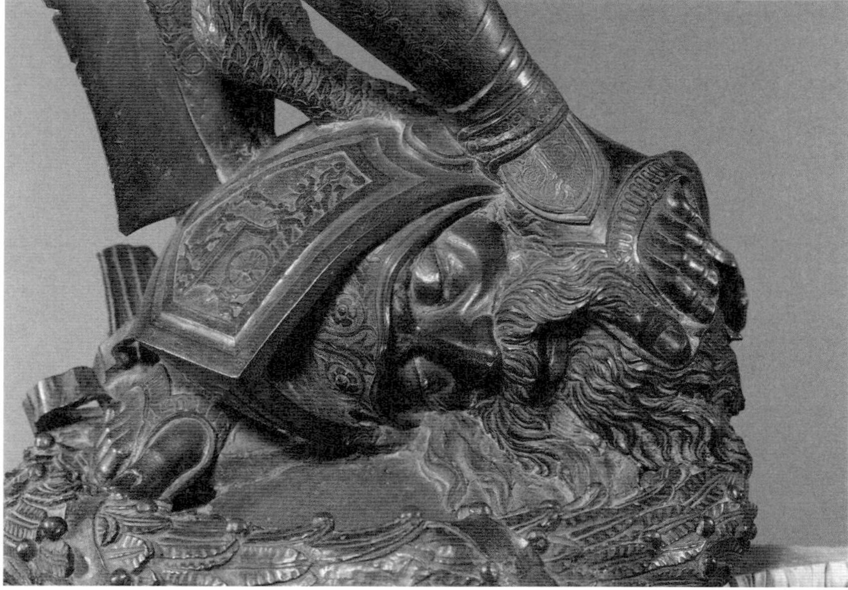

Fig. 4. Donatello, detail of *David*, head of Goliath, 1428–32

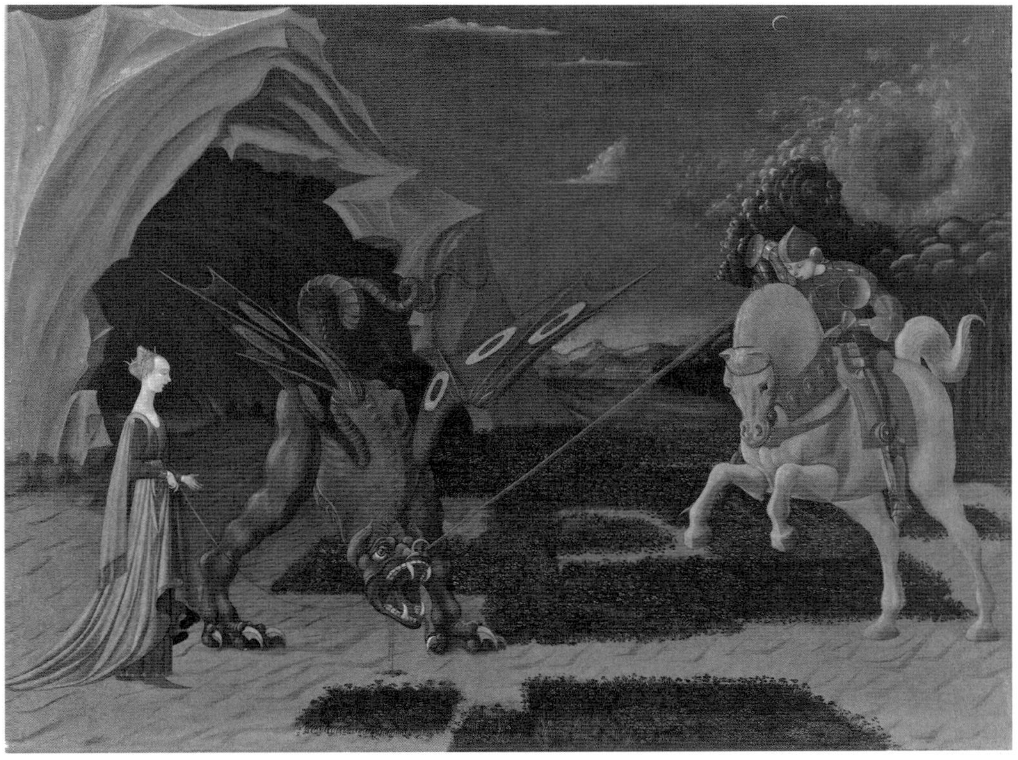

Fig. 5. Paolo Uccello (Italian, 1397–1475), *Saint George and the Dragon*, c. 1470. Oil on canvas, 21 7/8 x 29 1/4 in. (55.6 x 74.2 cm). National Gallery, London

In the spirit of poetic fun, let me share with you the middle section of U.A. Fanthorpe's poem, "Not My Best Side," about Paolo Uccello's painting *Saint George and the Dragon* in the National Gallery in London (fig. 5). This is Uccello's maiden speaking:

> It's hard for a girl to be sure if
> She wants to be rescued. I mean, I quite
> Took to the dragon. It's nice to be
> Liked, if you know what I mean. He was
> So nicely physical, with his claws
> And lovely green skin, and that sexy tail,
> And the way he looked at me,
> He made me feel he was all ready to
> Eat me. And any girl enjoys that.

> So when this boy turned up, wearing machinery,
> On a really *dangerous* horse, to be honest,
> I didn't much fancy him. I mean,
> What was he like underneath the hardware?
> He might have acne, blackheads or even
> Bad breath for all I could tell, but the dragon—
> Well, you could see all his equipment
> At a glance. Still what could I do?
> The dragon got himself beaten by the boy,
> And a girl's got to think of her future.

This is seemingly pure poetic fantasy and tells us little, if anything, about the painting, right? Well, not quite. The poetry is decidedly playful, and if you look at the capricious forms of Uccello's picture, the cunning contours of the cave opening, the monstrosity of the dragon, the decorative perspective of his wings, his curling tail, his great claws, and Saint George's toy horse, you see that they are all manifestations of a painter at play. What we might say, therefore, is that the poet enters with extreme license into the playful spirit of the picture. The maiden, thinking ever so coolly about her future, is appropriate to Uccello's aloof damsel holding her pet dragon by a leash—whatever the iconographical conventions might be.

I think it fair to say that, as a general rule, poets and novelists writing about art exhibit a far greater sense of humor or wit in their writings that celebrate art than do art historians, who are excessively serious. This is not to say that art historians lack a sense of humor in real life but when they turn to historical exegesis, they too often check their playfulness at the door. And when they recognize a playful detail, rather than evoke its charm, they flog it to death. The alienation of art history from art as a form of play is a striking feature of the discipline. Excessive seriousness trumps, if not crushes, playfulness almost every time.

There are many ways of writing well about art, particularly in the artful description of art, but such artful writing is not much cultivated in our academic institutions where we—to use the language of industrialized scholarly prose—"problematize" works of art, often at a cost. It is exceedingly difficult to describe works of art in precise, evocative, or inspiring ways. In the present circumstances, we would need a revolution in our institutions to effect a change. Who, dashing toward professional success—tenure or scholarly prominence—will pause long enough to do the work necessary to write beautifully and without unnecessary jargon in a prose that is seemingly effortless? Such work requires significant revision and polishing. Although the realization of an excellent prose style takes time, we should work toward the cultivation of vivid and engaging writing.

In our advanced undergraduate and graduate seminars on theory, methods, and historiography, in which students read classic texts that range from Vasari to Kant to Greenberg (and some of the absolutely terrible stuff I quoted earlier), we might well also insert into the curriculum some selected writings from novelists and poets and also such excellent journalists and critical essayists as Alex Ross or Anthony Lane. These would serve as models of vigorous, beautiful, and suggestive descriptions of works of art of various kinds—interpretations in a language that would be compelling, indeed a pleasure to read. In the history of English and American literature, for example, there is a great tradition of such writing from Hazlitt, Lamb, Thackeray, Browning, Hawthorne, and Dickens, not just Ruskin and Pater, as well as Woolf, Cather, Byatt, and Barnes, among others. One finds similar traditions of writing in other languages. Such prose or poetry might encourage students not merely to write in a clear, jargon-free exposition of facts and ideas but to write with a certain élan. This, I believe, would be a step in the right direction. And who could possibly object to that?

"Oil painting, before it was anything else, was a celebration of private property." *

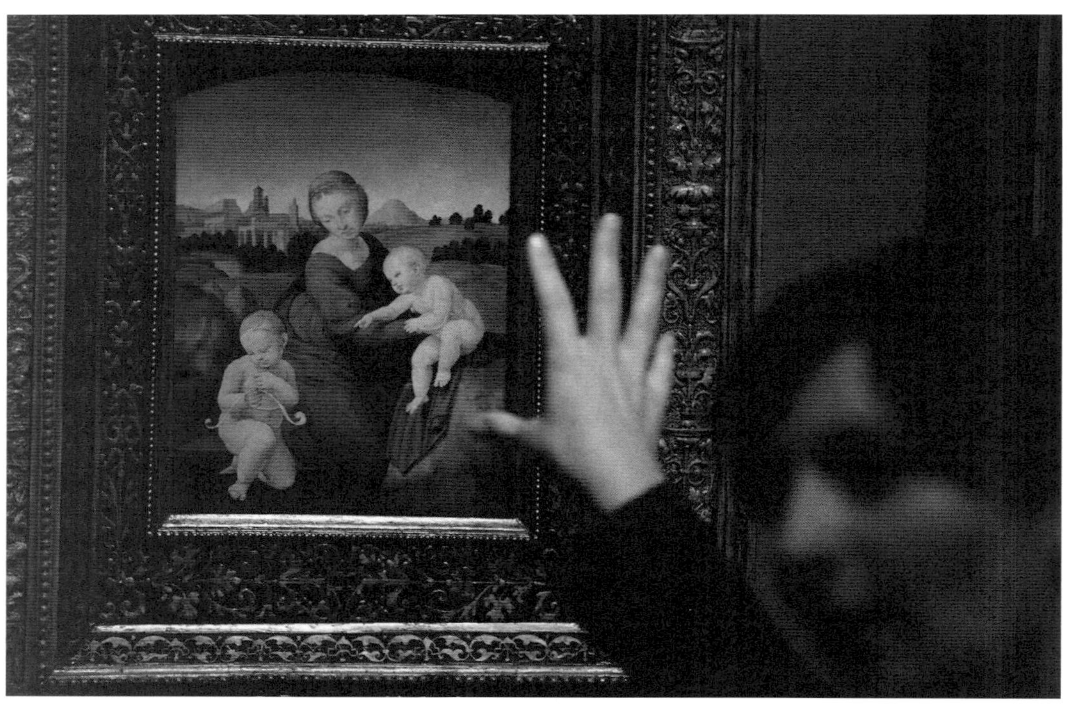

Fig. 1. The Royal Academy of Arts prepares for the *Treasures of Budapest* opening, Royal Academy of Arts, London, September 21, 2010. Oli Scarff / Getty Images News / Getty Images

The Case of the Errant Art Historian

Gloria Kury

Securing the Scene

Noon. Upstate New York. A darkened theater. Can you see the grimacing faces on the walls? Probably not. The phantasmagoria on the giant screen has you mesmerized. Naked women, naked men. People cradled in brocades, velvets, and furs. Gods and goddesses raping human beings. A dead man in a bathtub. Mutilated men tied to trees. A voice with the diction of another era speaks in tongues strange and incomprehensible. *Ut pictura poesis, di sotto in sù*, rococo, metamorphosis. A red dot traces patterns over the translucent pictures. A long shadow cuts across a beam of dazzling light. Jupiter's shower of gold impregnates Danae. The beam generates life on the iridescent screen in this secluded neo-Gothic room. A sun, a galaxy of stars shines on the faces of student-scribes, an alternative universe.

Noon. The time of the first *Idyll* of Theocritus. Thyrsis and a goatherd meet in the shade in Arcadia, a world not mythological, not real. Fictional? There, at noon in the shadow of a tree, art as art comes into being.

> When I filled my lungs with smoke, I let it go slowly, watching it swirl up toward the ceiling. "Lee," I said, "you don't know me so I'll tell you something. I hate phonies."
>
> —Mickey Spillaine, *One Lonely Night* (1951)

Hardboiled they are not, the art historians of crime fiction. They don't smoke, don't pack a rod in a shoulder holster, and they are frail. Blame the gene pool. One branch in the family tree? Dr. Brainard of the 1961 movie *The Absent-Minded Professor*. Another? Socrates, snub-nosed, a paunch; a lover not a master of wisdom. Crime fiction with art historians? A rogue's gallery of misfits, scoundrels, and Clark Kent / Supermen.

Tom Lynch. An alcoholic recently dismissed from the faculty of a New England college. Slow to publish, tries to lure students into sex, pastoral style, complaints to the dean. In a decayed English manor he lies, prowls, seduces his already pregnant hostess. All in a failed effort to find a Giovanni Bellini Madonna.

Jonathan Argyll. Cannot finish his dissertation. Falls asleep after he's a few pages into a scholarly monograph. In Venice admiring the facade of San Barnaba, steps back and back, falls into a dank canal. Does sort out various art crimes, with the help of his girlfriend, Flavia, and her boss, the head of the Italian Art Police.

Alejandro Ballesteros. Dissertation topic, Giorgione's *Tempest.* Written and accepted after five years of "errand boy service" to his advisor. "With the eagerness lovers have when they embark on marriage," he goes to Venice to see the painting. A fake is what he discovers, then more and more simulacra. When he locates the so-called real painting, it no longer possesses the aura of an original.

Robert Langdon. Meets some of the criteria for the tough hero. Strong swimmer, faces danger with courage and ingenuity. Impresses Harvard undergraduates with knowledge of "symbology." Childish though. Wears a Mickey Mouse watch, loves Disney's *Little Mermaid,* munches apples while teaching. Prefers writing books on the eternal feminine to connubial bliss or sadomasochism à la Mike Hammer.

Hammer would have hated them all. They're bookish and upper class. They're phonies. They pose and talk and talk some more. "Erwinning the Panofsky"—Michael Frayn's term for this kind of pontificating. Fatuous as Langdon surely is, he convinces his listeners. Most of the others do not.

They get trapped in a double bind. They think they have fooled people, when the reverse is true; they are the ones being fooled. They believe their own ideas and theories. A lost masterpiece, a fake, or a dead body, the lure doesn't matter. In the more genteel books, like the Robert Langdon or Jonathan Argyll mysteries, the art historian-detective eventually solves the mystery. In the others, detecting and art-historical knowledge lead to humiliation, unethical behavior, and/or crime.

Good guys or bad, are they inept art historians? Not exactly. Try Quixotic—would-be heroes caught in a web of illusions in which they are complicit if not always the spider doing the spinning; e.g. Kenneth Clark's Giorgione fiasco, London, 1937; the combined efforts of John Shearman, Perry Rathbone, and Hanns Swarzenski to purchase and smuggle a putative Raphael for the MFA, Boston, 1969. The type is not a mere caricature in a branch of pulp fiction. Michael Frayn turned it into *Headlong,* a finalist for the Man Booker Prize. John Banville's trilogy—*The Book of Evidence, Ghosts, Athena*—montages paintings, illusions, delusions, love, and crime in a portrayal of a murderer-turned-art historian.

"Glamour cannot exist without personal social envy being a common and widespread emotion."

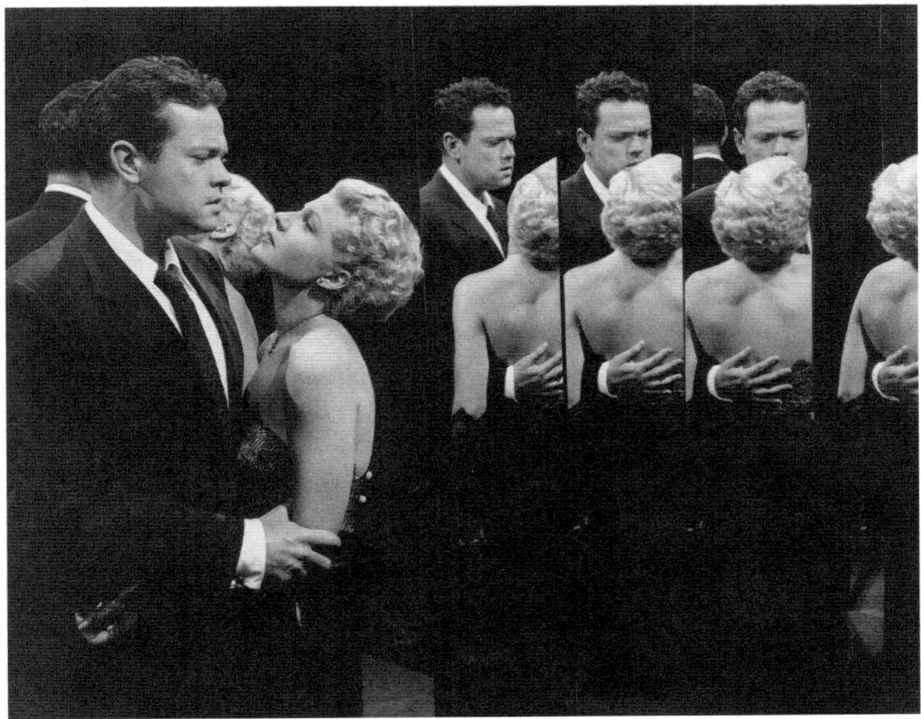

Fig. 2. Film still of Orson Welles and Rita Hayworth in Orson Welles's *The Lady from Shanghai*, 1947, 87 mins. © Underwood & Underwood / Corbis

1948. Almost anywhere in the U.S. A darkened theater. Marriage on the rocks, Orson Welles and Rita Hayworth appear together for the last time in a noir classic of 1947, *The Lady From Shanghai*. Welles directs and plays Mike O'Hara, Irish sailor; Hayworth Elsa Bannister, wife of a famous criminal lawyer. Elsa and her lover have played Mike as the fall guy in a plot to kill her husband. Within the darkened theater, there is another darkened theater, the Magic Mirror Maze. Reflections multiply, dissolve fixities of time and place. Which of the many Rita / Elsas corresponds to the real Rita / Elsa? Shots explode. The mirrors shatter. Orson / Mike escapes.

A day, c. 1600. A city-state in North Italy. A picture gallery in a palace. An aristocrat, sometimes identified as the fifth Duke of Ferrara, has pulled back a drape. A portrait of his deceased wife appears before him and the agent with whom he is negotiating the terms of a second marriage. No one but the duke is allowed to uncover the portrait. And his is the only voice in Robert Browning's famous poem of 1842:

> That's my last duchess painted on the wall,
> Looking as if she were alive. I call
> That piece a wonder . . .

The duke's monologue is a further unveiling. His words show him to be a person of refinement and subtle observation. He's also possessive, jealous, and arrogant. Once he mentions his "nine-hundred-years-old name," he strains to control the rage his first wife still arouses in him. Her offenses? She noticed ordinary people, enjoyed little pleasures, had a ready smile. He had to "stoop" to her and chose never to stoop. He didn't even kill her himself.

> I gave commands;
> Then all smiles stopped together. There she stands
> As if alive . . .

The drape once again enshrouds the duchess; memories of her smiles and murder linger momentarily. At the poem's conclusion, the duke is in his usual persona, the aristocratic collector. He gestures toward another prize.

> Notice Neptune, though,
> Taming a sea-horse, thought a rarity,
> Which Claus of Innsbruck cast in bronze for me.

For me, a sea-horse tamed, a wife murdered and fetishized in a portrait. For me, the perfect inscription for the petrified world of this Renaissance autocrat.

A set of questions came to the forefront of mid-nineteenth-century society, particularly in industrialized regions, but also in Russia. The questions did not go away and never received more than provisional answers. Questions about objects, about the ways objects do and do not represent the people who make them, the people who use them, write about them, or simply own them. Serfs and slaves—property or human beings? What about women? Was the world under threat from an increasing number of manufactured things, things Ruskin excoriated? Ugly, devoid of the animating and beautifying touch of the human worker, and false. False like idols, counterfeit currency, and phonies. False. The word came to carry heavy baggage for those concerned with things of aesthetic privilege.

Walter Benjamin looked back and asked if the collector is a gambler or magician. At the governor's ball in Dostoyevsky's *Possessed*—"the best sustained comic scene of all of literature"—a man mounts the stage. In a squeaky voice he proclaims:

> Shakespeare and Raphael are of greater value than the emancipation of the serfs, than nationalism, than socialism, than the younger generation, than chemistry . . . and perhaps even mankind itself! . . . they represent an achievement of beauty without which I wouldn't be able to go on living.

He starts to sob. Hubbub. A student shouts a shameful truth. The high-minded aesthete on stage used one of his serfs to settle a gambling debt. Next up? A man known to be really crazy. NB Stepan the sobbing, drunk idealist will later admit his life is nothing but a tissue of lies.

If you skip Browning, Dickens, Collins et al., the situation was less tragicomic in Britain. Ruskin and the Pre-Raphaelite Brotherhood decided "a finer optic" could detect the true from the false. They looked at fifteenth-century Flemish painting and Gothic cathedrals. Saw things exfoliating like gorgeous flowers. God-given yet made by human beings, petal by petal. Proust would follow—to Amiens Cathedral to "see the little man," to the Vermeer exhibition to see "the little patch of yellow." And pace Carlo Ginzburg, Sherlock Holmes was a very belated (1887) practitioner of looking "awry"; see Sargeant Cuff, *The Moonstone*, 1868.

J.A. Crowe and G.B. Cavalcaselle operated as art detectives, self-appointed and neo-Ruskinian. They traveled to look at paintings and drawings, took notes about details of facture and form. So armed, in 1871 they published *A History of Painting in North Italy*. It forever changed the field. Crowe and Cavalcaselle exposed the evils of a practice that was ancient—like prostitution, that other evil—but was still flourishing. The evil practice? Copying the paintings of acclaimed artists. Never mind that the practice had long served a number of perfectly legitimate purposes, it had become a crime tantamount to counterfeiting money. They thumped the pulpit of high art and vented and vented some more.

> It was not so much a mania, as the knowledge that value was attached to the greatness of a name [Giorgione] that caused the collectors to christen afresh the colossal impersonations of Pordenone, the semi-sensual figures of Pellegrino, etc. etc. . . . By this device, the public was

> first deceived and, in course of time, connoisseurs learned to confound the real with the unreal, the good with the bad, and one painter with the other.

By the time the passage ends, Giorgione has become a victim of theft and personal assault whose case now rests in the capable hands of two public defenders. Überconnoisseurs, Crowe and Cavalcaselle lay a claim to cleaning up the art market and restoring truth and beauty to the art of Giorgione.

A day, c. 1875. A city in Central Italy. A picture gallery in a seicento palace, recently opened to the public. An upper-class man, heavily bearded, prepossessing, stands in front of a portrait of a woman. He delivers a monologue in which he performs an act of unveiling that leads to an assertion of complete mastery over the portrait. This time the portrait is in a museum in Rome. This time the person giving the monologue has done his own staging, written his own lines.

> As I stood before this mysterious portrait . . . the spirit of the master met mine, and the truth flashed before me. "Giorgione, thou alone," I cried in my excitement, and the picture answered, "even so." Those eyes with their profound and yearning expression, beneath the slightly arched brows, that low straight forehead, that refined mouth, all testify to Giorgione, all are modeled as in the Knight of Malta. The painting has been retouched in the neck and other parts, but, on the whole, is well-preserved. . . . In conception it appears to be a very marvel of art and to Giorgione alone was it given to produce portraits of such astonishing mystic charm, of appealing to our imagination in the highest degree.

Trouble recognizing the portrait? Relegated long ago to maybe School of Licinio or another second-tier artist of the cinquecento. The man romancing the portrait and its presumed maker? Yet another art historian caught in a web of illusions. Trouble identifying him? That's because he's been heavily retouched in recent efforts to furnish art history with a canon of quasi-scientific, respectable founding figures—figures eligible for the professional caste being established in the late nineteenth century. In this instance the outcome is ludicrous. The speaker is the biggest phony in the art world of that era. Even admitted to being a phony in his own writing, even ignored friends who urged him to play it straight, friends like Sir Austen Henry Layard, archeologist, diplomat, and master of the role of Victorian sage.

No more clues. Giovanni Morelli, Prince of Connoisseurs.

Instead of publishing the outcome of his travels and detecting under his own name, he presented them as Johannes Schwarze's translation of the writings of a Russian amateur, Ivan Lermolieff. There are more reflections and deflections. Lermolieff explains he learned the principles of connoisseurship from "an elderly gentleman, apparently an Italian of the better class," met quite by chance in Florence on the steps of the Palazzo Pitti. Is this an early example of the polyglotism endemic to *Kunstgeschichte*? Be that as it may, don't skip Morelli's daggers. At the end of each major correction—each revelation of truth—appears a small printed dagger, one of those "telltale trifles" he claimed to use in his work as an überconnoisseur. Lermolieff-Schwarze-elderly gentleman-dagger-Morelli, a man who constructed a public persona resembling nothing so much as a reflection in a shattered mirror.

Morelli never wrote monographs or "school" histories. The gallery guide, the emended gallery guide, the guide as an undercover report on the operations of major museums is his genre. Each of his "studies" leads readers through a picture gallery—Dresden, Munich, Berlin, the Borghese, the Doria Pamphilj—giving an overview of the history of the collection, commenting on the installation, expounding precepts of connoisseurship, and assessing the museum's attributions. Not at all benign, he challenged the authority of the museums, particularly German museums. He loved exposing their errors.

The supreme example? Until Morelli looked into the shadows at the Dresden Gallery and recognized Giorgione's *Sleeping Venus*, the painting had "been labeled a copy (!) by Sassoferrato (!) of a Titian." Anger laced with heavy sarcasm follows.

> Of what avail is the culture we hear so much of these days, and of what use our annual exhibitions of pictures, or the lectures and countless publications of art, if we are wholly unmoved by one of the most sublime works of art ever produced, unless it be specially brought to our notice?

Wilhelm Bode detested Morelli. He was not alone.

It's not difficult to lift the masks, see contradictions. Those much-reproduced drawings of ears get no mention in Morelli's account of the *Sleeping Venus* (now, by the way, ascribed in part to Titian) and count for little elsewhere in his book. He called Crowe and Cavalcaselle "truffle hunters" for relying on

"A privileged minority is striving to invent a history which can retrospectively justify the role of the ruling classes."

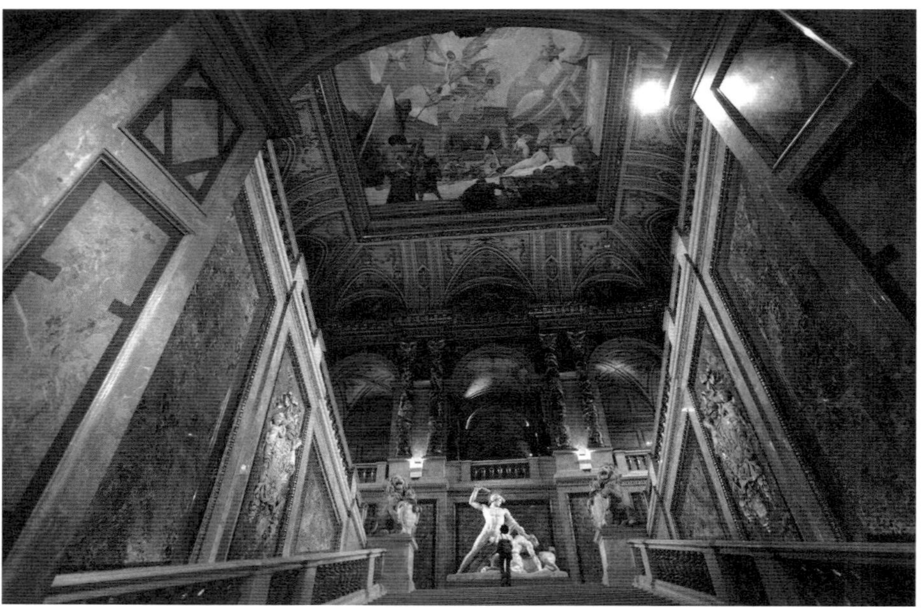

Fig. 3. A woman visiting the Kunsthistorishes Museum, Vienna, May 12, 2003, the day after Benvenuto Cellini's famous golden *Salt-cellar* had been stolen. ATTILA KISBENEDEK / AFP / Getty Images

documents, yet he recognized the *Venus* because of its mention in a sixteenth-century source. Morelli did advocate stocking the mind with a personal "museum without walls" based on direct experience, cross-referenced with documents and current judgments, but materialist he was not. He placed Giorgione at the apex of his hierarchy of Italian artists because no other artist of the Renaissance came so close to fulfilling Morelli's neoclassical, neo-Kantian ideal of truth and beauty.

Contradictions, wiliness? Of course. He played pure Giorgione against carnal Titian. Visited museums assuming he was entering magic mirror mazes. All, in his opinion, were rife with deception and fraud, though meant to be temples of high culture. Repaint? As much an abomination as maquillage on a novitiate. Worldly wise Morelli saw pictures as palimpsests built up through repairs, retouchings, or outright falsification. Important? Extremely. What also requires emphasis is the morality he brings to bear on the task, his posture as an honest outsider, a quixotic knight tilting with illusions and delusions—and this noteworthy contradiction. Morelli served as an advisor to people like Layard collecting Italian art. Money? He made it. Restoration? He engineered it; preferred a type that covered the entire painting with a lustrous unifying surface.

Hardboiled—that's Morelli. He joins idealism with tough infighting against fraud and doesn't mind getting his hands dirty. When he rails against German museums, he sounds like Mike Hammer on the mob. He sells repainted pictures? Mike again. Hitting below the belt, can't resist the pleasurable surge of power. Fallen angels; see *Paradise Lost.*

Given another life, I'd write a biography of Morelli. Suffice it to say here, his knowledge of Great Britain and association with British expats in Northern Italy have been overlooked. His closest friend was Layard. Through Layard he met Browning, then living in Asolo near Venice. Browning and Morelli both venerated Italy as "the very Europe of Europe" and admired one another's work. In "My Last Duchess," *The Ring and the Book*, and other monologue poems, Browning stages an art-filled panorama of Italian history—proto-cubist in its sudden shifts in perspective, and modern in its preoccupation with sex, violence, and crime. Insofar as Morelli is concerned, two more features of Browning's work merit mention: brilliant play with seeming "trifles"; and, in *The Ring and the Book*, a crime story with nine monologues, exposing the shortcomings of official authority in and through a display of competing realities.

Night, c. 1950. A road on the outskirts of New York City. "All I saw was the dame standing there in the glare of the headlights." She's just escaped from a mental institution; a stop at a gas station; easily conned police at a blockade; an accident; the mob gets them, tortures them; she won't tell the secret, Mike doesn't know the secret; she's killed. Mike Hammer discovers the secret and becomes her avenging angel.

Night c. 1860. A road on the outskirts of London. "There, as if it had that moment sprung from out of the earth or dropped from the heaven—stood the figure of a solitary Woman, dressed from head to foot in white garments." She's just escaped from a mental institution; she has a secret she won't tell Walter Hartright, the man on the road, or anyone else; she's killed. Walter Hartright, teacher of drawing, discovers the secret and becomes her avenging angel.

In New York City, in rooms, distant from one another in space, time, and function, men and women scheme to find a cache of drugs worth huge sums of money. They are puppets jerked by strings attached to the supreme puppet master. A pot of gold. Heroin. Without the avenging fallen angel, Mike, nothing close to justice would ever prevail. The dame's death would mean nothing.

The pot of gold in Wilkie Collins's novel is Laura Fairlie, the half sister of the mysterious woman on the road to London. She and her half sister are virtual doubles; one is legitimate, the other illegitimate. Which is the copy of the other? Laura escapes death but is imprisoned in the very institution from which her mentally disturbed half sister had escaped. After the bastard sister is murdered, she is assigned Laura's identity and buried in a grave marked with Laura's name; the estate goes to Laura's ruthless husband. Though eventually rescued from the mental institution, recognized, and married to her avenging angel, Laura's mental health is permanently impaired, her fortune wasted. She is a damaged replica of her former self.

Collins's novel layers doubles upon doubles, lies upon lies; presumed facts turn out to be fictions. Who's to blame? Obtuse and / or corrupt authorities. "The Law," warns Heartright, "is still, in certain inevitable cases, the pre-engaged servant of the long purse." It follows that Collins's novel would unfold in and through a magic mirror maze. One after another their facades crumple—stately homes, lawyers' offices, parish churches, a snug home in a new village, servants, masters. The price of each is exposed; the pot of gold aka Laura Fairlie multiplies, eventually resembling nothing so much as the reflections of that pricey bottle blonde Rita / Elsa at the climax of *The Lady From Shanghai.*

No matter if a person detests money-grubbers, escape from their pollution proves illusory. Laura's uncle and guardian, Mr. Fairlie, cannot abide the thought of a dealer's fingers on a watercolor. The draperies are never opened in his room at Limmeridge, the Fairlie manor; thick, soft carpets muffle sound. Its occupant never leaves; he receives as few visitors as possible. The family lawyer's urgings are to no avail when the scoundrel Perceval Glyde demands a marriage settlement that gives him immediate control of Laura's entire fortune. Fairlie cannot be bothered with financial matters; he accedes to Glyde, setting in motion the chain of events that will nearly destroy his niece and the Fairlie estate. The term *phony* is apt yet again. Sublimated wealth and displays of supposed aristocratic refinement are the lifeblood of this country gentleman. Fairlie spends his days in an easy chair, scrutinizing one or another of the objets d'art he has collected and arranged around himself as if they were as much a fortification as a spectacle of cultured taste. In Hartright's recollection, the room is a glimmering maze of bibelots and curiosities, among which, almost hidden, its rarest treasure, a selfish, vulgar man playing neurasthenic aesthete, is installed, ruler of all he surveys.

> One side . . . was occupied by a long bookcase of some rare inlaid wood . . . the top was adorned with statuettes in marble, arranged at regular distances one from the other. On the opposite side stood two antique cabinets, and between them, and above them, hung a picture of the Virgin and Child, protected by glass, and bearing Raphael's name on the gilt tablet at the bottom of the frame. On my right hand and on my left, as I stood inside the door, were chiffoniers and little stands, loaded with figures in Dresden china, with rare vases, ivory ornaments, and toys and curiosities that sparkled at all points with gold, silver, and precious stones . . . [and finally Fairlie] leaning back, listlessly composed, in a large easy chair, with a reading-easel fastened on one of its arms, and a little table on the other.

The glass over the Raphael and the "gilt tablet" with the master's name mean Fairlie's prize is probably a fake. Hartright's account of their conversation piles on evidence of his utter falseness. He strikes attitudes, confusing cranky narcissism with superior sensibility. To make Hartright feel like an uncouth intruder, he cuts him off: "Pray excuse me. But could you contrive to speak in a lower key? In the wretched state of my nerves. . . . " Fairlie proceeds to treat the new drawing master as a servant, but professes: "There is none of the horrid English barbarity of feeling about the social position of an artist in this house." The self-parody goes on. Fairlie sends Hartright to a window to see if "horrid children" are trespassing on the garden, then points to the cloud-enveloped putti in his sham Raphael: "Quite a model family! . . . Such nice round faces, and such nice soft wings, and—nothing else. No dirty little legs to run about on, and no noisy little lungs to scream with." The Madonna and Christ Child are not mentioned; neither here nor in any other scene in the novel does Fairlie probe aesthetic matters. He is always a poser associated with simulacra, reflections of art rather than art itself. To improve the taste of "the Goths and Vandals" in the region, Fairlie plans to donate photographs of his art treasures to a local institution. "Horrid place!"

Albeit a caricature, the pseudo-aristo Fairlie, wielding a magnifying glass, playing aesthete in his chamber, anticipates Bernard Berenson at the Villa I Tatti. Isolated on a hilltop, safe from the realities of workaday Florence, I Tatti was a theater where Berenson followed the example of other Anglo-American expats, treating himself to a neo-Renaissance rebirth. Jewishness, commercial wheeling and dealing, greed for wealth and status would fade into the background of a scene in which Berenson emerged as a world-famous connoisseur, an intellectual, and, eventually, the personification of the idealized version of the Florentine Renaissance still being sold to gullible tourists. Were he and I Tatti masterpieces of refined taste or well-oiled stagecraft? Take a look behind the scenes. BB could be but was not always honest in his work of finding, attributing, and selling art. Black-and-white photographs often served as the basis for attributions and sales. The getting and spending of money were omnipresent at I Tatti, the center of an international business, but not a topic to broach at cocktails or any other time. The supposed intellectual never published anything substantive after the early essays, written with Mary Berenson's help and never revised. The neo-Renaissance garden and the villa? The work c. 1910 of Geoffrey Scott and Cecil Pinsent, English champions of a chastened version of Renaissance culture (think Ospedale degli Innocenti, Fra Angelico) and enemies of everything vulgar (a lot of Italy—smells, beggars, Papists, crucifixes that kiss criminals—could not be recommended). However clichéd and backward-looking, it worked, this configuration of the connoisseur and the faux villa he rarely left. A fiction of art history framed on art for art's sake doctrines, it never could and never would conceal the realities out there in the larger world; see Gilbert Osmond in *The Portrait of a Lady* (1881).

Ezra Pound and Adrian Stokes read *Il Fuoco* (1900) as a guide to Venice and something more—an adaptation of the Browning-Morelli scripting of the predicament of the mirror maze when erotic passion and longing for possession transform art of the past into mirages, hovering near yet eluding a caressing hand or imploring look. Fair to say this is the predicament of the art historian / the writer on art then and now? That they therefore engage not merely in the study of the invented category Art but a category of Fiction as well? If so, attempts to cast the enterprise into legalistic or quasi-scientific "argument" will make it fall short of meeting the largest challenges the always and already volatile category poses. One point is clear. After Browning, after Pater and Nietzsche, some cognoscenti of the late nineteenth century would prefer the mirror maze to the museum. Art ceases being an inanimate artifact to dissect and classify when positioned amid mirrors, becomes intangible, not inanimate, gains allure, proves vision to be an unruly sense, and triggers transformative experience.

Not everyone is equipped for specular spectacle. Lucy Honeychurch in *Room with a View* cannot even recognize the Giotto frescoes in Santa Croce, the ones Mr. Ruskin praised. At the other end of the spectrum are the epiphanies in a species of semi-autobiographical fiction in which the Browning-Morelli dramatic monologue, mise-en-scène centered upon an artwork, is crossed with the novel. Proust's *In Search of Lost Time* (1913–27) is one masterpiece in this literature, another is Rilke's *The Notebooks of Malte Laurids Brigge* (1910). In *Il Fuoco*, Gabriele D'Annunzio portrays himself as Stelio, a patriotic poet who admires Wagner and Nietzsche and has as his companion an aging actress, Eleonora Duse / Foscarina. They are in Venice, for Stelio a place of incomparable splendor; his responses and musings are regarded as the most ardent glorification ever written for a city. It is not at all simplistic, not suitable for visitors on a holiday art junket. Melancholia is all pervasive. Beautiful Venice is a place of bygone glory and alienation, taken over, first, by Napoleon's troops and their Austro-Hungarian successors, later by tourists. How to find a way to shoot a bullet at the mirrors, burst forth heroic, reclaim this masterpiece for himself and the citizens of Venice? A public address in sitù in the presence of Venetian masterpieces. Call it an interpretation of the Venetian school of art. Promethean theft is not farfetched.

Night, c. 1900. Venice. A darkened room. The sala del gran consiglio in the Doge's Palace. Every surface boasts stupendous art. Gods and goddesses intermingle with human beings. D'Annunzio / Stelio, "the maker of images," lectures. He makes an "unrealization" of self through the interplay of idea and impersonation learned from Nietzsche. He becomes Dionysos, the god of masks and theater, and the suspension or reality into illusions and delusions where other identities and energies can be experienced.

At the beginning of his speech, the audience of Venetian citizens feels "ill at ease" with the "immense traces of past glory" surrounding them. This changes. The Renaissance "murdered" innocence—revealed "the boundless possibilities of life" and a "dream of endless pleasure." D'Annunzio / Steeli / Dionysos transforms the room into an intoxicating stream, a regenerating force seen and felt and heard.

> The strength that swelled the muscles of gods, kings, and heroes, the beauty of the naked goddesses, queens, and harlots painted on the great vault and high walls, flowed like visible music.

Next morning, "cruel awakening," faded illusions, ashes mixed with bits and pieces of the body called Innocence. A reflection of the virgin Ursula glimpsed in paintings in a museum Napoleon had created from S. Maria della Carità.

Art history? Noirish fiction, generally set in Europe, the U.K., and the U.S. in art galleries, museums, homes of the wealthy and / or nouveau riche, posh universities; a connoisseur or other art expert, well-mannered, smart dresser, heads a cast of characters apt to include collectors, art dealers, forgers, museum officials, prelates of churches with supposed treasures, penurious aristocrats with supposed treasures—any of these can be unscrupulous, demented, or a phony (the forger in Gaddis's novel *The Recognitions* is an honest forger); plots vary little: a work of art morphs into an object of irresistible allure, often fake, hidden, or lost and known only at secondhand through photographs, copies, legends, fantasies; search for the fetishized object leads to libraries, archives, travel to art capitals and collections throughout the world and is wont to precipitate deception, danger, and even death; though not unknown, sex scenes are infrequent, possibly because the "art" absorbs most, if not all, available erotic energy. The outcome is rarely happy.

In Lieu of Notes, Working Postmortem

"I begin with the desire to speak with the dead." Greenblatt / Ulysses / Aeneas did say that. I knew he would as soon as I saw the picture on the book's cover. Don't recognize the book? *Renaissance Self-Fashioning* (1980). Holbein's *Ambassadors* you have seen many times. Signed, dated, phantasmagoric in the way peculiar to the hyperreal and fashion photography. Satin, fur, bling galore, objects of conspicuous consumption thinly disguised as instruments of learning. Room 4, National Gallery, London.

At the right of the room, visitors cluster, genuflect. Obeisance to the two men, life-size and lifelike, and endowed with the bearing of those born to command? More likely looking for the ghost. It appears only and when the viewer steps far right, bends, and looks back at the picture at an oblique angle.

It's a trick, anamorphosis. There's no "phallic ghost," no ghost at all, just a large, ashen blotch low down, at the front of the picture. Virginia Woolf conceived the idea of "some continuous stream, not solely of human thought, but of the ship, the night, etc., all flowing together: intersected by the arrival of bright moths."

Too accepting of random events, too dependent on atmospheric unity? Too soft, yielding, and "feminine"? Lacan, Greenblatt, Lyotard et al. preferred to trace the outlines of a skull in the ashen blotch. No blood. On this point they are correct. The skull in the foreground—this predecessor of the corpse in the library—is as clean as the murder victim in the upper crust sort of detective fiction in which crime is a charade played to while away a rainy afternoon in a country house. Symbol, death's head, still belies the violence and gore foregrounded from ancient times forward in the representation of crime or of its punishment. Ulysses "batters" the brains of the Suitors; the ground "seethes" with their blood. The modern crime novel is considered a Calvinist genre, see *Confessions of a Justified Sinner* (1824) and, for comparison, go back to *Macbeth* (1603–7).

> Yet who would have thought the old man to have had so much blood in him?
>
> —*Macbeth*, 5.1

There is a place in the National Gallery masterpiece where pooling blood might once have marked corporeal presence. This preordained, if not consecrated place contains a dark shadow. Protestant surrogate for sacrificial blood? Reminder of the necessity of divine grace to win salvation from the "utter depravity" into which humanity is born? Whatever you think of the theology (and its morphing into a symbolic order maintained in and through "the gaze"), this is a noir scene. The first, and already worthy of Raymond Chandler.

The skull occupies the here and now, or so its shadow implies, but not the here and now of the picture's aristos. The skull conjures a space-time continuum that jams rectilinear systems. The shadow is angled as if cast by an intruder, and the shadowed intruder is always and already a burglar and / or rapist and / or murderer. Punctum is the term Barthes gave to this place where a picture comes alive and turns violent: "It points to the spectator . . . slaps you in the face, it hurts you badly, to the point even of killing you."

Who or what is in control here? The punctum / skull or "the Ambassadors" or the spectator? The Queen or the mirror on the wall? The portrait or Dorian Grey? The monster or Victor Frankenstein? "The symbolic order"?

> Now the blues grabbed my both legs Sunday morning
> A chair near throwed me down
>
> —"Blues Trip Me This Morning"

Slaves in Mississippi had firsthand knowledge of the way "the symbolic order" can so easily twist into "utter depravity." The sound of the flattened notes shows Lacan's theory to be cold, dry, and academic—as sterile as Edward Casaubon's *Key to All Mythologies* (unfinished, of course). People with hearts and souls under assault should stay clear of the phallic ghost. He's a fugitive from surrealist psychodrama.

Funny, Greenblatt's first priority was speaking with the dead, as if they were waiting for him. What about the more loquacious members of the family, the undead? Count Dracula? He has "long" conversations with his guest, British solicitor Jonathan Harker. The Count warms "wonderfully" to the subject of Transylvanian history, speaking of past events, "especially of battles," as if "he had been present." Fascination stiffens into fear when Harker realizes he is a prisoner in the castle "on the very edge of a terrific precipice" in the Carpathian Mountains. Tension builds. The Count seems more and more bizarre. But Harker discovers the truth about his host with "peculiarly sharp white teeth" only after a catastrophe in the "kingdom of the eye." At a window high up in the castle Harker sees an "expanse, bathed in soft yellow moonlight," "distant hills" melt into the light, shadows in valleys and gorges of "velvety blackness." Magisterial vision gives him a reprieve from "horrible imaginings." A slight turn of Harker's head, an oblique look, everything changes. He sees the vampire.

> As I leaned from the window my eye was caught by something moving a story below me, and somewhat to the left . . . at first I could not believe my eyes. I thought it was some trick of the moonlight, some weird effect of shadow, but I kept looking, and it could be no delusion. I saw the fingers and toes grasp the corners of the stones . . . and thus using every projection and inequality move downwards with considerable speed.
>
> What manner of man is this, or what manner of creature, is it in the semblance of a man? I feel the dread of this horrible place overpower me. I am in fear, awful fear . . . I am encompassed about with terrors that I dare not think of.
>
> This is the nineteenth century brought up-to-date with a vengeance. And yes, unless my senses deceive me, the old centuries had, and have, powers of their own that mere "modernity" cannot kill.

This passage pivots on a fatal conflict. "Modernity," which has brought the nineteenth century "up-to-date with a vengeance," is forced to confront an anathema it cannot banish, the vampire and belief in supernatural forces. They also operate with "vengeance." An earlier scene turns on a related polarity: an immutable realm of wealth and aristocratic possessions versus the same realm when it succumbs, as it must, to time and change. Harker recalls that at Hampton Court (not incidentally the palace of Henry VIII, another monster remembered for sacrificing women to a need for perpetual life / a royal lineage) the furnishings are "worn and frayed and moth-eaten." But through some miracle or curse, time has spared or not entered Dracula's fortress. It abounds in "extraordinary evidence of wealth"; Harker is served dinner on a "beautifully wrought" gold table-service; though "centuries-old," he notes, the furnishings have "the most beautiful fabrics," all "in excellent order." Umberto Eco's concept of the "hyperreal" in period rooms in museums or in sites like Colonial Williamsburg is relevant here. There is as well consanguinity in the figures of the Count and the collector Mr. Fairlie. Fairlie lives off the "blood" of an innocent victim, is consubstantial with treasures arrayed in a petrified world, sealed from sunlight as if a pharaoh's tomb.

Add the chess-playing automaton in Walter Benjamin's allegory of history to this list of affronts to reason: the skull that pops into view, neither three-dimensional or two-dimensional, as if it were a ghost haunting room 4 of the National Gallery; the long afterlife of the blood of murder victims; in Dracula's castle, objects and creatures that mock the laws of time and change, collapse the boundary between dead things and living beings. This boundary is first and foremost in Benjamin's account of the automaton. At the start we are shown defeated challengers to its powers, at the end the grotesque figure pulling strings.

> It is well-known that an automaton once existed, which was so constructed that it could counter any move of a chess-player with a counter-move, and thereby assure itself of victory in the match. A puppet in Turkish attire, water-pipe in mouth, sat before the chessboard, which rested on a broad table. Through a system of mirrors, the illusion was created that this table was transparent from all sides. In truth, a hunchbacked dwarf who was a master chess-player sat inside, controlling the hands of the puppet with strings.

In Benjamin's allegory the hunchbacked dwarf represents theology, the puppet "historical materialism." (For more on automata, puppets, and allegory, treat yourself to Kenneth Gross, *Puppet: An Essay on Uncanny Life*.) As allegories should, this one has provoked extensive commentary, though Benjamin scholars have not considered the many differences between the real automaton and the one summoned for the purposes of his allegory. From 1770 to 1854, when destroyed by fire, the automaton, also called the Turk, was displayed in Europe and North America and played many experts. Benjamin's claims to the contrary, the Turk was defeated from time to time; there were no mirrors, no "hunchbacked dwarf" hidden under the table. Instead various chess masters, none said to have been hunchbacked or exceptionally short, crawled into a chamber within the base of the table to lend their skill to foiling challengers, Benjamin Franklin among them. There was as well "a presenter," and in some cases a second table was added as a safeguard against tricks in the automaton table. The tricks? A system of magnets linked the pieces atop the board to pieces hidden under it. A numerical code in the presenter's control provided a fallback if a sceptic like Napoleon demanded a second table.

During the performance the automaton produced a cat's cradle of moves and counter moves, each blurring the distinction between mechanical contraption and human player. As the game proceeded on the checkered board, the chess pieces were repositioned in response to the previous move. A true battle of skill and a miniature simulacrum of warfare ensued. The more difficult the game, the more the pieces became extensions of the players, and, vice versa, the players grew increasingly absorbed into the rooks, knights, and other chess pieces. Then, too, the figure of the Turk is half-human, half-thing. It is a puppet, also a disguise and deception.

The chess-playing machine used human intelligence to reveal the limits of human intelligence, so much so it baffled the chess-playing elite for decades. A product of Enlightenment proclivity for invention, it is equally a marker of the dawning of a century when things were manufactured, admired, and consumed in ever larger quantities. The logic of chess and the logic of invention are demonstrated in the Turk. So too is the restricted purview of human reason, the psyche's susceptibility to things. In Stoker's novel a vampire forces men trained in science and law to resort to crucifixes, garlic, and silver stakes, all primitive weapons against the supernatural. The Turk inflicted a similar wound. A dead thing animated a scene, fed off its human audience. Works of art that endure for centuries, fascinate, lead to human folly and crime? Pater's "vampire," the *Mona Lisa*?

> She is older than the rocks among which she sits;
> Like the vampire,
> She has been dead many times,
> And learned the secrets of the grave.

Pater is more original and noir than generally conceded. Not at all hard to fast forward from his undead *Mona Lisa* to a later assault on squeamish / schoolmarmish sensibilities.

> I inhaled some of my drink. "It's not that kind of story," I said. "It's not lithe and clever. It's just dark and full of blood."
>
> —Raymond Chandler, *Farewell My Lovely* (1940)

Noir L.A. is an "underbelly" with grotesques. Ever see Moose Malloy, "alligator shoes with white explosions on the toes," "about as inconspicuous as a tarantula on a slice of angel food"? Is that Moose standing on the left in the picture in room 4?

Humanism, civic and/or hobby horse of academe, does not admit the grotesque except in dados, and then preferably of the all'antica sort. Benjamin (is he prefigured at the right in that picture?) cautions against this hierarchy:

> Once the ethical subject has been absorbed in the individual, then no rigorism—not even Kantian rigorism—can save it and preserve its masculine profile. Its heart is lost in the beautiful soul. And the radius of action—no, only the radius of the culture—of the thus perfected beautiful individual is what describes the circle of the "symbolic."

Defense of the Lacanian subject notwithstanding, Žižek is astute to call attention to the significance of noir in assessing models of historical interpretation. In noir, Žižek observes, the clue is "indicated by a whole series of adjectives: 'odd–queer–wrong–strange–fishy–rummy–doesn't make sense,' not to mention stronger expressions like 'eerie,' 'unreal,' 'unbelievable,' up to the categorical 'impossible.'" It is indispensable to the analyst of the dream work as well as to the detective investigating a crime. Yet more significant is the awareness here of omnipresent danger in a sphere of confused signs. If the picture in room 4 is the opera princeps of noir, "The Purloined Letter" of 1844—a notably smoke-filled story—is a sequel that has everything to do with correcting the high–church-apostolic succession narratives of origins currently being constructed for art history; see also Wind's complaint in *Art and Anarchy* that rational analysis is causing art to lose "its sting."

In an entry to his 1893 journal, Gide confesses to "rather" liking works of art that double upon themselves, like "The Murder of Gonzago," the play "to prick the conscience of the King" in *Hamlet*, and like the painting on the easel seen from the back in *Las Meñinas*. But none of these "is altogether exact."

> What would explain better what I'd wanted to do in my *Cahiers*, in *Narcise* and *La Tentative*, would be a comparison with the device from heraldry that involves putting a second representation of the original shield en abyme within it.
>
> The second shield, with its own bearings, can enhance the meaning and structure of the first shield. It can also modify and complicate that shield. The same is true of "The Murder of Gonzago" and the painting in *Las Meñinas*. Each work of art reflects the other, frames and reframes it.

"You can't set out to trap a likeness. It comes on its own or it doesn't. It moves in sideways."

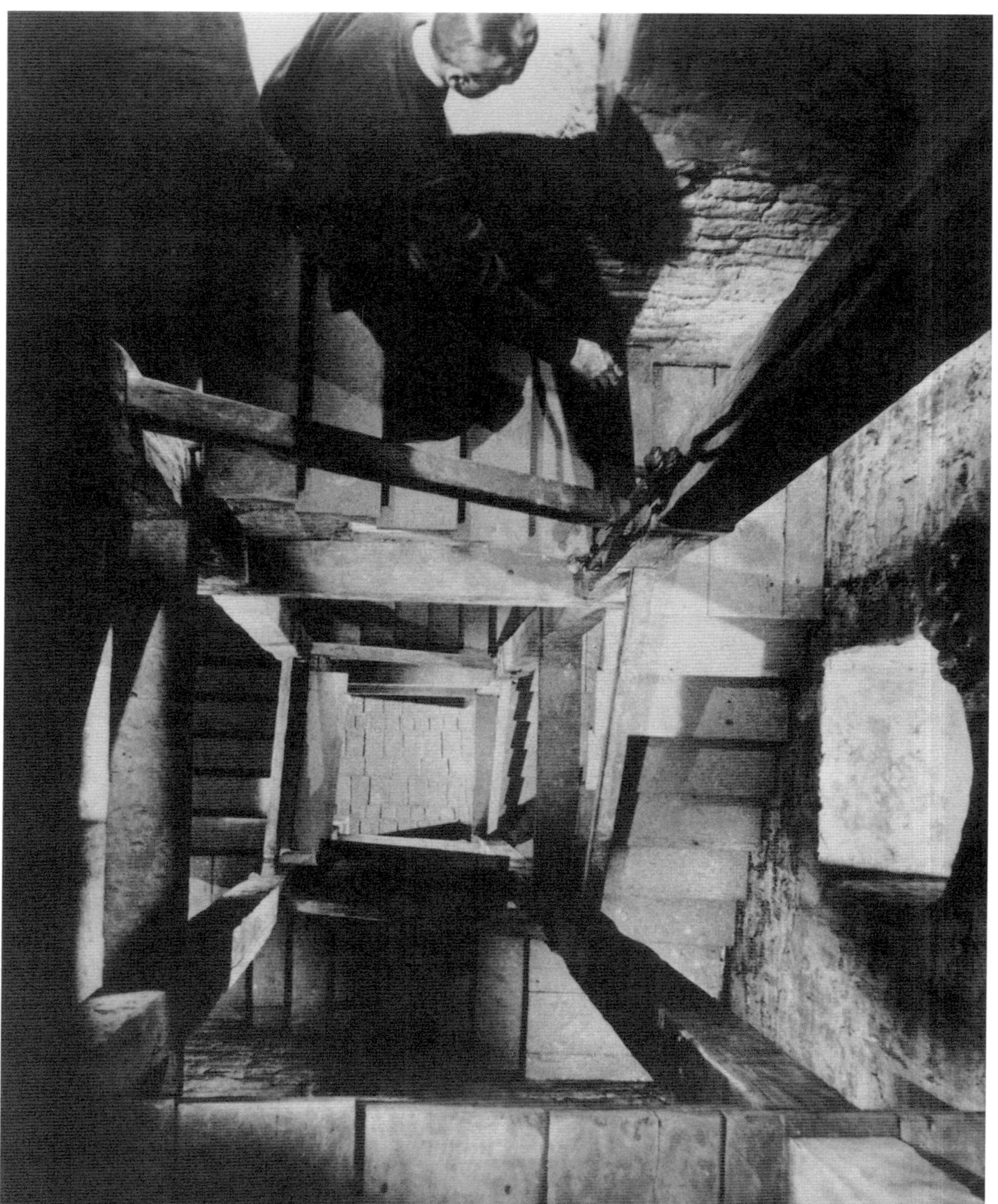

Fig. 4. Film still of James Stewart in Alfred Hitchcock's *Vertigo*, 1958, 128 mins. Paramount Pictures/Archive Photos/Getty Images

At Decon's height, "mise en abyme" meant an intricate sequence of internal reflections that destabilize meaning, defer, and multiply it. The result? The detecting of previously unimaginable networks of intertextual references. Think text as puppet with hundreds of strings, many invisible to ordinary sight. Or liken the Decon critic to a vampire feeding off the corpse of world literature. Not for the fainthearted. Lucien Dällenbach comments that mise en abyme usually harbors shadows, is hostile to rectilinear structures of any type, and, more often than not, induces metaphysical vertigo. Peer into the reflections suddenly open to view. They appear unending and enveloping. Try to find an exit or solid truth. Stand alongside Orson / Mike in the Magic Mirror Maze. The illusion of depth and mystery is certain to appear. It lends glamour and excitement, occasionally a sense of transgression and danger, to the Decon critic's otherwise pedantic task of explicating a work of literature or art. Is the Maze still art history's preferred mise-en-scène?

Mission San Juan Bautista, c. 1958. Sixty miles south of San Francisco. In a reenactment of an earlier event, acrophobic detective James Stewart / Scottie forces Kim Novak / Madeleine / Carlotta / Judy to climb the stairs to the top of a bell tower. He learns the truth. The real Madeleine did not jump from the tower. With the help of Kim Novak aka Madeleine / Carlotta / Judy, Madeleine's husband had killed his wife, then faked her suicide. A shadow—a nun walking past the tower—catches Judy's eye. She falls to her death. Did the undead Madeleine lure Judy into the abyss? Consult *Vertigo* (1958), based on Boileau-Narcejac's novel, *D'entre les morts* (1954).

Those seductive lectures in the darkness of classrooms-cum-theaters? They present art's history in the manner of a film shot with dolly zooms, the source of "the vertigo effect" in Hitchcock's masterpiece. The object of the gaze remains constant in size in this trick of cinema, while the camera executes a continuous change in the angle of vision, creating distortions in perspective. Zoom in, zoom out and keep track of the distortions visited upon the works of art being discussed. Show a detail many times larger than it is in reality. Offer images scanned from a reproduction in a book, a reproduction often Photoshopped before being translated into the CMYK system and inked onto paper, usually though not always glazed and available in myriad textures and types of white. That slight sparkle in all the projected pictures? From the coated surface of the screen. End with a soft fade of a cathedral or one of Rembrandt's late self-portraits. For the audience the mise-en-scène / mise en abyme keeps going. The dark, truncated figure at the podium recalls the chess-playing Turk. Who or what maneuvers the pictures, animates the strange figure wielding a laser light, voice resounding through a lavalier mike? Nothing innocent, nothing straightforward in this familiar scene of erudite pedagogy. Fiction or nonfiction? The categories merge and as they do yield an important truth. By training and practice an art historian is always errant, always in a state of vertigo.

Expert Witnesses

Part One. Securing the Scene

* All quotations accompanying illustrations are from John Berger, *Ways of Seeing* (London: BBC and Penguin Books, 1972).

Banville, John. *Athena.* London: Martin Secker and Warburg, 1995.

———. *The Book of Evidence.* London: Martin Secker and Warburg, 1989.

———. *Ghosts.* London: Martin Secker and Warburg, 1993.

Berger, John. *Ways of Seeing.* London: BBC and Penguin Books, 1972.

Brown, Dan. *The Da Vinci Code.* New York: Doubleday, 2003.

Browning, Robert. "My Last Duchess." 1842.

———. "The Ring and the Book." 1868–69.

Cavalcaselle, Giovanni Battista, and Joseph Archer Crowe. *A History of Painting in North Italy.* London, 1871.

Collins, Wilkie. *The Woman in White.* London, 1860.

———. *The Moonstone.* London, 1868.

D'Annunzio, Gabriele. *Il Fuoco.* Milan, 1900.

Dostoyevsky, Fyodor. *The Possessed (The Devils).* 1872.

Frayn, Michael. *Headlong.* New York: Metropolitan Books, 1999.

Gaddis, William. *The Recognitions.* New York: Harcourt, Brace, 1955.

Ginzburg, Carlo. "Morelli, Freud, and Sherlock Holmes: Clues and Scientific Method." *History Workshop Journal* 90, no. 9 (1980).

James, Henry, *The Portrait of a Lady.* Boston and London, 1881.

Lowry, Elizabeth. *The Bellini Madonna.* London: Quercus, 2008.

Morelli, Giovanni (Johannes Schwarze and Ivan Lermolieff). *Die Werke italienischer Meister in den Galerien von München, Dresden und Berlin: Ein kritischer Versuch [von Ivan Lermolieff, aus dem Russischen übersetzt von Dr Johannes Schwarze].* Leipzig, 1880.

———. *Die Galerien Borghese und Doria Pamfilj in Rom.* Leipzig, 1890.

Pears, Iain. *The Titian Committee; An Art History Mystery*. London: Gollancz, 1991.

———. *The Raphael Affair; An Art History Mystery*. London: Gollancz, 1990.

Prada, Juan Manuel de. *La Tempestad (The Tempest)*. Barcelona: Planeta, 1997.

Rilke, Rainer Maria. *The Notebooks of Malte Laurids Brigge*. Champaign, Ill.: Dalkey Archive Press, 2008. Originally published as *Die Aufzungnungen des Malte Laurids Brigge* (Munich, 1910).

Spillaine, Mickey. *Kiss Me, Deadly*. New York: E. P. Dutton, 1952.

———. *One Lonely Night*. New York: E. P. Dutton, 1951.

Theocritus. *Idylls*. 1st half of 3rd century BCE.

Virgil. *Eclogues*. 37 BCE.

Welles, Orson, dir. *The Lady From Shanghai*. Film. France 1947, US 1948.

Part Two. In Lieu of Notes, Working Postmortem

Barthes, Roland. *Camera Lucida: Reflections on Photography*. New York: Hill and Wang, 1981. Originally published as *La Chambre claire: note sur la photographie* (Paris: Gallimard, 1980).

Benjamin, Walter. "On the Concept of History." *In Selected Writings* 4. Ed. Howard Eiland and Michael Jennings. Trans. Rodney Livingstone et al. Cambridge: Harvard University Press, 2003. Originally published posthumously as *Geschichtsphilosophische Reflexionen* Los Angeles: Institut für Sozialforschung, 1942).

———. *The Origin of German Tragic Drama*. London: Verso, 1998. Originally published as *Ursprung des deutschen Trauerspiels* (Berlin: Rowohlt, 1928).

Chandler, Raymond. *Farewell My Lovely*. New York: Alfred A. Knopf, 1940.

Dällenbach, Lucien. *The Mirror in the Text*. Chicago: University of Chicago Press, 1989. Originally published as *Le récit speculaire* (Paris: Seuil, 1977).

Eliot, George. *Middlemarch*. 1871.

Eco, Umberto. *Travels in Hyperreality*. New York: Harcourt Brace Jovanovich, 1986. Originally published in *Sette anni di desiderio* (Milan: Fabbri-Bompiani Sonzogno, 1983).

Foister, Susan et al. *Making & Meaning: Holbein's "Ambassadors."* London: National Gallery Publications, 1997.

Gide, André. *Journals: 1889–1913*. Paris: Editions Gallimard, 1939. First published in English (New York: Alfred A. Knopf, 1947).

Greenblatt, Stephen. *Renaissance Self-Fashioning*. Chicago: University of Chicago Press, 1980.

Gross, Kenneth. *Puppet: An Essay on Uncanny Life*. Chicago: University of Chicago Press, 2011.

Hervey, Mary F. S. *Holbein's "Ambassadors": The Picture and the Men*. London, 1900.

Hitchcock, Alfred, dir. *Vertigo*. Film. 1958.

Hogg, James. *The Private Memoirs and Confessions of a Justified Sinner*. London, 1824.

Lacan, Jacques. *Seminar XI*. Given and recorded in Paris, École normale supérieure, 1964. Published in English as *The Four Fundamental Concepts of Psychoanalysis* (New York: Norton, 1978).

Lyotard, Jean-François. *Leçons sur l'analytique du sublime.* Paris: Editions Galilée, 1991. Published in English as *Lessons on the Analytic of the Sublime: Kant's Critique of Judgment* (Stanford: Stanford University Press, 1994).

———. *La Condition postmoderne: rapport sur le savoir.* Paris: Les Editions de Minuit. Published in English as *The Postmodern Condition: A Report on Knowledge* (Minneapolis: University of Minnesota Press, 1984).

McClennan, Tommy. "Blues Trip Me This Morning." Recording. c. 1939.

Pater, Walter. *The Renaissance: Studies in Art and Poetry.* 1873.

Poe, Edgar Allan. "The Purloined Letter." *The Gift.* 1844.

Stoker, Bram. *Dracula.* 1897.

Wind, Edgar. *Art and Anarchy.* London: Faber and Faber, 1963.

Woolf, Virginia. *The Letters of Virginia Woolf.* London: Hogarth, 1975–80.

Žižek, Slavoj. *Interrogating the Real.* London: Continuum, 2005.

———. *Looking Awry.* Cambridge, Mass.: MIT Press, 1991.

PART TWO

NOT WHO YOU THINK I AM

Face to Face with Fiction: Portraiture and the Biographical Tradition

Caroline Vout

> I, too, am drawn to the avid contemplation of Roman and all other portraits because they give life to historical persons, freed from the bonds of mortality.
>
> —Richard Brilliant, *Portraiture* (1991), 7

Face to Face with Nero

What kind of life does a portrait give? I begin my answer with a portrait of Nero (fig. 1; Roman Emperor, 54 to 68 CE)[1] and the words of the classical art historian Diana Kleiner:

> Although Nero never reached the age where he could be depicted as old, however, the aging process is incorporated in his portraiture. He is portrayed as the bland Julio-Claudian prince in 51, as a more mature youth in 54 and 55, and as a corpulent and debauched megalomaniac between 59 and 68. The vicissitudes of Nero's life are, therefore, mirrored in his portraits. . . . In fact, in the Worcester portrait Nero's eyes seem smaller, almost entirely lost in the mountain of flesh of his cheeks and chin.[2]

Kleiner is not unique in seeing a life devoted to excess. More recently, her pupil Eric Varner has taken a more artist-based approach, which reframes rather than revises:

> The heavier, emphatically modeled facial features of Nero's final two portrait types are clearly modeled on the images of Hellenistic rulers, especially Ptolemaic portraits. These fleshier faced images are intended to communicate the concept of τρυφή or *luxuria* (royal luxury and beneficence).[3]

These reactions are understandable. With Nero's enforced suicide in 68 CE came the end of the Julio-Claudian dynasty and—after a year of civil war—an emperor,

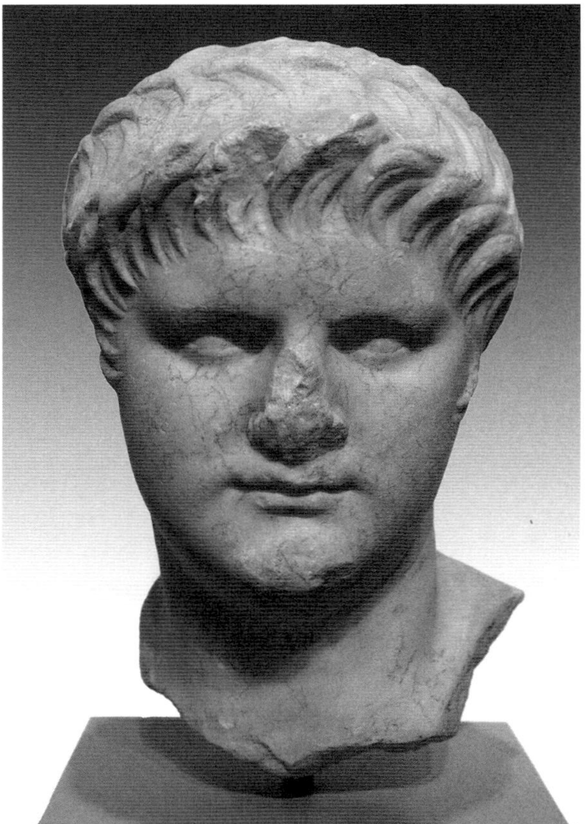

Fig. 1. Portrait of the Emperor Nero, 64–68 CE. Marble, 14 15/16 × 8 13/16 × 9 1/2 in. (38 × 22.4 × 24.1 cm). Worcester Art Museum, Worcester, Massachusetts, Museum purchase, inv. 1915.23

Vespasian, who aimed at "keeping it in *his* family." Laying the foundations for a new dynasty necessitated continuity and rupture. Nero bore the brunt of rupture, enabling the first Julio-Claudian ruler, Augustus, adopted son of Julius Caesar, to live on as a role model for continuity. Nero's portraits were cast down or recut, the grounds of his Golden House given back to the people, and rumors about his reign ratified forever. Almost all of the extant literature about Nero is posthumous: he is famed for sleeping with, and murdering, his mother; playing the lyre while Rome burned; lighting his gardens with blazing Christians; and for being overly self-conscious about his image.[4] "What an artist the world is losing!" are his last words, according to second-century biographer, Suetonius.[5]

Individuals versus Artworks

I am not the first to draw attention to how, as Harry Berger puts it, "the art-historian's ekphrasis is influenced and indeed overdetermined by the archive";[6] in other words, how our inherited knowledge about a person's life and loves dictates a response to his portrait, thus short-circuiting the need for visual analysis. Kleiner's ekphrasis makes Nero's portraits an index of the mind and soul of the individual (negative), while Varner's is indicative of how he was deliberately portrayed (positive). Yet each lets the literature lead. Image and archive were massaging each other in antiquity already: those who attacked Nero's portraits aimed for the eyes, nose, and lips, as though depriving a real man of his senses.[7]

All of this duly recognizes the portrait as a stand-in for the person—as Richard Brilliant says, an "oscillation between object and human subject" that "gives portraits their extraordinary grasp on our imagination."[8] But it risks reducing them to the status of pale imitation, rather than according them discursive power in their own right. It also risks turning their subjects from "the centre of attention" to passive victims. Even if we do as Berger asks, and take account of the sitters' investment in creating the "fiction of objectivity," the denouement comes once the last brushstroke or chisel-mark has been made, when there is a finished product to represent, then and for eternity. I have written elsewhere about how this conclusion elides the effect that an emperor's damaged or recut images might have when compared not to flesh but to other images, or indeed to their prior perfection.[9] Some of these remained on public display, less individuals than artworks.

This reassertion of portrait as artwork enables us to sidestep the vexing question of *mimesis* or faithfulness. "I cannot see the man for his likeness," claimed English artist and art critic Roger Fry of one of John Singer Sargent's contemporary portraits.[10] It is a sentiment that might equally be applied to the posturing Nero; and one that takes on particular force, given the impossibility, now and in antiquity, of knowing what the emperor looked like. Even when alive, he was inaccessible to all but a fraction of his subjects; subjects in Asia Minor, for example, might have nothing to compare his portraits to but a host of other images. This lack of a flesh-and-blood reference point meant that these portraits did not stand in for Nero so much as bring a new emperor into being. Although there must have been official models of some kind in circulation, most extant images were not imposed from on high but sponsored by local communities: in one sense, they were copies, but in another sense, each Nero they body forth assumes a life of its own to threaten the real ruler's standing. Take, for example, the rumors of maternal incest that beset his reign: how far were these prompted by early coinage, which showed busts of him and his mother eyeball to eyeball (fig. 2), cheek to cheek?[11] After his death in 68 CE, an imposter sprung up in Greece, terrifying the locals with his "facial similarity"—whether to Nero or to his portraiture, Tacitus leaves open.[12]

In *Power and Eroticism in Imperial Rome*,[13] I took a number of sculptures (most importantly, perhaps, the portraits of Antinous, the young male lover of Hadrian, Roman emperor from 117 to 138 CE) to explore how their visual details and viewing contexts fired imaginations and stimulated fantasies to enhance imperial charisma. Here I want to think harder about the nature of these

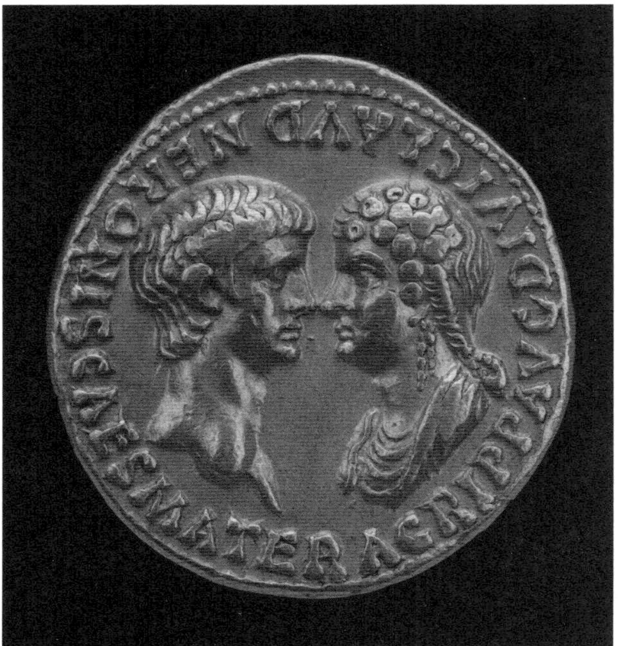

Fig. 2. Aureus showing Nero and his mother, Agrippina the Younger, 54 CE. Gold. British Museum, London, 1864, 1128.252

fantasies: moving beyond offering suggestive "readings" of the Delphi Antinous or Nero's Worcester portrait to explore the ancient visual environment that gave shape and pace to these stories. To quote novelist A. S. Byatt, "Portraits in words and portraits in paint are opposites, rather than metaphors of each other. . . . A painting exists outside time and records the time of its making. . . . Even the description in visual language of a face or body may depend on being unseen for its force."[14] If verbal and visual portraits are opposites, where does that leave ekphrasis?

Childhood Innocence

In the antiquities museum in Parma, Italy, is a marble portrait of a boy, with "round fleshy face and even features,"[15] found in the basilica at Velleia in 1761 (fig. 3).[16] He wears the *toga praetexta* and disk, or bulla, which show that he is freeborn and prepubescent, yet he already performs his masculinity.[17] Originally, his arms would have been outstretched, one of them perhaps holding a scroll. He would have stood in a niche, next to a series of male and female figures, the majority of them swathed in fabric (fig. 4). It is the similarity of their posturing that secures his place as a mini-adult.

What kinds of stories does this statue invite, not of its subject's past but its subject's present and future? The answer lies to a large extent in the identities of its sculpted companions, all members of the imperial family, from Augustus to Nerva (emperor briefly from 96–98 CE), and in the overlaps with portraits beyond the basilica, which turn them from individuals into recognizable types. The boy's features are not unique among surviving statuary but are shared by two other

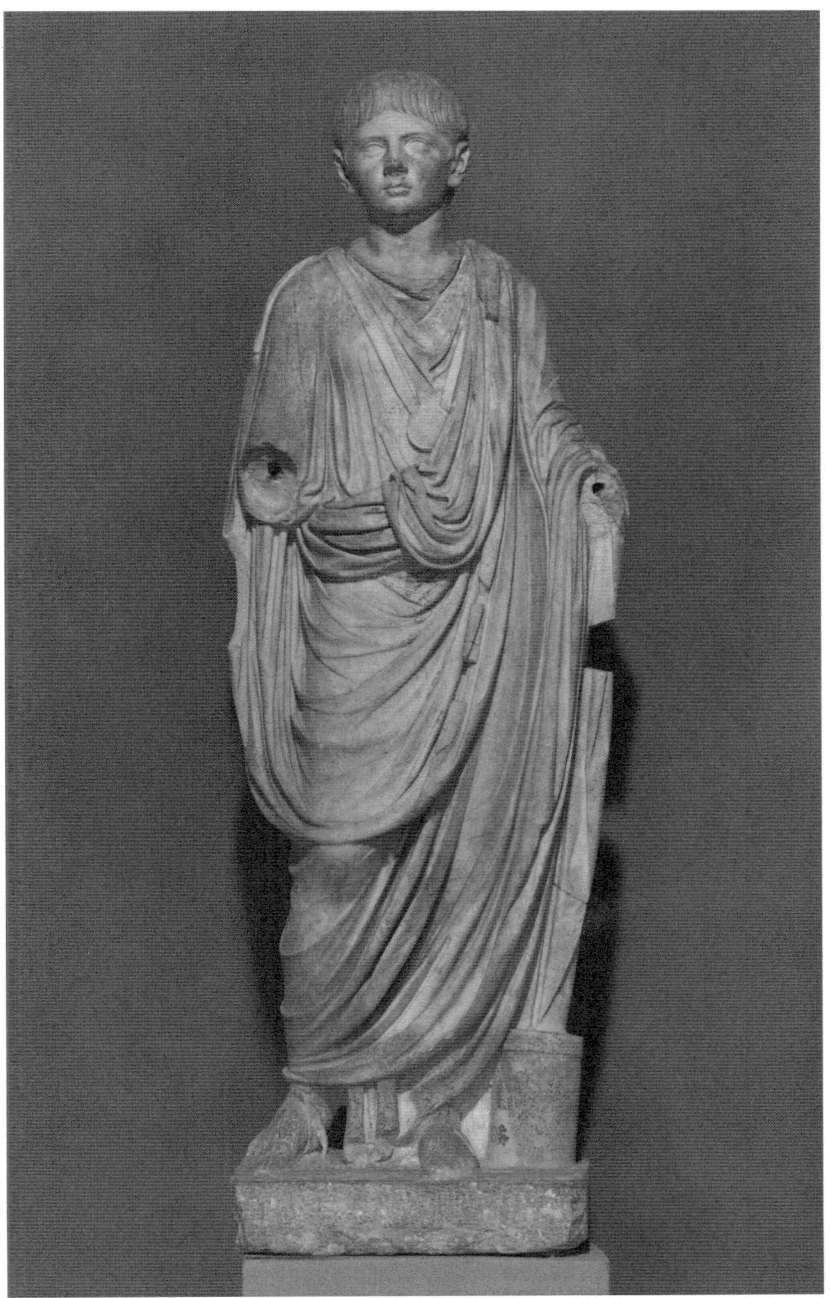

Fig. 3. Statue of Nero as a boy, from the Roman basilica at Velleia, Italy, c. 48–51 CE. Marble, height 60 1/4 in. (153 cm). Museo Nazionale di Antichità, Parma, inv. 1952.826

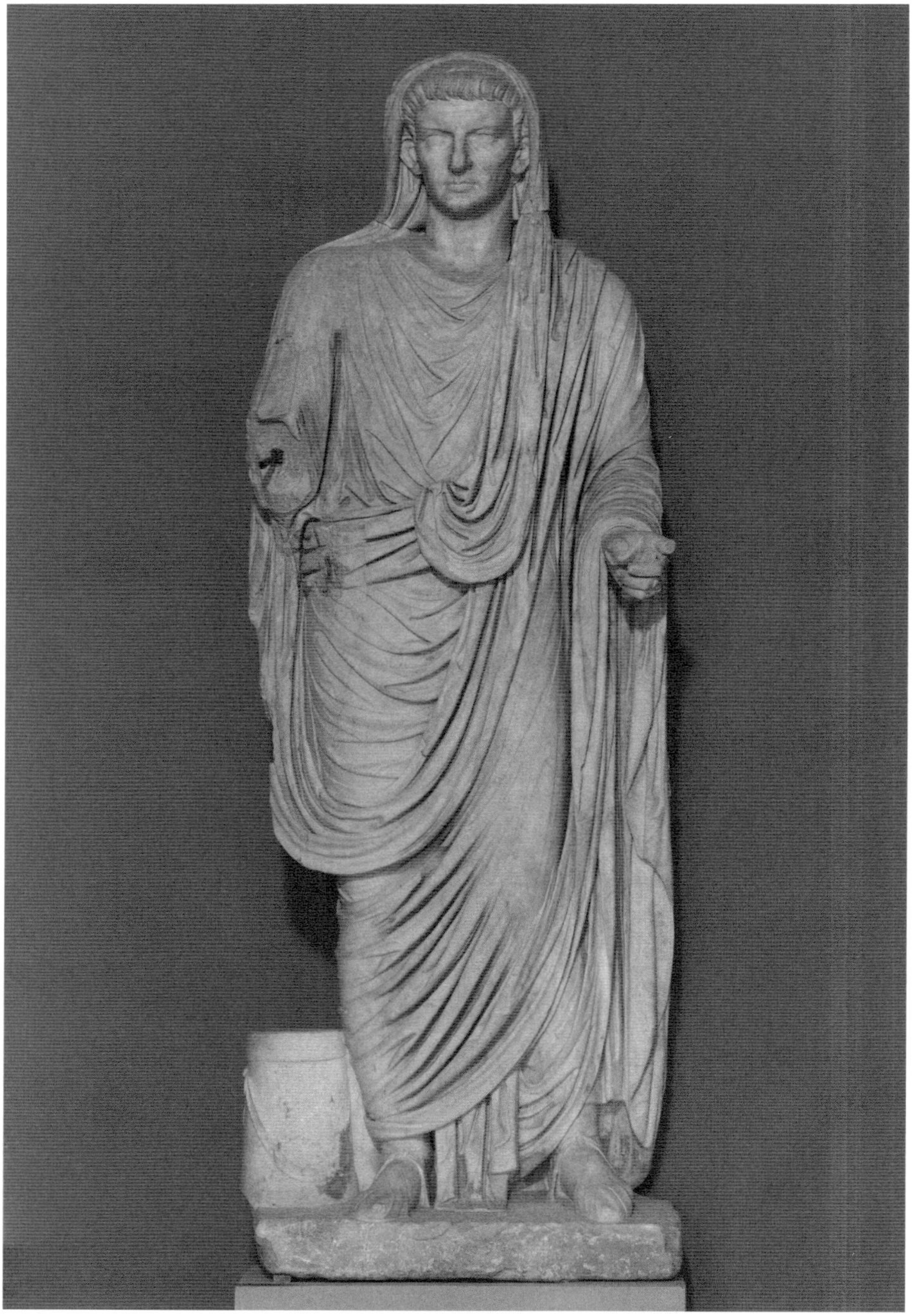

Fig. 4. Statue of Claudius, recut from Caligula, from the basilica at Velleia, Italy, c. 45 CE. Marble, height 87 in. (221 cm). Museo Nazionale di Antichità, Parma, inv. 1952.834

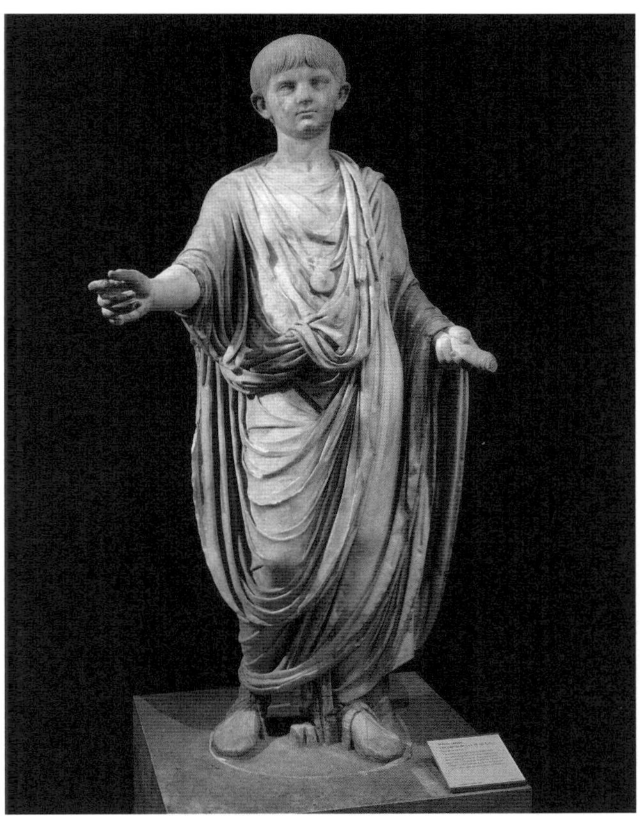

Fig. 5. Statue of Nero as a boy, wearing the bulla or seal, 50 CE. Marble, height 54 3/8 in. (138 cm). Musée du Louvre, Paris, inv. MA 1210

togate statues, one from Asia Minor and the other probably from Rome (fig. 5),[18] as well as by several heads. Although there has been some argument about their grouping and identity, most scholars agree that they represent Nero as epitomized in 50–51 CE after his adoption by the emperor Claudius.

At Velleia, Nero and his mother Agrippina joined her new husband, Claudius, and his son Britannicus, adapting an earlier phase of statuary that went back to the start of the Principate. Together, these figures represented a new chapter in the Julio-Claudian dynasty and looked to its longevity in the shape of the two young princes. Within a year of Nero's accession in 54 CE, his stepbrother Britannicus was dead—gossip held that he and Claudius had been poisoned by the emperor. Five years later, Nero added his mother to the list; her last words, according to Cassius Dio, being that her assassin should strike her womb in acknowledgment of the monster that she had created.[19] The "corpulent and debauched megalomaniac" was at his height, "the vicissitudes of his life mirrored in his portraits." And yet this family snapshot remained on display, both a catalogue of recent crimes and testament to a young boy full of promise.

Velleia is not unusual in continuing to display portraits of the young Nero.[20] Even in Rome, his name is not erased from two important public contexts, an inscription originally accompanying a statue group of himself, Agrippina, and Claudius's mother, and a Claudian family monument close to the Ara

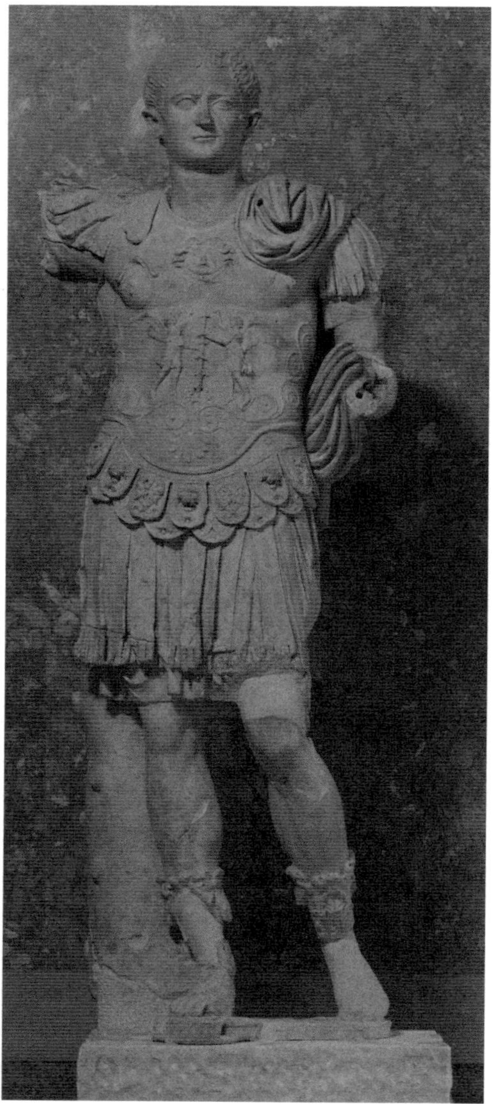

Fig. 6. Statue of Nerva, recut from Nero, from the basilica at Velleia, Italy. Marble, height 80 3/8 in. (204.3 cm). Museo Nazionale di Antichità, Parma, inv. 1952.827

Pacis.[21] In each of them, he was no doubt depicted as a child. What is it about the child's body that made these Neros inviolate? This question becomes particularly moot at Velleia where, after Nero's death, the display is augmented again, and with portraits recut from earlier imperial statuary. The most interesting of these for our purposes is a portrait of Nerva that has been recast from an image of Nero—not Nero the boy but Nero the mature despot (fig. 6).[22] Its status as the Basilica's only cuirassed statue suggests that it was brought from elsewhere, but its presence raises the stakes about the young Nero, which kept company with a Claudius that was itself recut from a portrait of Caligula (emperor, 37–41 CE).[23] Some scholars think that Agrippina too had been reworked from a statue of Claudius's former wife, Messalina, while the awkwardness of the join between the boy's head and body suggests that there was reuse there also.[24] If recycling were this normal, why not replace the problem child with someone more suitable? Despite Vespasian's moves to distance himself from Nero, and from Otho and Vitellius, who were briefly acclaimed emperors in between and had fostered Nero's image, here Nero endured, competing with emperors old and new and with his own negative reputation.

Compare and Contrast

Putting Nero's statue from Velleia next to his Worcester head offers us an extreme example of three related issues that affect the stories that Roman portraits stimulate: their longevity, their replication, and their adaptation. When Kleiner speaks of the evolution of Nero's portrait from "bland Julio-Claudian prince in 51," to "mature youth in 54 and 55," and so on, she fails to take account of the arrested development that comes of continued display. When a new portrait-type was issued—to mark ten years of Nero's reign, for example—not all earlier images were confiscated anymore than all of his images were warehoused on his demise. Throughout his reign, he was seen as child, adolescent, and adult *simultaneously*. After his death, some of his portrait-types remained on public view—largely those that showed him in boyhood, as we have seen, and those that were reworked into portraits of Nerva and other emperors, with just enough of Nero's hair or fleshy chin and neck to assert his having been there. Before and after: wasted potential. Occasionally, Nero was denied existence altogether, his portraits recut not into subsequent rulers but into images of Augustus, thereby reversing the course of history.[25] The resulting loss of mature portraits enhances their celebrity and the celebrity of Nero himself (creating a space for imposters as well as a fashion for coins from the last years of his reign as late as the second century).[26] It is in the dearth of heads like the Worcester head that the fictions of a tyrant's life are generated.

But even before the destruction of Nero's portraits, when he was still in power, this sense of something missing was as important to the stories they told as their physical presence. By this I am not just referring to the person that the Worcester head is and is not but to its failure to epitomize all possible images of Nero, some of them versions of the same portrait-type in marble or bronze, large scale or miniature, and others of different moments in his career. The experience of seeing Nero as a boy and as a mature man simultaneously is not the same as seeing Obama's life in pictures. They may show stages of life, but in a world in which Augustus could live to be seventy-six years old yet never appear much older in the visual record than in his statue from Primaporta (fig. 7),[27] and in which it was common for statues to be made with detachable heads and hair so as to build instability into their identity,[28] the visual environment was not so much "freed from the bonds of mortality" as actively working to subvert them. These portraits did not simply record the time of their making or function as "indexes of the act of portrayal that produced them."[29] Although ancient authors and modern artists are interested in imagining the creative process that resulted in images of Alexander the Great and his mistress,[30] there are no such stories about Augustus or Nero meeting with their portraitists. Their portraits were made to be remade;[31] were already reworkings of that seminal moment back in Alexander's tent when in-

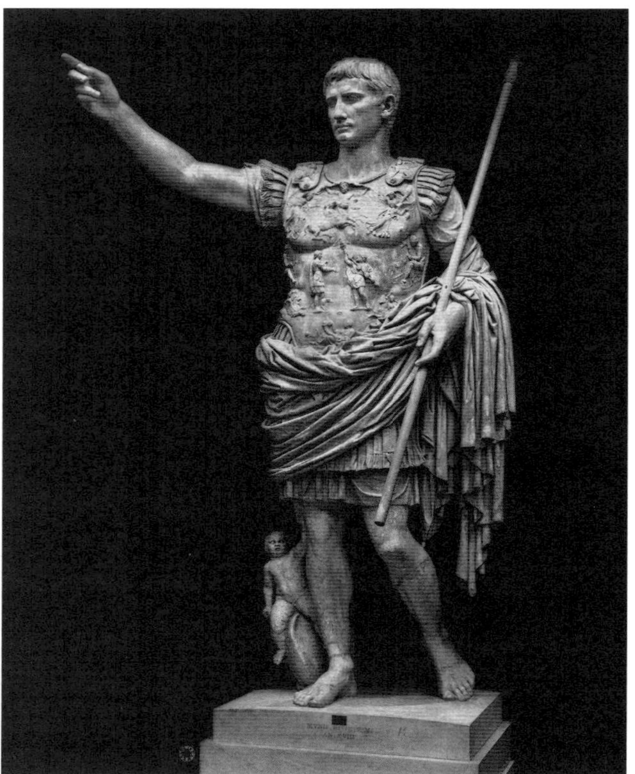

Fig. 7. Augustus as Imperator, from the Villa of Livia, Primaporta, early 1st century CE. Marble, height 80 1/4 in. (204 cm). Braccio Nuovo, Museo Chiaramonti, Vatican Museums, inv. 2290

dividual charisma was given a form to outshine community identity. Nero was not given a life in his images but in ensuing acts of comparison.

"Who are we looking at when we gaze upon any one of her many portraits?" asks the catalogue of the recent exhibition, *Francis Alÿs: Fabiola* (fig. 8), a Belgian artist's installation of over three hundred versions of a lost nineteenth-century portrait of a fourth-century Christian saint. The question's emphasis is again on "the many," and stems from accepting that the polyphony of portraits "destabilizes the prospect of a settled referent."[32] As the authors go on to explain, "the images resemble one another, not the sitter."[33] They thus threaten the sitter's integrity, not to mention his or her investment in any act of posturing, turning possible acquaintance on the part of the viewer into a series of encounters that pull and push against each other. In the process, Fabiola and Nero are made more enigmatic, inscrutable even, as befits the personalities of people worth knowing. It is not unlike the multiple images of Athena that stood on the Athenian Acropolis, each of which was revered as the god, whether wooden and portable or colossal and chryselephantine. The goddess was everywhere and nowhere. This competition between images meant that each could be an epiphany.[34]

At Velleia, it is not only Nero past and prospective that asks to be assimilated. His face and hairstyle make him as much a young Claudius as they do a Nero, so much so that some scholars have erroneously called him "Britannicus" or "Germanicus."[35] No matter that Nero is Claudius's son by adoption only, and

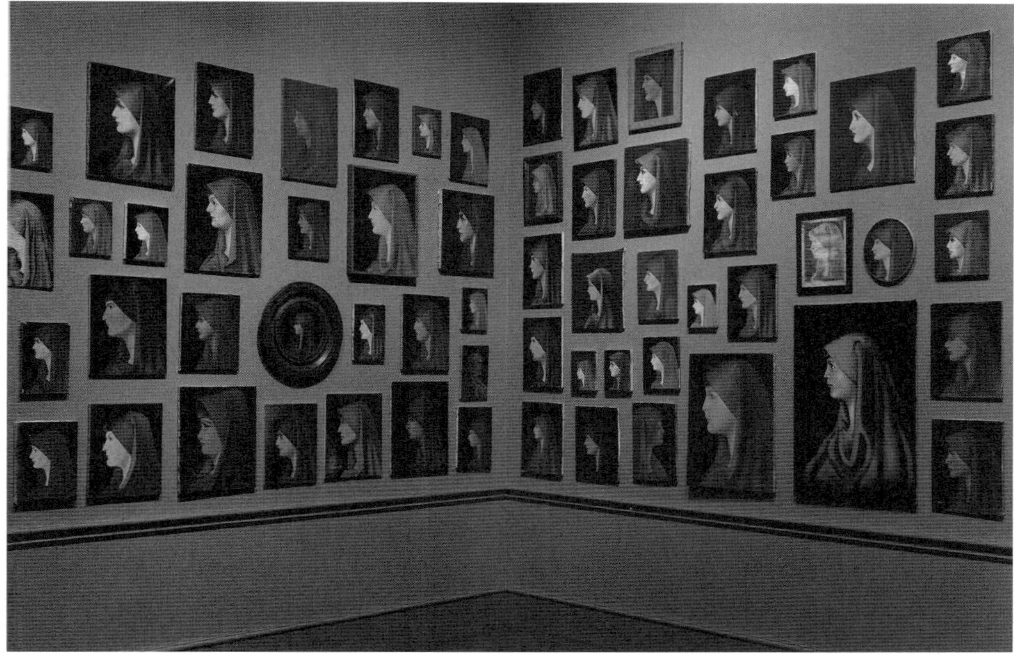

Fig. 8. Installation of Francis Alÿs's (Belgian, b.1959) exhibition "Fabiola," 2008. Los Angeles County Museum of Art

the implied genetic coding counterfeit. Culling the portrait of the young Nero from a family group is less a comment about his reign than about the mechanics of imperial succession. Which plotline are we more invested in? Nero's tyranny; Claudius's newly acquired divinity; or the durability of the Principate?

Portraits as Fictions

Sometimes, "portraits seem the opposite of fiction, fixed in time and space, not running with the curve of a story or a life," claims the jacket of Byatt's book. But if portraits are the opposite of fiction, they are also the opposite of fact. They weather, but do not age; body forth individuals that assume the physical attributes of others (whether in the sweep of the fringe or, more literally, in the recarving of an existing portrait); and hold their own in rapidly shifting circumstances. It is not only that the boy Nero and mature Nero/Nerva can share the same space. Dio Chrysostom, writing just after Nero's demise, complains that on Rhodes, rather than recarve statues, they often changed only the inscription, with the result that a young man could be commemorated by an image of an old man, and a puny man by that of a boxer, while Plutarch records how, in Athens, a statue of Pergamene dynast, Attalus, had been reinscribed "Mark Antony."[36] The link between image and referent is often far from logical. In Sicyon in the third century BCE, according to Plutarch, there had been great opposition to the idea of destroying a tyrant's portrait because of its beauty.[37] For all that scholars, myself included, have recently stressed that the blurring of flesh and marble defines portraiture as genre, the reality of marble is that it has its own narrative.

This paper has been about the possibilities and limits of this narrative. The emphasis that many of us now put on the moment of viewing over that of production makes us vulnerable to charges of excessive fictionalization. But the facts (fictions?) we fabricate when faced with a portrait are not groundless. They equate to our experience of the portrait and to the ways in which portraiture works as visual biography. Seeing a portrait is different from seeing the person in more ways than one. Did Nero have spindly legs, spotty skin, and a pot belly, as Suetonius maintains?[38] It is a question we might ask of the real Nero. "Was he, like Peter Pan, eternally prepubescent?" is not, or at least not with similar earnestness. But then the statue at Velleia is not Nero any more than the Worcester head is Nero: Nero resides in sets and sequences of images. We create him out of difference. This is why Kleiner's account is so inadequate ("he is portrayed as the bland Julio-Claudian prince in 51, as a more mature youth in 54 and 55, and as a corpulent and debauched megalomaniac between 59 and 68"). It is the *move* from bland to mature to corpulent that is the move from tendentious view to compelling story.

How do we ensure that these stories are told? "I have seen stone sculpture of him . . . and it well portrays the harshness and bitterness of character which are ascribed to him," wrote Plutarch of one Roman statesman.[39] Like Kleiner, Plutarch renders the portrait illustrative. It is stripped of its agency the moment it is extracted from the visual tradition. The same is true of historians who write biographies of the ancients today.[40] They raid publications like Gisela Richter's *The Portraits of the Greeks* and Jocelyn Toynbee's *Roman Historical Portraits* through to the *römische Herrscherbild* series, which groups portraits together, regardless of when and where they were produced, to establish types and persons.[41] Any member of the corpus will make a nice image for the cover, but will it serve *as evidence*—to rival Tacitus and Suetonius?

The blame is not only on historians' shoulders: in presenting our catalogues in the way that we do and obsessing about issues of attribution, we, as art historians, fail to realize that what we claim to be the most scientific activity—the compilation of a catalogue raisonné—is the most accommodating and productive of fictions, and that its claims about the identity of its examples,[42] and the uniqueness and completeness of the corpus, are the ultimate tall tales. All of us need to be braver in acknowledging this; only then will extant portraits be properly served—not as epitomes of person x or y but as data in a live tradition. The life story of that person is not on its pages as it is in the pages of Suetonius, but in the gaps between images. I have used this word a few times already, but as Jas′ Elsner has recently reiterated, all art history is ekphrasis, and dramatized within it, a "way of looking."[43] The sophistication is not in description but in "how we tell it."

1. Portrait of the Emperor Nero, 64–68 CE. Marble. Worcester Art Museum, Worcester, Massachusetts, inv. 1915.23. See Eric R. Varner, *Mutilation and Transformation: Damnatio Memoriae and Roman Imperial Portraiture* (Leiden and Boston: Brill, 2004), 68–69, with bibliography; and Ulrich W. Hiesinger, "The Portraits of Nero," *American Journal of Archaeology* 79 (1975): 120–21.

2. Diana E. E. Kleiner, *Roman Sculpture* (New Haven, Conn., and London: Yale University Press, 1992), 139.

3. Varner, *Mutilation and Transformation*, 49. Also relevant here is H. P. L'Orange, "Le Néron constitutionnel et le Néron Apothéosé," *From the Collections of the Ny Carlsberg Glyptothek*, vol. 3 (Copenhagen: Munksgaard, 1942): 253; and *Apotheosis in Ancient Portraiture* (Oslo: H. Aschehoug, 1947), 57.

4. Nero's reputation is such that he has spawned a formidable literature. Most useful among these for paying due attention to the ancient sources are Miriam T. Griffin, *Nero: The End of a Dynasty* (London: Batsford, 1984); Jas′ Elsner and Jamie Masters, eds., *Reflections of Nero: Culture, History, and Representation* (London: Duckworth, 1994); and Edward Champlin, *Nero* (Cambridge, Mass., and London: Belknap Press, 2003).

5. Suetonius, *Life of Nero*, 49.1: "Qualis artifex pereo!"

6. Harry Berger, Jr., "Fictions of the Pose: Facing the Gaze of Early Modern Portraiture," *Representations* 46 (Spring 1994): 88.

7. See Peter Stewart, *Statues in Roman Society: Representation and Response* (Oxford: Oxford University Press, 2003), 275.

8. Richard Brilliant, *Portraiture* (London: Reaktion Books, 1991), 7.

9. Caroline Vout, "The Art of Damnatio Memoriae," in *Un discours en images de la condamnation de mémoire*, ed. Stéphane Benoist and Anne Daguet-Gagey (Metz: Collection du CRUHL no. 34, 2008), 153–72.

10. Fry made this statement of Sargent's portrait of General Sir Ian Hamilton: quoted by Noel Annan, *New York Review of Books*, May 29, 1984, 4.
11. Confronted heads of Nero and Agrippina II: see aureus and denarius, struck 54 CE by the mint of Rome with the legend AGRIPP AVG DIVI CLAVD NERONIS CAES MATER. British Museum, London. Harold Mattingly, *Coins of the Roman Empire in the British Museum* (London: Oxford University Press, vol. 1, 1923), 200, nos. 1 and 2. And, for cojoined busts of Nero and Agrippina (i.e., not eye to eye but cheek to cheek), aureus and denarius, 55 CE, NERO CLAVD DIVI F CAES AVG GERM IMP TR P COS: Mattingly, *Coins of the Roman Empire*, 201, nos. 7 and 8. See also Hiesinger, "Portraits of Nero," 114.
12. Tacitus, *Histories* 2.8.1: the Latin for "facial similarity" here is "similitudinem oris."
13. Caroline Vout, *Power and Eroticism in Imperial Rome* (Cambridge, U.K.: Cambridge University Press, 2007). Also relevant here is Caroline Vout, "Hadrian, Hellenism, and the Social History of Art," *Arion* 18, no. 2 (Summer 2010): 55–78.
14. Antonia S. Byatt, *Portraits in Fiction* (London: Chatto and Windus, 2001), 1.
15. Kleiner, *Roman Sculpture*, 136.
16. Museo Nazionale di Antichità, Parma, inv. 1952.826. See Cesare Saletti, *Il Ciclo Statuario della Basilica di Velleia* (Milan: Ceschina, 1968), 49–52; Hiesinger, "Portraits of Nero," 116–17; Charles Brian Rose, *Dynastic Commemoration and Imperial Portraiture in the Julio-Claudian Period* (Cambridge, U.K.: Cambridge University Press, 1997), 71 and 121–26; and Varner, *Mutilation and Transformation*, 79–80.
17. Excellent on the ways in which Roman masculinity was not born but earned and repeatedly tested in public are Maud W. Gleason, *Making Men: Sophists and Self-Presentation in Ancient Rome* (Princeton, N.J.: Princeton University Press, 1994); and Erik Gunderson, *Staging Masculinity: the Rhetoric of Performance in the Roman World* (Ann Arbor: University of Michigan Press, 2000).
18. Detroit Institute of Arts, Acc. no. 69.218 and Louvre, Paris, inv. 1210.
19. Cassius Dio, *Roman History* 62.13.5.
20. See, for example, the two young togate statues with bulla from the headquarters of the Augustales at Rusellae, now in the Archaeological Museum at Grosseto: Rose, *Dynastic Commemoration and Imperial Portraiture*, 116–18.
21. *CIL* 6.921 = 31203 = *ILS* 222 and *CIL* 6.40424: see Harriet I. Flower, *The Art of Forgetting: Disgrace and Oblivion in Roman Political Culture* (Chapel Hill: University of North Carolina Press, 2006), 213, who further notes that erasure of Nero, young or old, is inconsistent; and Varner, *Mutilation and Transformation*, 80.
22. Museo Nazionale di Antichità, Parma, inv. 1952.827: Rose, *Dynastic Commemoration*

and Imperial Portraiture, 122; and Varner, *Mutilation and Transformation*, 80n295 and 251, cat. 2.50.

23. Claudius: Museo Nazionale di Antichità, Parma, inv. 1952.834. Rose, *Dynastic Commemoration and Imperial Portraiture*, 121–23; and Varner, *Mutilation and Transformation*, 232, cat. 1.27.

24. With regard to the Agrippina statue (National Antiquities Museum, Parma, inv. 830), see Varner, *Mutilation and Transformation*, 258, cat. 3.4, and Nero's neck, 79n293.

25. Ibid., 238–40.

26. K. Dahmen, "Ein Loblied auf den schönen Kaiser. Zur möglichen Deutung der mit Nero Münzen verzierten römischen Dosenspiegel," *Archäologischer Anzeiger* (1998): 319–45. Also relevant here is Champlin, *Nero*, 30–34; and Flower, *Disgrace and Oblivion*, 209–12.

27. Augustus as Imperator, from the villa of Livia, Primaporta, early 1st century CE, but based on a bronze statue of 20 BCE. Vatican Museums, inv. 2290.

28. See Stewart, *Statues in Roman Society*, 47.

29. Berger, "Fictions of the Pose," 99.

30. For Alexander's control of his own portrait-image, see Pliny, *Natural History* 7.125 and 37.8; Plutarch, *Moralia* 335A–B; and *Life of Alexander* 41. For his desire that Apelles paint his mistress, see Pliny, *Natural History* 35.86. Also relevant here, for defining the limits of what was permissible for a dynast's public persona, are the stories of Alexander's negotiations with an architect about the possibility of casting Mount Athos in his image: Plutarch, *Moralia* 335 D, Plutarch, *Life of Alexander* 72.4, Strabo, 14.1.23, and Vitruvius 2. pref. 2. Unsurprisingly, these stories seize the imagination of later artists: for example, Sebastiano Ricci (Italian, 1659–1734), *Apelles Making a Portrait of Pancaspe*, 1700–1704, oil on canvas, 244 x 246 cm, Ospedali Riuniti, Parma; Giovanni Battista Tiepolo (Italian, 1696–1770), *Alexander the Great and Campaspe in the Studio of Apelles*, 1740, oil on canvas, 41.9 x 54 cm, J. Paul Getty Museum, Los Angeles; Jacques Louis David (French, 1748–1825), *Alexander Presenting Campaspe to Apelles*, 1748–1825, oil on wood, 96 x 136.2 cm, private collection; Fischer von Erlach (Austrian, 1656–1723), *Entwurff einer Historischen Architectur*, 1725, plate 18; and Pierre Henri de Valenciennes (French, 1750–1819), *Mount Athos Carved as a Monument to Alexander the Great*, 1796, oil on canvas, 41.9 x 91.4 cm, The Art Institute of Chicago.

31. Although the artist Dioskourides is famed for having cut Augustus's seal-portrait, there is little suggestion of a dialogue between them. The lack of stories about Roman emperors and their portraitists does not mean that the ancient sources do not talk about painting and sculpture in connection with imperial power. Far from it. Imperial power is often defined by emperors' treatment of art. However, when portraits are mentioned, their own

or otherwise, these authors usually talk about changing their shape: see, for example, Dio Cassius, *Roman History* 54.35.2 and 75.16.2; and Suetonius, *The Divine Augustus* 52. In different ways, the literary reputations of both Augustus and Nero construct *them* as artists. Also interesting here is Pausanias 2.17.3, where a statue of the hero Orestes is rededicated as Augustus.

32. David Morgan, "Finding Fabiola," in *Francis Alÿs: Fabiola: An Investigation*, ed. Stephan Bann et al. (New York: Dia Art Foundation, 2008), 11.

33. Ibid., 18.

34. Excellent here is Verity Platt, *Facing the Gods: Epiphany and Representation in Graeco-Roman Art, Literature and Religion* (Cambridge, U.K.: Cambridge University Press, 2011).

35. Hiesinger, "Portraits of Nero," 115–16.

36. Dio Chrysostom, *Orations* 31.153–56; and Plutarch, *Life of Antony* 60.2. Also relevant here is Cicero, *Letters to Atticus* 6.1.26; and Julia Shear, "Reusing Statues, Rewriting Inscriptions and Bestowing Honours in Roman Athens," in *Art and Inscriptions in the Ancient World*, ed. Zahra Newby and Ruth Leader-Newby (Cambridge, U.K.: Cambridge University Press, 2007), 221–46.

37. A painted portrait of the tyrant Aristratus by Melanthus and pupils, with a helping hand from Apelles: Plutarch, *Life of Aratus* 13.1–3.

38. Suetonius, *Life of Nero*, 51.

39. Plutarch, *Caius Marius* 2.1.

40. More sophisticated than this in some senses were the illustrated histories of the seventeenth and eighteenth centuries, which saw portraiture as crucial evidence. See, for example, the preface of François de Mézeray's *Histoire de France* (Paris, 1685), which makes a distinction between portraiture and narrative: "[portraiture] traces the features and displays the exterior and majesty of the body, while narrative relates actions and depicts characters." See Francis Haskell, *History and its Images: Art and the Interpretation of the Past* (New Haven, Conn., and London: Yale University Press, 1993), 26–80.

41. Gisela M. A. Richter, *The Portraits of the Greeks* (London: Phaidon, 1965); and Jocelyn M. Toynbee, *Roman Historical Portraits* (London: Thames and Hudson, 1978). For *Das römische Herrscherbild* series, see, e.g., Dietrich Boschung, *Die Bildnisse des Augustus* (Berlin: Mann, 1993); and Max Wegner, *Hadrian, Plotina, Marciana, Matidia, Sabina* (Berlin: Mann, 1956).

42. An excellent text on accepting anonymity and how to work with it is Shiela Dillon, *Ancient Greek Portrait Sculpture: Contexts, Subjects and Styles* (Cambridge, U.K.: Cambridge University Press, 2006), esp. 1–14.

43. Jas´ Elsner, "Art History as Ekphrasis," *Art History* 33 (2010): 10–27.

“I Am Not Who You Think I Am”: Attributing the Humanist Portrait, Identifying the Art-Historical Subject

Maria H. Loh

Prologue: Five Florentines in Search of an Author

The attentive visitor to the Louvre will find the anonymous *Five Florentine Renaissance Masters* just to the left of the door that leads out of the Salon Carré and into the melodramatic pull of the Grande Galerie. Five painted portrait busts are assembled upon the thin pictorial space of an old wooden board (fig. 1). The composition is framed at either end by a man facing in, appearing pensive on the left and in abrupt profile on the right. In the center, the steely gaze of a bearded figure glares out at the viewer, the confrontational nature of his expression undoubtedly heightened by the strong cast shadow (the only one of its kind in the painting) that cuts across his shoulder. Two additional bodies, one older and one younger, are inserted between the others; both are in three-quarter view and both glance toward the left (suggestively looking toward the past). Beneath the lumbering parade of faces, five names have been inscribed onto the fictive stone frame: GIOTTO, PAOLO.VCCELLO, DONATELLO, ANTONIO.MANETTI, FLIPPO.BRVNELLES. These five Florentines stand as mute witnesses before the threshold in the museum that separates the carefully curated summation of Giorgio Vasari’s *prima* and *seconda età* in this first room and the grand narrative in the hallowed hall to come.

In the first edition of his *Lives of the Artists*, written in 1550, Vasari attributes a painting featuring portraits of Giotto (c. 1267–1337), Donatello (1386–1466),

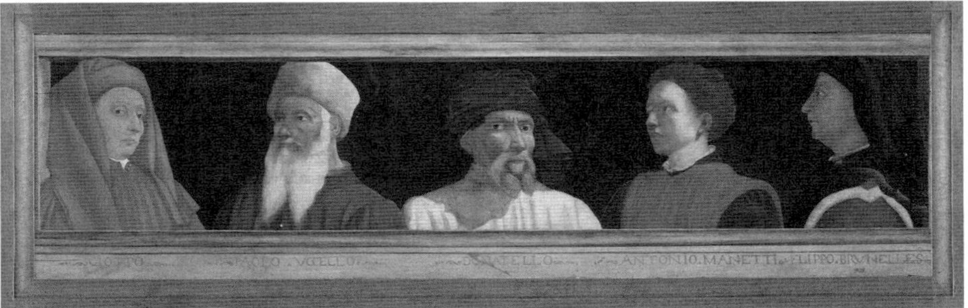

Fig. 1. Anonymous, *Five Florentine Renaissance Masters*, first half of the 16th century. Oil on panel, 8 3/8 × 25 3/4 in. (21.3 × 65.5 cm). Musée du Louvre, Paris

Filippo Brunelleschi (1377–1446), Paolo Uccello (1397–1475), and Antonio Manetti (1423–1497) to the early fifteenth-century prodigy Masaccio (1401–1428).[1] According to Vasari, the painting ended up some decades later in the hands of Giuliano da Sangallo, a Florentine architect and friend of Michelangelo. Vasari seems to have been undecided about the panel's attribution, and in the second edition of the *Lives*, written eighteen years later, he reattributes the painting to Uccello, whom we see in the painting with the formidable forked white beard, depicted second from the left in a gray hat.[2] *Five Florentine Renaissance Masters* then became the main character in an extended art-historical family romance in which the legitimacy of the named fathers was doubted in spite of the documented genealogies on hand.

This paradoxical image—an image possessing a surplus of authors yet lacking a stable author—will serve as a case study for a larger consideration of the fraught discursive process through which desire is often manipulated into truth and fiction becomes history. This essay will examine the Louvre panel from the perspective of the connoisseur's thesis, the historian's antithesis, and the fabulist's synthesis. What follows, however, is not a straightforward dialectical dance in which the pursuit for truth is shown to be nothing more than self-aware fiction; instead, I would like to consider the Louvre painting from three points of view, all of which claim, each in its own way, to be "based on a true story."

The Connoisseur's Thesis

Art historians have tried to champion the authorship of *Five Florentine Renaissance Masters* as a work by either Masaccio or Uccello based on Vasari's mixed attributions.[3] The inconsistent quality of the painting failed, however, to convince scholars—after all, how could Masaccio (the appointed founder of Quattrocentro plasticity) or Uccello (the designated inventor of Quattrocento perspective) possibly have been responsible for this disjunctive image of five men who crowd into this strange space with their baggy headgear, wide shoulders, missed glances, and inexplicable light sources? Jenö Lanyi remarked that the painting was "uneven and opalescent for these many anomalies." The only logical explanation he could provide was that it was a "pseudo-picture . . . a copy showing fragments of an earlier original."[4] Yet he was unable to let go entirely of Vasari's textual evidence and of his own desire for the panel to somehow be an original work of art. According to Lanyi's close analysis, one of the portraits (the one identified as "Giotto") was a fifteenth-century copy after a lost self-portrait by Masaccio.[5] Thus, even if this was the face of Masaccio as he saw himself, the portrait in the Louvre panel was

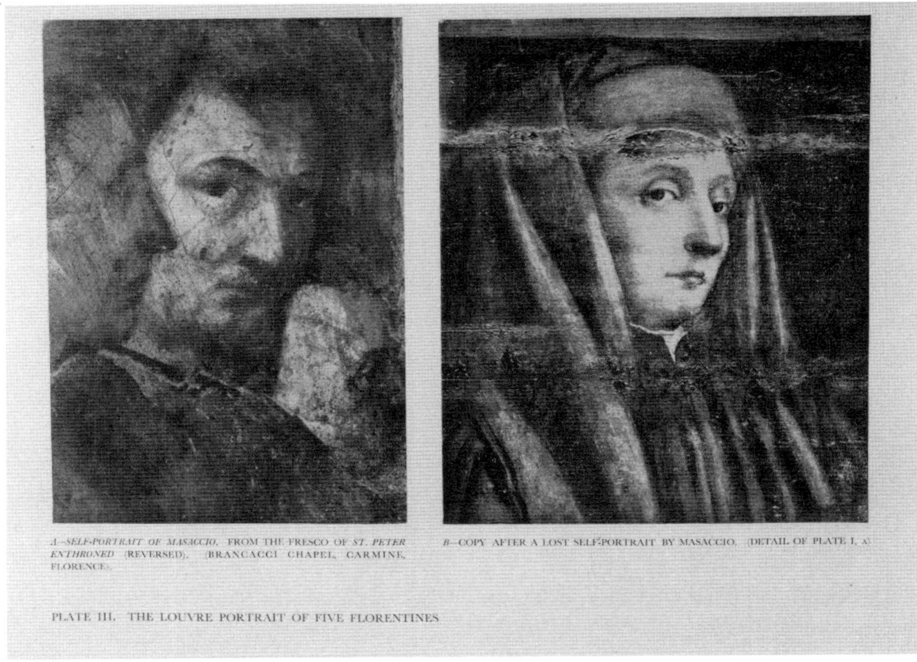

Fig. 2. Plate III from Jenö Lanyi, "The Louvre Portrait of Five Florentines," *The Burlington Magazine for Connoisseurs* 84, no. 493 (April 1944), 93

made by another fifteenth-century artist. For Lanyi, the value of *Five Florentine Renaissance Masters* resided in its authenticity as an object dating to the time of the figures represented—it was vintage, a true relic of the Quattrocento, even if not an original in the hand of Masaccio. Lanyi's compromise was to relegate the painting to the dubious category of what we might call the almost-authentic—a historical half-truth "based on a true story"—or, in Lanyi's own words, a "pseudo-picture."

The crux of Lanyi's argument rests upon a physiognomic comparison he made between the figure of "Giotto" and an alleged, although undocumented, self-portrait looking out from Masaccio's fresco of *Saint Peter Enthroned* in the Brancacci Chapel in Florence (fig. 2). In an age before instant, simultaneous, and ubiquitous digital reproduction, when art historians had to rely upon the nebulous quality of black-and-white photographs and memory, it would appear that Lanyi wanted far too much for this face to *be* Masaccio's—his desire filled in the blanks, morphed the features of the face, and determined the conclusions of his interpretation. Lanyi's thesis is, without a doubt, somewhat shaky. If the face of "Giotto" belongs to Masaccio, then why did Vasari's printmakers use this same portrait

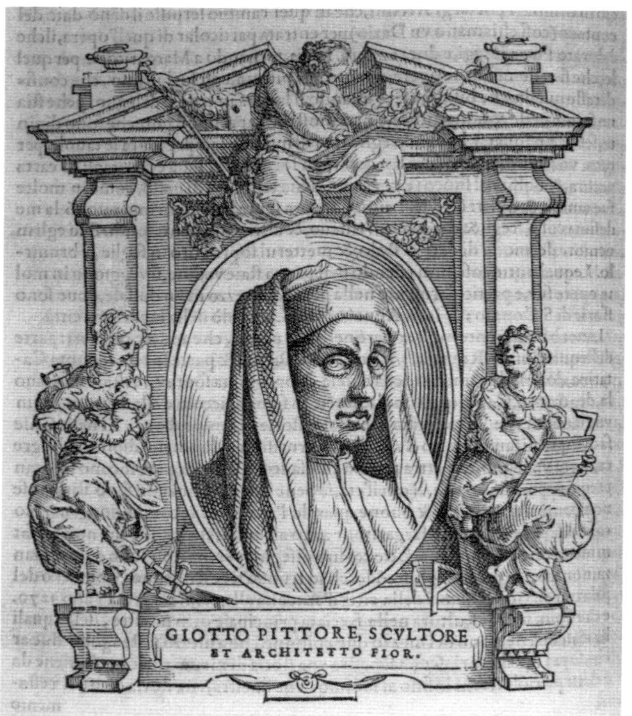

Fig. 3. Portrait of Giotto di Bondone (c. 1267–1337) from Giorgio Vasari, *Lives of the Artists* (1568). Private Collection / The Bridgeman Art Library

at the beginning of Giotto's biography in the 1568 edition of the *Lives* (fig. 3)? Likewise, if this is Masaccio's face, who is the young man gazing out of Masaccio's biography some pages later (fig. 4)? It also remains unexplained why Lanyi chose to focus on a detail from Masaccio's fresco of *Saint Peter Enthroned* as the bearer of the master's true likeness. This figure corresponds to Alberti's *ammonitore* who beckons the viewer into the pictorial fiction, but not all such figures are necessarily hidden self-portraits. Lanyi's conclusion is especially odd since Vasari clearly identified the young bearded man, the last Apostle on the right in *The Tribute Money*, as a self-portrait of Masaccio painted "with the aid of a mirror" (fig. 5).[6] It is entirely possible that Vasari himself made a mistake, as he is known to have done in other instances, but, in all fairness to the Florentine biographer, one would imagine that he would have been especially scrupulous with the portraits of the founding fathers of Florentine art.[7]

It would seem that everything about this painting has frustrated and will continue to frustrate the evidentiary methodology of connoisseurship. Already in 1923 Mary Pittaluga is heard saying: "It seems to me that the work, itself in repainted condition since the sixteenth century, now makes any attribution impossible," yet each of her male colleagues at the time and since have insisted on being in the right despite the obvious impasse.[8] Joseph A. Crowe and Giovanni B. Cavalcaselle infamously saw the panel as "an old copy from the time of Pontormo," and Paul Schubring believed it to have been repainted by Giuliano Bugiardini.[9] While Lanyi admitted that there was much uncertainty about the authorship and origin of the panel, he absolutely rejected the theory that the painting might be

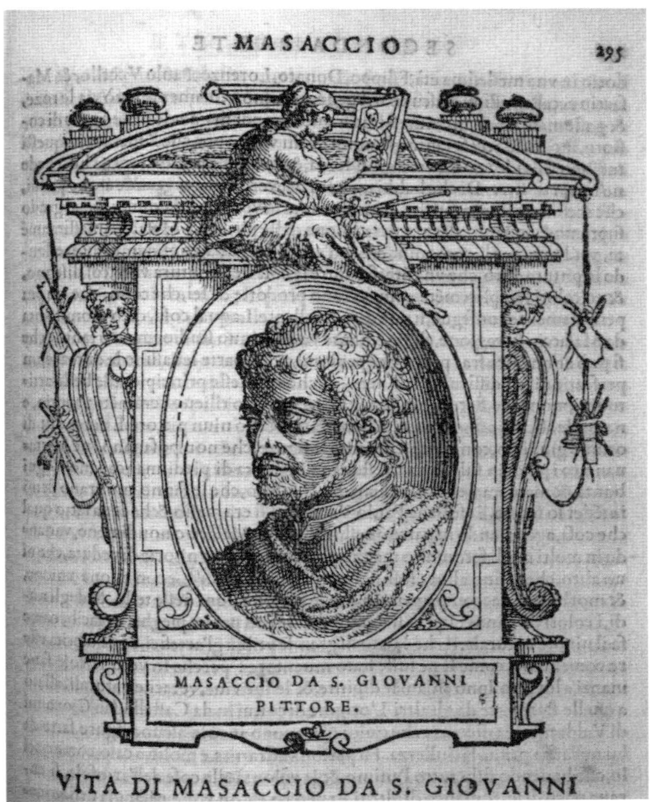
MASACCIO 295

MASACCIO DA S. GIOVANNI
PITTORE.

VITA DI MASACCIO DA S. GIOVANNI

Fig. 4. Portrait of Masaccio (Italian, 1401–1428) from Giorgio Vasari, *Lives of the Artists*. Private Collection / The Bridgeman Art Library

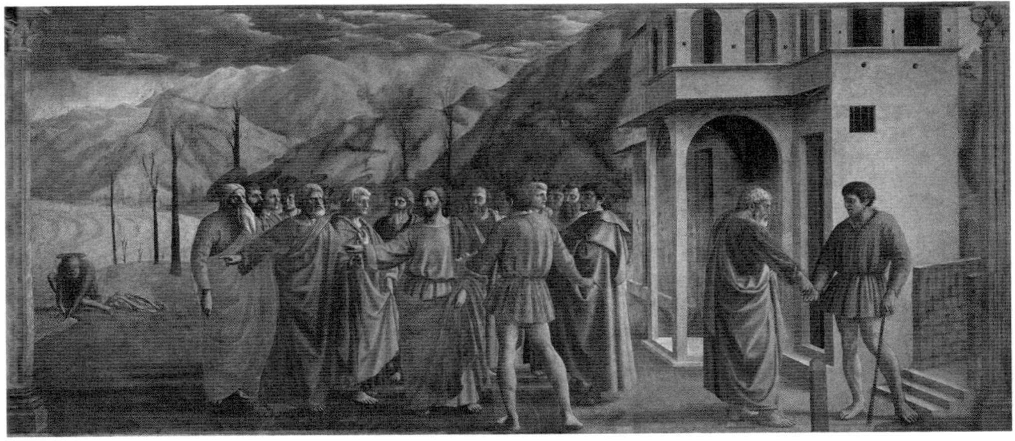

Fig. 5. Masaccio, *The Tribute Money*, c. 1427. Fresco, 90 1/2 x 236 1/4 in. (230 x 600 cm). Brancacci Chapel, Santa Maria del Carmine, Florence

a sixteenth-century pastiche.[10] John Pope-Hennessy is among the few to express uncertainty; in his catalogue raisonné of Uccello, the reader is confronted instead with a motley crew of contenders: "a collaboration between Masaccio and Uccello" (Boecke); "shop of Paolo Uccello" (Lipman); "late work, certainly executed after 1450 and possibly after 1460" (attributed to various authors).[11] Another early twentieth-century footnote proposed Antonello da Messina as the unlikely author of the painting.[12]

Here we are faced with a vertiginous matrix of competing desires. It bears reiteration that the aim is not to discount this literature but to highlight the subjective aspect of what claims to be an objective science. In spite of a collective desire for *Five Florentine Renaissance Masters* to be a true relic of the Quattrocento, today the anonymous panel hangs almost unnoticed in the corner of the Louvre (as authorless works often do), slightly too low for the eye line of the modern spectator (a curatorial oversight or perhaps a carefully choreographed caesura), left floating in the ambivalent and expansive era known as the "first half of the sixteenth century."[13] This is both a generous and convenient rubric that achieves little else beyond rejecting the scholarship that came before, reinforcing the authority of the museum over the academy, and justifying the current location of the painting in this liminal space.

The Historian's Antithesis

It has been argued that the connoisseur's desire is not simply to be proven right but to enter into "an intimate relation with the sensuous substance of the work, the most intimate intercourse since that of the artist making it."[14] Perhaps the real story lies in the blind spot generated by this desire. To a certain extent, the unresolved case of *Five Florentine Renaissance Masters* seems to confirm the claim put forth by Gary Schwartz that connoisseurship remains "the id of the art-historical ego."[15] If this is the case, do we dare define the archival and documentary drive of contextualization as art history's grumpy superego?

The social historian would argue that the eye alone does not suffice, and that every attribution requires some level of verifiable—textual or material—evidence.[16] The peculiar circumstance here is that the evidence has proven itself to be inconsistent and unreliable. Still, if we pay attention to Vasari's descriptions of *Five Florentine Renaissance Masters* in both editions, what do they tell us about how men of the past might have lived with such images? Not what did such an image mean or how and for whom was it produced but how did the image itself produce meaning? What was Vasari's desire?

The shift in attribution from Masaccio to Uccello is often interpreted as a qualitative judgment by which a work is downgraded from one artist and reattributed to a lesser artist (a classic move of what David Carrier referred to as "connoisseurship of quality").[17] The assumption that Uccello was considered a lesser artist may have arisen during the twentieth century. In spite of the personality flaws that Vasari includes in his biography of Uccello (excessive diligence and a tendency to strive beyond his abilities), there is little doubt that he rated the artist highly—this can be demonstrated by looking at the visual evidence. In Vasari's fresco of *Cosimo the Elder Surrounded by Humanists and Artists* in the Palazzo Vecchio in Florence (fig. 6), he included Uccello among the background figures. This scene was a pendant to the more often discussed image of *Cosimo I de' Medici between His Artists* painted in the second half of the 1550s (after the first edition of the *Lives* and shortly before the establishment of the Accademia del Disegno in 1563 and the second edition of the *Lives* in 1568). Let me be clear here: it does not matter to me whether or not this *is* Uccello's face (for this would fall into the very trap that connoisseurs often make in their attempts to identify the artist among the crowd).[18] Instead, for all practical purposes, this figure was identified *as* Uccello and therefore *became* Uccello in the master narrative Vasari sought to construct in and through this image. For an artist like Vasari painting in the late 1550s, the assembled group represented the epitome of artistic excellence that that earlier generation had to offer; these men were, according to Vasari's retrospective assessment, Cosimo il Vecchio's rising contemporary art stars.

Masaccio is not included in the group portrait with Cosimo, although he enacts a similar role in Vasari's 1550 text. In the passage from the first edition of the *Lives* where Vasari discusses *Five Florentine Renaissance Masters*, he notes that Masaccio was "the most modern artist" of all the Old Masters since Giotto; this work, he concludes, was a "testament" of his appraisal of contemporary Florentine art—to a promising young artist like Masaccio, these men represented the very best in their respective fields (at least in Vasari's mind as he was writing in the 1540s). Among the illustrious five, Giotto is the only figure who would be considered a historical precursor; the only one who was not a contemporary of the young Masaccio. According to this version of the story, and in keeping with the inscriptions and the two attributions, *Five Florentine Renaissance Masters* becomes a monument made by a young artist (Masaccio) recognizing his peers (Uccello, Donatello, Manetti, and Brunelleschi) and acknowledging his illustrious predecessor (Giotto). Or, to follow Lanyi's thesis to its logical conclusion, this is a painting made by an unknown contemporary artist from the fifteenth cen-

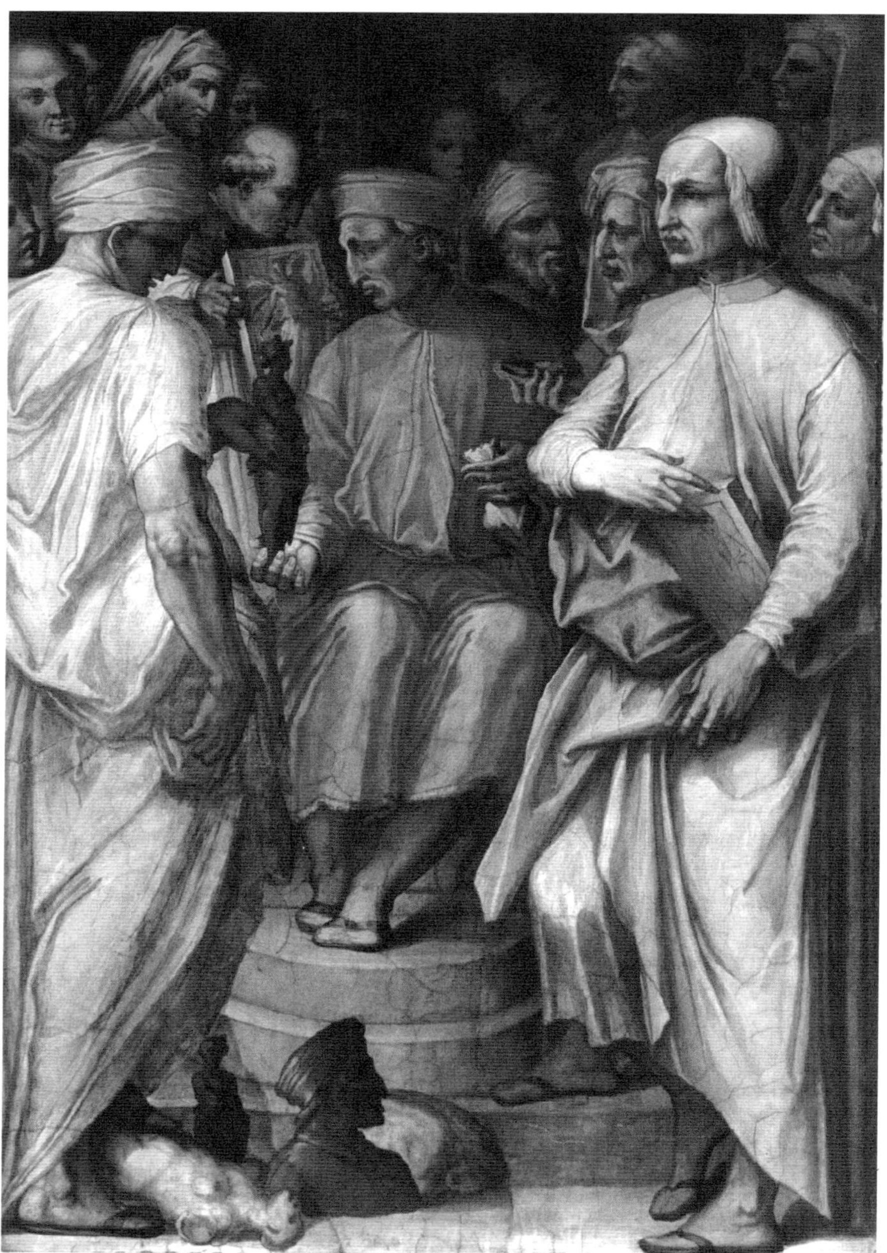

Fig. 6. Giorgio Vasari (Italian, 1511–1574), *Cosimo the Elder Surrounded by Humanists and Artists*, 1556–58. Fresco. Sala di Cosimo il Vecchio, Palazzo Vecchio, Florence

tury depicting five of his/her peers (Masaccio, Uccello, Donatello, Manetti, and Brunelleschi). According to either scenario, the Louvre painting was a testament to the perception of its maker's modernity and presentism. If the panel is indeed a fifteenth-century Florentine work, then the use of oil paint also signals a calculated experimentation with what was then a new media (in contrast to the more traditional egg tempera). If Masaccio painted it himself, it would be an ego-document; if Uccello painted it, it would be a collective portrait of an artistic generation.[19]

Looking at the Louvre panel, I can't help but draw a structuralist analogy to David Robbins's *Talent* (fig. 7). We find Robbins in the lower-right corner of this collection of the eighteen black-and-white photographs that he made in the form of agent's casting cards of his artistic contemporaries in the mid-1980s: some of the names, such as Jenny Holzer, Cindy Sherman, and Robert Longo, still resonate today; their faces are easily located through the inscriptions on their portraits. In the center of the grid on the right-hand side we see Jeff Koons with his winsome smile oozing with self-confidence in a knowing manner not unlike that of Donatello in the Louvre panel. This is not a gratuitous comparison but a timely reminder that our five Florentines were once perceived, in their moment, as contemporary artists too.

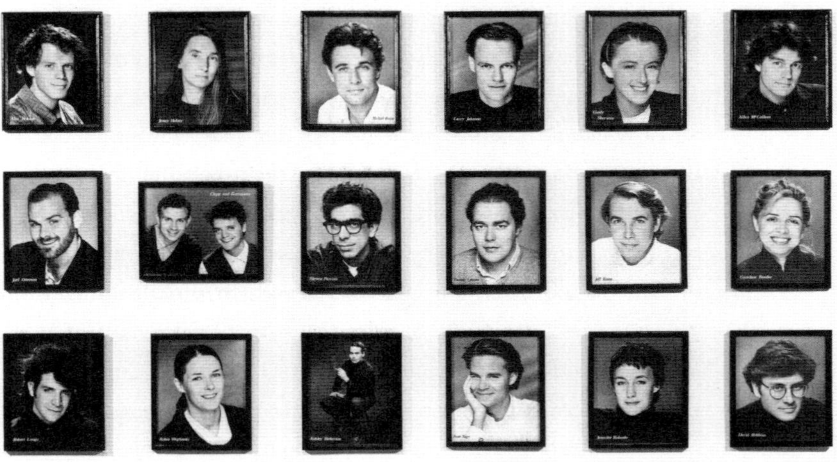

Fig. 7. David Robbins (American, b. 1957), *Talent*, 1986. Portfolio of 18 black-and-white photographs, 10 × 8 in. (25.4 × 20.3 cm) each. Courtesy of the artist

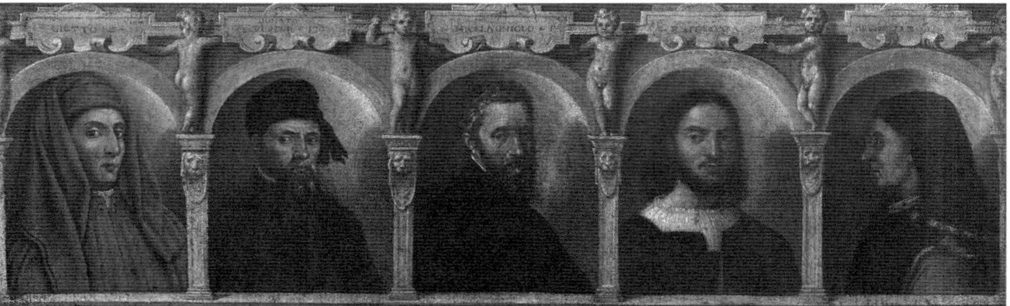

Fig. 8. Attributed to Francesco Salviati (Italian, 1510–1563), *Portraits of Five Artists, Giotto, Donatello, Michelangelo, Raphael, and Brunelleschi*, 16th century. Oil on canvas, 9 1/4 x 27 5/8 in. (23.5 x 70.1 cm). © The Fitzwilliam Museum, Cambridge, U.K.

A concern with the perception of modernity within its historical context may offer an explanation to Vasari's subsequent change of heart: if, in 1550, Masaccio represented the most modern of the Old Masters since Giotto, perhaps when Vasari was revising his text in the 1560s (after completing the group portrait in the Sala di Cosimo il Vecchio), Uccello had become a more current candidate for this honor. Vasari provided no explanation as to how or why the transfer of authorship occurred, but in both accounts it would appear that the panel remained in Florence as a curious, marvelous object passed down from one generation of painters to the next. It became the "top five" of a larger canon in the making by artists for artists to come. This generational intention is evident when we turn to another work attributed to the Florentine painter Francesco Salviati (1510–1563) that is clearly related to the Louvre panel and in which Uccello and Manetti have been updated by two fresher faces—those of Michelangelo and Raphael (fig. 8). This drive to renew and reconfigure the canon explains, in part, the persistent appeal of the Louvre panel, regardless of its authorship. From a historicist perspective, the modernity thesis would offer a contextual explanation for the production of canons of greatness at different moments in time (such a reading would also broaden the connoisseur's narrow desire to explain the reattribution on the grounds of qualitative criteria). But to simply close the conversation here with a tidy contextualist explanation would be to underestimate the poetic resistance of the image.

The artwork serves as a fetish, a relic, a magic portal that enables the connoisseur or historian to commune with or otherwise revisit the past as it was. Portraiture, in particular, stimulates this vitalistic tendency through the implied subjectivity of the silent faces that gaze out at us. At first glance, *Five Florentine Renaissance Masters* seems to be a simple celebration of the arrival of the artist as a renaissance humanist. However, the more one looks at it, the more one is affected by a resounding sense of paradox; certainty gives way to doubt, and even the assertiveness of the identifications begins to break down.[20] While the authority of the written word usually functions to reassure the interpreter, here the excess of information inadvertently causes meaning to become unstable, complicating the intersection of visual evidence, archival documentation, and received wisdom. This anxiety is even enacted in the very gestures of writing and depiction. The letters of the final two names—like the bodies to whom they attach themselves—are squeezed rather clumsily together as the painter ran out of space. Even this attempt at clarity results in an awkward jumble. Moreover, haunting the commemorative impulse that compelled a subsequent author to make the identifications permanent (most likely in the sixteenth century) is a sense that *time is out of joint.* Like the "that has been" that characterized the sting of photography for Roland Barthes, these names serve as a reminder that the bodies that may have been attached to them are no longer alive, but their images confront us nevertheless in our moment of viewing.

Here I would like to invoke W. J. T. Mitchell's infamous question: "What do pictures want?," although this should be rephrased as: What do art historians want this picture to want? Standing before *Five Florentine Renaissance Masters,* I want to ask these historical subjects: Are you who you claim to be? Who has named you thus? Why are you assembled here in this manner? If this picture could speak for itself, what would it say? As in all role-playing scenarios driven by desire and fantasy, the response is inevitably: "I am who you want me to be," even if "I am not who you think I am." Somewhere in between these two extremes is the parenthetical remark: But I am nevertheless "based on a true story." It is the possibilities that arise from this liminal position to which I now turn.

The Fabulist's Synthesis

> Eccentric as he was, Paolo loved talent in artists, and in order that he might leave a memorial of them to posterity, he drew the portraits of five of the most distinguished on a long panel and kept it in his house. One was Giotto, as the light and father of art, then Filippo di ser Brunelleschi for architecture, Donatello for sculpture, himself for perspective and animals, and his friend Giovanni Manetti for mathematics, with whom he frequently talked and argued on questions of Euclid.[21]

This is the passage in Vasari's second biography of Uccello that both multiplied and divided the authorship of the Louvre panel. What is often overlooked is the second slip that Vasari makes concerning the first name of Manetti, who is transformed from Antonio in 1550 to Giovanni in 1568.[22] The modern spectator is left with the niggling question: Who is Manetti anyway? He is missing from Vasari's lineup in the *Lives* (indeed, Vasari provides no portrait of Manetti in his 1568 edition).

The young man on the right whose red tunic reiterates the color scheme initiated by Giotto's robe turns to address his forefathers. His head uncovered, he stands confidently among this venerable group as its youngest member. He is usually identified as Antonio di Tuccio Manetti, the Florentine mathematician and architect, as well as Brunelleschi's first biographer. Why Vasari made this double slip (first with the authorship of the panel and then with Manetti's name) cannot really be known. This multiplication of the two Manetti, however, brings me to *The Fat Woodworker (Novella del Grasso legnaiuolo)*, a fifteenth-century novella written by the same mathematician of Vasari's muddled identification, our Antonio Manetti, the young man as identified on the Louvre panel.

The Fat Woodworker is a bizarre and wonderful tale about identity theft that revolves around yet another Manetti—nicknamed il Grasso, or the Fat One—who is the hapless victim of a deeply antihumanist prank mounted by none other than Brunelleschi, with the collaboration of Donatello.[23] In the short story, this illustrious gang of Florentine artists sets out to punish their friend, whose only crime was that he failed to show up to one of their dinner parties, by convincing him that he had been transformed somehow from a simple craftsman into a wayward Florentine nobleman named Matteo Mannini who was being pursued by his creditors. In spite of Manetto's repeated protests "non sono chi tu credi" (I am not who you think I am), he is arrested and imprisoned by Brunelleschi's network of accomplices.[24] While in prison, Manetto comes to (what can only be described as) the brutally Greenblattian conclusion that his veridical self has been irreparably refashioned by external forces beyond his control, and he is left with no other choice than to accept the impossible: he is now, at least in the eyes of Florence, Matteo.[25] It is in this moment of resignation that Brunelleschi's crew then inverts the prank and returns to addressing him as Manetto. When the poor woodworker discovers that he is the butt of the biggest joke of the century, he leaves Florence for Hungary, where he becomes yet another Manetto in the court of the king: Maestro Manetto di Firenze.

The subject in infinite regress is hardly restricted to the domain of modernist and postmodernist fiction; it was in fact a favorite theme emerging from what Manetti's commentators refer to as the culture of the prank: "la burla," "la beffa," and "la facezia."[26] Yet in his biography of Brunelleschi, the historical Manetti (our young man in red) insisted that the popularity of this story was attributed to its claim "che la fu storia vera" (that it was based on a true story).[27] The novella ends with the successful and wealthy Manetto returning to Florence years later where he confronts Brunelleschi, who recounts the chain of events that took place all those years ago:

> The Fat One smiled while hearing this story. He smiled at the thousand wonderful things within the story and within himself. He smiled at his confusion about whether he was dreaming or remembering dreams when he thought of the past. And he smiled about things that no one else knew about.[28]

Art-Historical Alter Egos

Two closing remarks: First, the Louvre panel can be read in a similar manner to the novella—as an embellished history involving contemporary artists whose names were known to its audience. Second, this passage communicates the beautiful resistance that images possess to totalizing explanations and pushes me to wonder whether our five Florentines are smiling at our confusion about whether we are dreaming or remembering dreams when we think of the past, and whether they are smiling about the things that we will never know but will nevertheless pursue.

Bill Brown has written that the "story of objects asserting themselves as things, then, is the story of a changed relation to the human subject and thus the story of how the thing really names less an object than a particular subject-object relation."[29] In the final analysis, the connoisseur, the historian, and the fabulist do not stand in staunch methodological opposition to one another. If connoisseurship is the id and history the disciplinary superego of art history, as has been suggested, perhaps fiction is where we find the healthy ego. This division, however, would be too clear-cut and simplistic; I would wish to see a more complex art-historical subject in which all three approaches function as methodological drives within the same art historian, who is always-already and at once the connoisseur, the historian, and the fabulist, struggling to cope with the anxiety of an unknowable past that speaks to us in hushed tones: *I am not who you think I am, but I am, nevertheless, based on a true story.*

I would like to thank the Leverhulme Trust for supporting this research at an early stage, Michael Hatt, Mark Ledbury, and the participants at the Clark Art Institute conference "Fictions of Art History" for the opportunity to present this material and for their critical feedback, Stefano Cracolici for helping me disentangle the various Italian versions of the *Novella*, and Marta Zboralska for her research assistance. All translations are mine unless otherwise indicated.

1. Giorgio Vasari, *Le Vite de più eccellenti pittori, scultori e architettori nelle redazione del 1550 e 1568*, ed. Rosanna Bettarini and Paola Barocchi (Florence: Sansoni, 1971), 2:134: "da Giotto in qua, di tutti i vecchi maestri Masaccio è il più moderno che si sia visto; e che e' mostrò col giudizio suo, quasiché per un testamento, in cinque teste fatte da lui, a chi per lo augumento fatto nelle arti si avesse ad avere il grado di quelle, lasciandocene in una tavola di sua mano, oggi in casa Giuliano da San Gallo in Fiorenza, i ritratti quasi vivissimi, che sono questi: Giotto per il principio della pittura, Donato per la scultura, Filippo Brunellesco per la architettura e Paulo Uccello per gli animali e per la prospettiva; e tra questi Antonio Manetti per eccellentissimo matematico de' tempi suoi" (1550 ed.). The five names correspond to the inscriptions on the Louvre painting, even if the sitters are slightly out of sequence. This minor aberration might be explained if we take into consideration that Vasari ordered the five Florentines in accordance with his hierarchy of professions (painting, sculpture, architecture, nature and perspective, and mathematics) rather than as the artist had depicted them in the panel.
2. Ibid., 70: "Amò Paulo, se bene era persona stratta, la virtù degli artefici suoi, e perché ne rimanesse a' posteri memoria ritrasse di sua mano in una tavola lunga cinque uomini segnalati, e la teneva in casa per memoria loro: l'uno era Giotto pittore, per il lume e principio dell'arte, Filippo di ser Brunelleschi il secondo, per l'architettura, Donatello per la scultura, e se stesso per la prospettiva et animali, e per la matematica Giovanni Manetti suo amico, col quale conferiva assai e ragionava delle cose di Euclide" (1568 ed.).
3. For the attribution history from 1923 to 1944, see Jenö Lanyi, "The Louvre Portrait of Five Men," *The Burlington Magazine* 84, no. 493 (April 1944): 87n2; for subsequent studies, see John Pope-Hennessy, *Paolo Uccello: Complete Edition* (London: Phaidon, 1969), 157–59.
4. Lanyi, "Louvre Portrait," 88.
5. Lanyi attempts to build a case around physiognomic resemblance, submitting a reversed reproduction of an alleged self-portrait in Masaccio's Brancacci Chapel frescoes. Ibid., plate IIIa. The Masaccio attribution was first suggested by Hermann Beenken, "Zum Werke des Masaccio," *Zeitschrfit für Bildende Kunst* 63 (1929/30): 112–19.
6. Vasari, *Vite*, 130: "Ma tra l'altre notabilissima apparisce quella dove San Piero per pagare il tributo cava per commissione di Cristo i danari del ventre del pesce; perché, oltra il vedersi quivi in un Apostolo che è nello ultimo il ritratto stesso di Masaccio fatto da lui medesimo a lo specchio, che par vivo vivo, e' vi si conosce lo ardire di San Piero nella dimanda e la attenzione degli Apostoli

nelle varie attitudini intorno a Cristo, aspettando la resoluzione con gesti sì pronti che veramente appariscon vivi" (1550 ed.).

7. See Sharon Gregory, "'The Outer Man Tends to Be a Guide to the Inner': The Woodcut Portraits in Vasari's *Lives* as Parallel Texts," *The Rise of the Image: Essays in the History of the Illustrated Book*, ed. Rodney Palmer and Thomas Frangenberg (Aldershot, U.K.: Ashgate, 2003), 56–57, which discusses such slippages in the text.

8. Pittaluga quoted in translation in Lanyi, "Louvre Portrait," 87n2; Mary Pittaluga, *Masaccio* (Florence: Le Monnier, 1923), 164.

9. Joseph A. Crowe and Giovanni B. Cavacaselle, quoted in Pope-Hennessy, *Uccello*, 157; Paul Schubring, *Cassoni: Truhen und Truhenbilder der italienischen Frührenaissance* (Leipzig: K.W. Hiersemann, 1915), 242.

10. Lanyi, "Louvre Portrait," 87: "There can be no accepting such a negative judgment, which, while adding nothing to the argument, robs the work of all value and would make all further enquiry into its historical importance illusory." Stefano Borsi, *Paolo Uccello* (London: Thames and Hudson, 1994), in contrast, questions whether it might have been commissioned by the Sangallo in the early sixteenth century.

11. Pope-Hennessy, *Uccello*, 158–59; Wilhelm Boecke, "Uccello-Studien," *Zeitschrfit für Kunstgeschichte* 2, no. 4 (1933): 249–75; Jean Lipman, "The Florentine Profile Portrait in the Quattrocento," *Art Bulletin* 18, no. 1 (1936): 54–102.

12. See Giorgio Vasari, *The Lives of the Painters, Sculptors, and Architects*, trans. A. B. Hinds (London: J.M. Dent and Sons, 1927), 1:238n1: "Now in the Louvre; critics attribute it to Antonella da Messina."

13. See "Cinq maîtres de la renaissance florentine," 1ère moitié 16e siècle, inv. 267, http://www.culture.gouv.fr/public/mistral/joconde_fr.

14. David Ebitz, "Connoisseurship as Practice," *Artibus et historiae* 9, no. 18 (1988): 208.

15. Gary Schwartz, "Connoisseurship: The Penalty of Ahistoricism," *Artibus et historiae* 9, no. 18 (1988): 202.

16. For the historical argument, see Schwartz, "Connoisseurship," 204–5; for slightly nuanced versions of this, see David Carrier, "In Praise of Connoisseurship," *Journal of Aesthetics and Art Criticism* 61, no. 2 (2003): 159–69; and Richard Neer, "Connoisseurship and the Stakes of Style," *Critical Inquiry* 32, no. 1 (2005): 1–26.

17. Carrier, "In Praise of Connoisseurship," 162.

18. See the who's who in Filippo M. Tuena, *Il Tesoro dei Medici: collezionismo a Firenze dal Quattrocento al Seicento* (Florence: Giunti Editore, 1987), 55.

19. Although if Uccello is the author, he appears here older than his contemporary Donatello:

"Paolo, vielli avant l'heure," wrote Mario Salmi, *Paolo Uccello, Andrea del Castagno, Domenico Veneziano* (Paris: A. Weber, 1937), 32.

20. For examples, see Pope-Hennessy, *Uccello*, 157; Christiane L. Joost-Gaugier, "Uccello's «Uccello»: A Visual Signature," *Gazette des Beaux Arts* 84, no. 6 (1974): 237; Patricia Emison, *Creating the "Divine" Artist: From Dante to Michelangelo* (Leiden: Brill, 2004), 285.

21. Vasari, *Lives of the Painters*, 238.

22. Paul Joannides, *Masaccio and Masolino: A Complete Catalogue* (London: Phaidon, 1993), cat. R4, explains this "slip of the pen" referring to Manetti's Christian name.

23. Robert Martone and Valerie Martone point out in their introduction to *The Fat Woodworker by Antonio Manetti* (New York: Italica Press, 1991), xv–xvi, that the Manetto of the story may correspond to either the Florentine woodworker and pupil of Brunelleschi, yet another Antonio Manetti (called "Ciaccheri"), or the Florentine intarsia worker, Manetto di Jacopo Ammannatini.

24. Antonio Manetti, *Vita di Filippo Brunelleschi preceduta da la novella del Grasso*, ed. Domenico de Robertis (Milan: Polifilo, 1976), 9.

25. Stephen Greenblatt, *Renaissance Self-Fashioning: From More to Shakespeare* (Chicago: University of Chicago Press, 1983). Pursuing a similar line of argument, Manfredo Tafuri, *Interpreting the Renaissance: Princes, Cities, Architects*, trans. Daniel Sherer (New Haven, Conn.: Yale University Press, 2006), 1, described *The Fat Woodworker* as a "bewildering system of replications, a treacherous conspiracy, a cruel and irreal comedy." For Tafuri, the novella could be compared to the claustrophobic spatial world created in the woodworker's intarsia, where artificial codes (i.e., the symbolic language of perspective) replaced the original natural code, and where the reliability of lived experience was supplanted by the authenticating powers of representation.

26. Giuliano Tanturli, in the introduction to *Vita di Filippo Brunelleschi*, xliii; André Rochon, "Une date importante dans l'histoire de la beffa: La Nouvelle du Grasso legnaiuolo," *Formes et signification de la «beffa» dans la littérature italienne de la Renaissance*, vol. 2 (Paris: Université de la Sorbonne Nouvelle, 1975), 211–376; Giorgio Manganelli in the introduction to *La novella del Grasso legnaiuolo*, ed. Paolo Procacciali (Parma: Fondazione Pietro Bembo, 1990), xv; and Antonio Lanza in the introduction to *La novella del Grasso legnaiuolo*, ed. Antonio Lanza (Florence: Vallecchi Editore, 1989), 7.

27. Antonio Manetti, *Vita di Filippo Brunelleschi*, 47.

28. Martone, *Fat Woodworker*, 52. The Martone translation is based on a different manuscript than the one used in the 1976 translation; Manetti, *La novella del Grasso*, 42, where the text suggests that it is Brunelleschi (and not il Grasso) who smiles upon hearing the tale: "gli disse questa novella ridendo continovamente, con mille be' casi drentovi, che erano stati in lui proprio, che non si potevano sapere per altri, e dello essere el Grasso e del nonn essere, e s'egli aveva sognato, o se sognava quand'egli ramemoriava el passato; di condizione che Filippo non aveva mai pel passato rìsone sì di buon cuore

come fece questa volta." Multiple written versions existed with such variations; on these philological issues, see *La novella del Grasso legnaiuolo*, ed. Paolo Procacciali (Parma: Fondazione Pietro Bembo, 1990): "Regesto delle Edizioni."

29. Bill Brown, "Thing Theory," *Critical Inquiry* 28 (2001): 4.

Fictional Deceptions: A True Story

Joanna Scott

The Unreal Reality of Masks

In his introduction to the memoirs of the Italian playwright Carlo Gozzi, the nineteenth-century English writer John Addington Symonds invites his reader to imagine a procession of masked commedia dell'arte performers crossing a stage.[1] First comes a fop wearing a woolen cap, short trousers, red slippers, with half his face concealed by a black domino. This is Pantalone, the Venetian merchant, who, Symonds tells us, is "good-hearted, shrewd, canny, yet preserving a certain childlike simplicity." He is followed by the Doctor, a "walking caricature of learning," who wears "a hideous black mask smudged with red patches, like skin-disease or wine-stains" (fig. 1). Next come the two Zanni twins from the countryside of Bergamo: Arlecchino, a rustic servant, who is "light-headed, gluttonous, gay, pliable, credulous, ingeniously naïve," and his "roguish, clever, cowardly" brother Brighella. More servants and peasants follow, including the famous black-masked, beak-nosed Pulcinella, a cast of women that includes Columbina, Rosetta, and Smeraldina, and a "fantastic extravagant troop of soldiers" led by their swaggering Capitano.

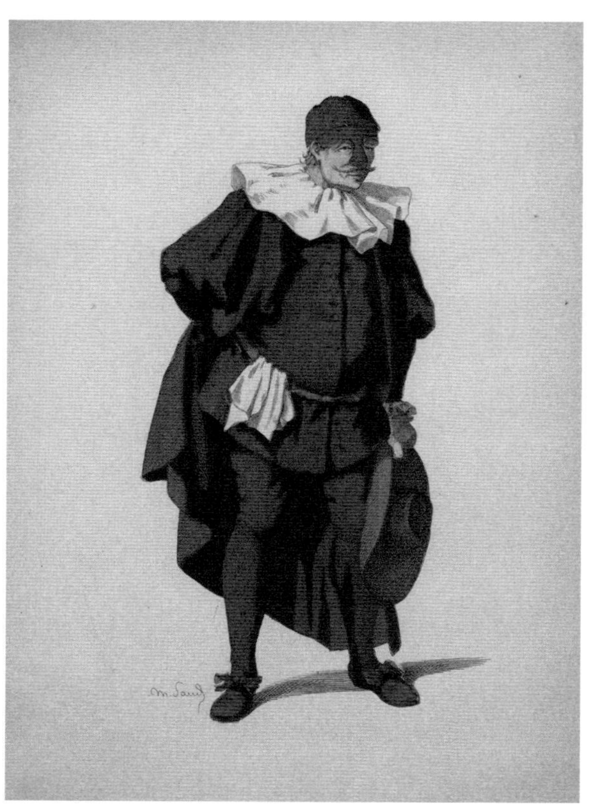

Fig. 1. Maurice Sand (1823–1889), *Il Dottore*, 1653. Engraved by A. Manceau. Published in *The Memoirs of Count Carlo Gozzi* (New York: Scribner and Welford, 1890), 1:160. The Getty Research Institute, Los Angeles (2565–899)

Wearing their signature masks, these stock characters were easy to recognize. But as Symonds presents the tradition, commedia dell'arte was celebrated more for its surprises than its predictable performances. Audiences did not go to the theater just to see their favorite characters act out stories they already knew; they went to see how the stories would be varied, and how each mask would be remodeled by the actor who wore it.

> The *Commedia dell'Arte* combined fixity of outline in the masks with illimitable plasticity in the details communicated by the genius and personality of their sustainers. The mask, the traditional character, was something which a comedian assumed; but he dealt with it as he found it suited to his physical and mental qualities. Each distinguished actor re-created the part he represented. The improvised extempore rule of the game allowed him boundless license. . . . Parts crossed and intercrossed. Pulcinella borrowed something from Arlecchino; Brighella patched himself with rags from Coviella's wardrobe.[2]

In this account of the connection between comedians and their masks, Symonds links the success of a performance to the mask's dynamic potential. By combining *fixity of outline* with *illimitable plasticity*, the traditional commedia dell'arte mask was more than a label announcing a familiar identity; the mask gave the performer an identity to reshape and change, to play with and against. It focused the audience's attention on the surface, and yet at the same time it hinted at the secrets it concealed. The performer and the character met in a contest that was played out in the dialogue between body and mask.

In Symonds's version of its history, commedia dell'arte did more than repeat well-worn skits. The familiar characters were *re-created* with each performance, and the restrictions related to each part were offset by the performer's "boundless license." The mask signaled both a revival and an invention, and the actors were judged by their skilled variations. Thanks to the identifiable masks, the audience knew what to expect; at the same time, it was understood that the comedians would play their parts in unexpected ways.

As every American who has ever answered the door on Halloween knows, masks can be startling. A mask draws attention to itself, though not only because of its exaggerated features. Its attraction comes from being a paradoxical thing. When it is hanging on a hook in the costume section of the local Walmart, even the most grotesque mask looks hopelessly lifeless. When it is worn by a living, breathing human being, however, and we see it moving in connection with a moving body, a familiar mask becomes unpredictable. A mask is as effective at protecting secrets as it is at exposing obsessions. It provides an opportunity for both conformity and rebellion. It indicates that there is a script to follow and at the same time reminds us of the performer's freedom to improvise. The mask's concealment can be artistically liberating, but it can also be morally dangerous, as the Venetian Doge realized at least as early as the year 1268, when, in what has been described as the first known legal reference to masks in Venice, they passed a law forbidding masqueraders from throwing eggs.[3]

Symonds attributes the success of the commedia dell'arte to its variations and surprises. A more recent advocate of the tradition, Jacques Lecoq, who is best known as a performer and teacher of physical theater, wonders about the controlled aspects of the performances.

> The commedia dell'arte is a magical territory in theater, one that has always inspired dreams and imagination. For two centuries, this great reservoir of actor-improvisers traveled from Italy all around Europe. The actors kept the same roles and gave a sense of perpetuity to the characters. How many men wore Harlequin's mask? . . . How did they perform? Did they really improvise?[4]

His answer to this last question is telling: he insists that "the actors did not improvise." The performances may have been reliably identical from one night to the next. What distinguished them was the richness of their original "lazzi," or jokes.

> Every author, whether he creates a gesture or a spoken or written text, improvises the first time that he moves in the space or puts pen to paper. Even if he has an initial idea, he must at some point throw himself into the unknown. From this starting point, the actor-improviser-author rehearses and refines his creation, testing it and finally performing it for an audience, who sees only the finished product.[5]

In his version of the history of traditional commedia dell'arte, Lecoq bundles the actor, improviser, and author together and offers a basic explanation for how an idea or impulse is translated into a finished work of art. Creative expression must begin as a confrontation with "the unknown" and initially demands an improvisational effort. The creation is polished through rehearsals or revisions. The "finished product" involves deliberate choices that the artist has tested and refined.

While visiting Padua in 1948, Lecoq participated in an effort to revive the tradition of commedia dell'arte, and the Italian sculpture Amleto Sartori made him a leather mask. When Lecoq went to try on the mask, he was disappointed. It sat too tightly on his face, and the leather was too soft. Only when Sartori remade it with firmer leather was Lecoq satisfied. "That's when I realised that you need a distance between a mask and a face to make the mask play," he reports.[6]

A good mask, he goes on to explain, must be made "so that it can perform." It should not lose its "vitality" when it is turned to profile. It should be a shape and not a painting, and preferably of one color that does not shine in the light. Finally, a good mask should not have an obvious, permanent expression, Lecoq insists. He claims that he cannot even imagine "a mask that laughs all the time." The shape of the features may be fixed, but the mask should move and change as the actor moves and changes. "It's not enough to just look at a mask and identify the propositions of its shape and intent; to really make it work, you have to wear it and experiment with the movements that it suggests."

Lecoq identifies five types of masks for his students to use in training: the undecorated neutral mask, the expressive mask with exaggerated features, the counter-mask that combines opposing expressions, the nonfigurative larval mask, and lastly, "the smallest mask in the world"—the clown's red nose. The masks have different uses, Lecoq says, but regardless of their shape or size, they all help to focus attention on the essential. They make it impossible to rely on the habits of ordinary life. They turn an ordinary person into a performer and illuminate "the elements of vivacity that life has not yet revealed." They force "an actor to raise his game"[7] so that every movement has dramatic intention (fig. 2). It is up to the wearer to make the lifeless object come alive "and help the audience to discover the mysterious relationship between masks and life."[8]

In his celebration of traditional commedia dell'arte, John Addington Symonds pays tribute to the paradoxical nature of the mask. In his more detailed examination of the theatrical uses of the mask, Jacques Lecoq explores how an actor-improviser-author puts that paradox into performance.

Picasso coined the phrase "trompe l'esprit" to describe how an image can convince us to treat the unreality of art as something real.[9] With trompe l'esprit, we do not just mistakenly see a three-dimensional reality of a staircase or a corridor in an illusory two-dimensional trompe l'oeil; we experience the illusion *as* reality.[10] More important than the ostensible resemblance is the deliberate way the artist manipulates perception. Picasso used the phrase in reference to the development of papier collé, but it could also be used to describe the effect of a dynamic mask on a viewer. By exposing the materials that have been used to create the image, a mask, like a collage, gives us a chance to understand the constructed nature of experience.

Picasso's *La repasseuse*, or *Woman Ironing*, painted in Paris in the spring of 1904, can be seen as a transitional piece, coming at the end of his blue period and pointing toward the development of Cubism (fig. 3). The bent figure of the woman looks like it has been cut to fit her outline, as though her surface were made of cardboard and could be lifted away. Her appearance is separate from the self that it hides, and its artificial angularity conveys the crushing effect of the oppression she endures. The masking band of shadow across her eyes evokes a prisoner's blindfold. While we do not know who she is, the flatness of the figure suggests an unrepresented dimension that we can only imagine.

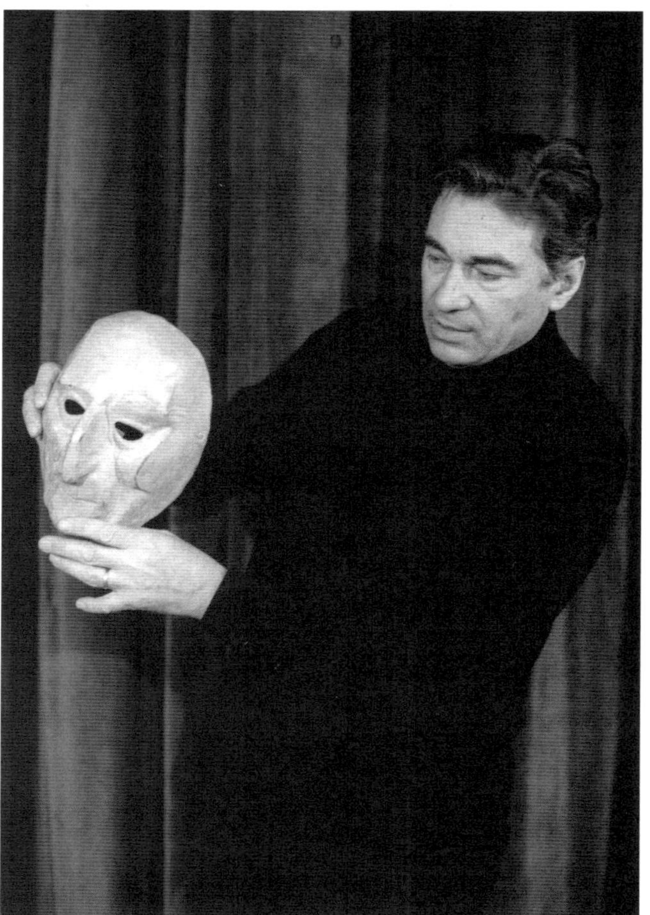

Fig. 2. Jacques Lecoq handling an expressive mask of Amleto Sartori. © Patrick Leqoc

There are more obvious manipulations announcing themselves in Picasso's ironic sculpture *Bull's Head*, from 1942 (fig. 4). Though wildly different,

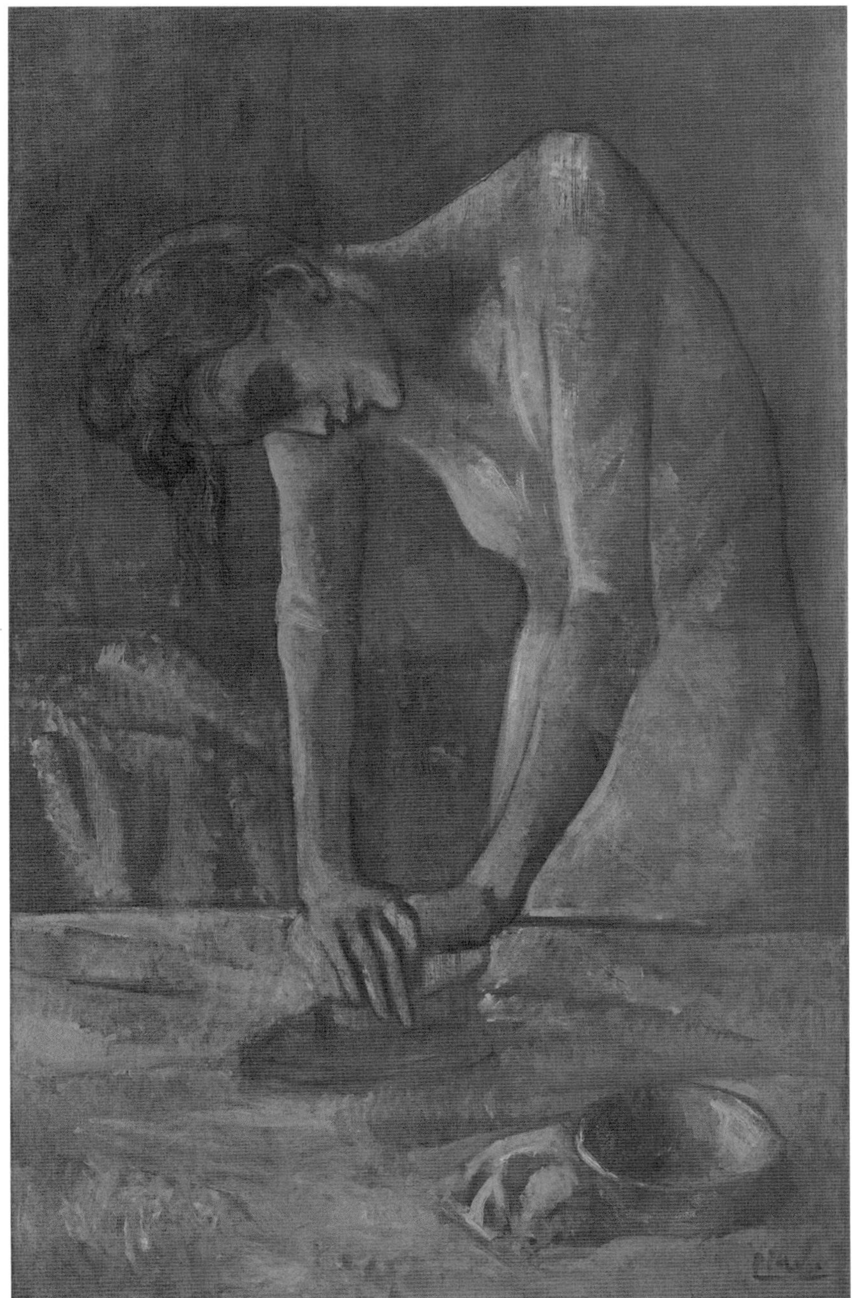

Fig. 3. Pablo Picasso (Spain, 1881–1973), *Woman Ironing (La repasseuse)*, Paris, spring 1904. Oil on canvas, 45 3/4 x 28 3/4 in. (116.2 x 73 cm). Solomon R. Guggenheim Museum, New York, Thannhauser Collection, Gift, Justin K. Thannhauser 78.2514.41. © 2012 Estate of Pablo Picasso/Artists Rights Society (ARS), New York

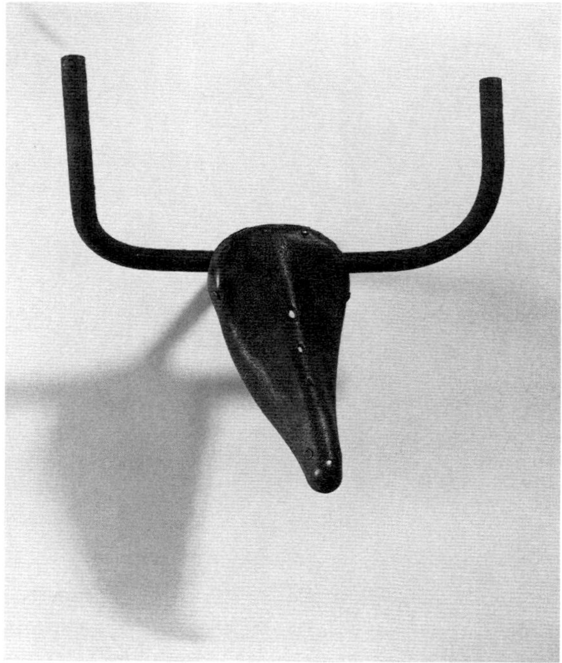

Fig. 4. Pablo Picasso, *Bull's Head (Tête de taureau)*, Paris, spring 1942. Leather bicycle saddle and metal handlebars, bronzing, 13 1/8 × 17 1/8 × 7 1/2 in. (33.3 × 43.5 × 19.1 cm). Musée National Picasso, Pablo Picasso Bequest, 1979. © 2012 Estate of Pablo Picasso/Artists Rights Society (ARS), New York

Bull's Head shares with *Woman Ironing* a mask-like surface that expresses the subject it purports to represent and at the same time exposes its artificiality. Bronzed, fused bicycle parts do not equal a bull's head any more than oppression equals the true identity of the woman ironing. But in their manipulations and containments, the false surfaces reveal the intended subjects in the same way that masks reveal the selves they are designed to conceal.

Picasso spoke about the origins of the sculpture, describing how he found in "a pile of jumble an old bicycle saddle next to some rusted handlebars. . . . In a flash they were associated in my mind."[11] It was as if the finished work was there waiting for the artist to catch up to it. He had only to solder the parts together and then bronze them to give them unity, he said. It all sounds so easy. For some critics, in fact, *Bull's Head* might be too easy. Is it "no more than a clever and surprising joke?" Alan Bowness asks. Or is it, as Jon Green argues, on the "cutting edge of tragicomic"?[12]

One answer can be found in Picasso's own description of the effect of bronze: "What is wonderful about bronze is that it can give the most incongruous objects such a unity that it is sometimes difficult to identify the elements that make them up. But it is also a danger. If you only see the bull's head and not the saddle and handlebars from which it is made, then the sculpture loses its interest."[13] In this sense, the bull's head functions as a mask, communicating an identity that is both singular and generic.

In its dynamic relationship with its subject, a mask is the visual embodiment of meaning that is constructed partly from within and partly from without. A *good* mask is blatantly false and at the same time unabashedly expressive. It starts out telling a story we think we already know, and it ends up telling a story we have never heard before.

The Unreal Reality of Fiction

Fiction writers share with masked performers the challenge of creating something that can be experienced as a convincing illusion, a trompe l'esprit. The assertions of truth that fill a fictional narrative are inherently contradictory. For many writers, this is a problem best ignored while they get on with their stories. For others, the status of truth within a fictional frame becomes in itself an important subject to consider.

"In the second half of the 1960s I traveled repeatedly from England to Belgium," begins the narrator of Sebald's *Austerlitz*.[14] Really? No, not really, since the narrator is no more than an arrangement of words stuck inside a book. And that poem titled "Pale Fire," consisting of nine hundred and ninety lines divided into four cantos—was it actually composed, as Nabokov's Charles Kinbote claims, by John Francis Shade?[15] The answer must be emphatically no, not because Kinbote will himself call into doubt his own assertions but because, in reality, there is no such person named Charles Kinbote. He is a ghost of a concept made of language, as unreal as the "old coffee-brown, black-veiled woman who made her living by telling stories" and who opens Isak Dinesen's "The Blank Page" with a tale of her own.[16]

"You want a tale, sweet lady and gentleman?" Dinesen's old woman asks. "Indeed I have told many tales, one more than a thousand, since that time when I first let young men tell me, myself, tales of a red rose, two smooth lily buds, and four silky, supple, deadly entwining snakes."[17] If she is "well paid and in good spirits," she will tell a story. Under similar circumstances, most authors will oblige. They will offer a pack of lies to entertain us. And with their slippery narrative techniques they might confuse us and mix in some truth with their trickery.

Certainly one of the pleasures strong fiction can offer is its ability to persuade us of the legitimacy of its artificial reality. We talk about the spell fiction casts, its dreamlike qualities, the willing suspension of disbelief. We talk about the feeling of immersion in the imagined world of a novel. We enjoy the forgetfulness that goes along with an absorption in reading. But all these pleasures are not only connected to the artificiality of any fiction; they are made possible because of fiction's invented status. A work that presents itself as a concoction succeeds for the same reasons that Lecoq's "good mask" succeeds: it has vitality and dramatic

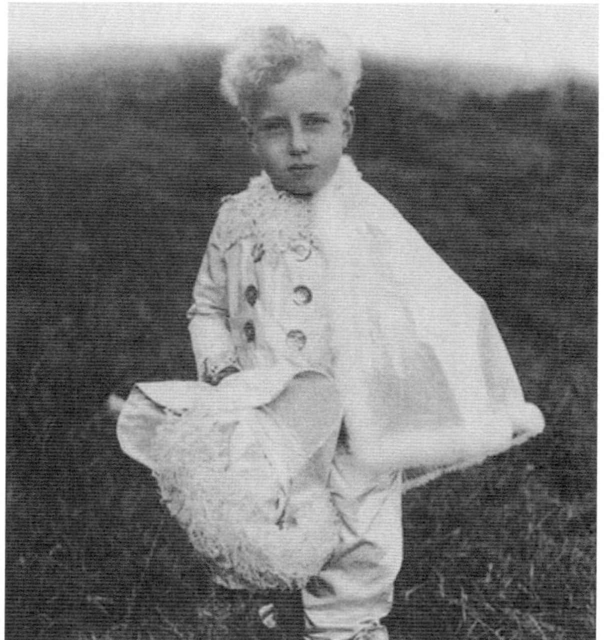

Fig. 5. Photograph of an unknown child from the cover of W. G. Sebald, *Austerlitz*, trans. Althea Belle (New York: Random House, 2001)

intention. And in the hands of an able writer, it gives its audience an opportunity to discover the mysterious relationship between the made-up story and the purpose that infuses it.

Most stories are designed to persuade readers that their purpose is worthy. But since fiction, like any masquerade, is bound up with deception, it is important to consider the role of skepticism in the experience of reading. Sebald's narrator, for instance, is not asking us to believe that the photograph, ostensibly of his main character Austerlitz as a child, actually proves that Austerlitz exists (fig. 5). Rather, he is asking us to believe that the image makes an enriching contribution to the fictional story of Austerlitz, in the same way that a gesture or the tilt of a head can animate a mask.

At every point, a work of fiction reminds us of the paradoxical relationship between its false claims and its potential meanings. It is malleable and can change and move to accommodate both the author's and reader's changing awareness. Its success is best measured by its dynamic qualities. A good story prompts us to imagine its invention. Even as the unfolding narrative makes us wonder about what is to come, it invites us to consider how it came into being. It is necessarily in disguise. And whether it wears a huge, enveloping mask or the bulb of a clown's nose, it is always, to some degree, absurd.

Reading the Disguise

To say that fiction is defined by its falseness might seem too close to a tautology for comfort. Yet, unlike a theatrical performance, fiction does not have explicit visual markers to remind its audience of its artificiality. However tinged with irony and self-consciousness the language might be, the boundaries between the real and the imagined can get blurry as a story goes on. This is part of the fun, especially for writers interested in testing the limits of fiction. Even when a narrator tells us that the unreal story is unimpeachably "true," he is preparing us for an encounter with paradox.

Defining fiction as "consciously false," Frank Kermode has distinguished between the useful absurdities of fiction and the dangerous deceptions of myth: "Fictions can degenerate into myths whenever they are not consciously held to be fictive. In this sense, anti-Semitism is a degenerate fiction, a myth; and *Lear* is a fiction."[18] In Kermode's analysis, myth and fiction are differentiated by the way they communicate their falseness. They might make all sorts of truth claims, but unlike myth, fiction does not ask us to believe in it.

Its obvious deception is not just a given of fiction. It has been and remains one of the most productive impulses in the genre. Whether Daniel Defoe's fictional editor assures us that *Robinson Crusoe* is "a just history of fact; neither is there any appearance of fiction in it" or Nabokov's Kinbote claims that *Pale Fire* "was composed by John Francis Shade (born July 5, 1898, died July 21, 1959)," a narrative made up of unreal characters invites us to pay attention to the persuasive powers of language and, by implication, to examine the role of belief. As Kermode says, "Fictions are for finding things out." Fiction is able to do this because of its conscious falseness rather than in spite of it. Whenever a fictional narrator says, *Reader, this really happened*, the reason for the claim must be considered. What does an author gain when he declares his fiction "a just history of fact"? What does such a claim tell us about the nature of fact when it is made by a fictional character? It tells us, at the very least, to think skeptically as we read on.

One of the most instructive passages to consider in these terms is the culminating encounter in Henry James's story, "The Jolly Corner," when the main character, Spenser Brydon, sees, or thinks he see, an occult version of himself. Brydon, who has returned to New York after an absence of thirty-three years, spends most of the story prowling through his family's vacant townhouse. The setting has a stage-like quality to it. The rooms are dimly lit by Brydon's small lamp, the suspense is described as "a single mouthful, as it were, of terror and applause," and he imagines that "a spectator" would have taken him for "a solemn simpleton playing at hide-and-seek."[19] What begins as an exploration of the building becomes a frantic search for himself: he imagines that he is stalking the man he would have become if he had stayed in New York—or maybe his *alter ego* is stalking him. He keeps turning around and retracing his steps, "as if he might so catch in his face at least the stirred air of some other quick revolution." He thinks of himself as the hunter; a moment later, he is sure that he is being hunted. As he tries to outmaneuver a prey he has yet to see, he compares himself to "Pantaloon, at the Christmas farce, buffeted and tricked from behind by ubiquitous Harlequin."[20]

It is consistent with the other theatrical metaphors in the story that when Brydon is on the verge of being overwhelmed by the tension of his self-generated suspense, the narrator invokes commedia dell'arte. It follows that at the moment of confrontation, his apparition is simultaneously exposed and hidden:

> Rigid and conscious, spectral yet human, a man of his own substance and stature waited there to measure himself with his power to dismay. This only could it be—this only till he recognised, with his advance, that what made the face dim was the pair of raised hands that covered it and in which, so far from being offered in defiance, it was buried as for dark deprecation. So Brydon, before him, took him in; with every fact of him now, in the higher light, hard and acute—his planted stillness, his vivid truth, his grizzled bent head and white masking hands, his queer actuality of evening-dress, of dangling double-eye-glass, of gleaming silk lappet and white linen, of pearl button and gold watch—guard and polished shoe.[21]

Brydon has been yearning for this encounter, but when it happens, or when, in his delirium, he imagines it happens, he is grateful for the mask that the apparition is making with his hands. He sees the hands as "splendid" and "strong," despite the fact that on one hand, two fingers "were reduced to stumps, as if accidentally shot away." For Brydon, the mask is a welcome, though, as it turns out, only temporary concealment. Just as he is thinking that he has been saved from confronting his alternate self directly, the hands open and drop, revealing a face that is defined as "grotesque" primarily because it is unfamiliar. As "the face of a stranger," it so shocks Brydon that he collapses: "His head went round; he was going; he had gone."

Fainting is a melodramatic device for a modern writer like James to use to close a climactic scene. But melodrama is in keeping with the spirit of the masquerade that permeates the story. Brydon has situated himself in an entrapping farce and is willing to see only what he is able to imagine. To remove the mask and look directly on a truth that it has supposedly been concealing involves a degree of exposure that cannot be described or adequately comprehended.

At the moment the face is revealed, the narrator offers no visual details. What Brydon sees is "unknown, inconceivable, awful, disconnected from any possibility—!" Later, after he has awoken, he can only consider what he missed: "I was to have known myself," he says, the convoluted tense expressing his inability to see his alternative self directly.

Spenser Brydon faints because he cannot believe that a vision of himself exists independent from his imagination. If he learns anything about himself from the encounter, it is through the apprehension of the mask. The indescribable face can only be perceived as a hideous absence. In contrast, the mask of the hands, with the two stumps in place of fingers, generates questions and hints at a mystery. At the moment of crisis, Brydon reads the mask much as we read the story. By interpreting the partial evidence that the mutilated hands present, he imagines what he cannot see.

The "poor hands" that initially shield Brydon from himself share with Lecoq's "good mask" the power to reveal meaning through the vibrantly paradoxical strategy of concealment. The language James uses to describe the hands tells us much more about Brydon than the negating abstractions describing the face. Only when Brydon believes he is seeing himself in disguise does he see himself with any clarity; when he believes he is seeing the uninhibited truth, he goes blank.

Fiction can seem a tempting mode for other genres to mimic. From the perspective of a writer who is responsible for conveying meaning through facts and careful argument, a novelist has an enviable freedom. For all the freedom that an invented narrative allows, however, it comes with its own peculiar set of demands. Fiction writers are expected to adhere to the pretenses they have established and keep the mask on at all times. They give expression to the meanings they want to convey through the false claims made by their fictional characters. Their language is full of lies and innuendo, and readers are rarely fooled.

Fiction invites us to believe that its invented, dynamic, linguistic expression is perfectly suited to its subject. At its best, it is as engulfing as a dream while at the same time it thrives on our skepticism. It shares its deceptions with theater.

More precisely, it shares its potential with commedia dell'arte. It can make the most familiar situation surprising. Through the supple movement of its prose, it gives new meaning to old words, making our well-worn language startling and strange. It leaves behind the haunting impression of trompe l'esprit rather than certain knowledge. And, to its lasting credit, it is close to useless as a means of conveying information, since no matter what it says, it cannot be trusted.

1. Carlo Gozzi, *The Memoirs of Count Carlo Gozzi,* trans. John Addington Symonds (New York: Scribner and Welford, 1890), 1:44–50.

2. Ibid., 48.

3. Pompeo Molmenti, *Venice: Its Individual Growth from the Earliest Beginnings to the Fall of the Republic,* trans. Horatio F. Brown (Chicago: A. C. McClurg and Co., 1906), 1:217.

4. Jacques Lecoq, *Theatre of Movement and Gesture,* ed. David Bradley (London and New York: Routledge, 2006), 100.

5. Ibid., 101.

6. Ibid., 103.

7. Ibid.

8. Ibid., 107.

9. Jon D. Green, "Picasso's Visual Metaphors," *Journal of Aesthetic Education* 19, no. 4 (Winter 1985): 61–76.

10. "When Picasso remarked that there is no *trompe l'oeil, only trompe l'esprit,* he was expressing a corollary to a principle formulated some three hundred years earlier by Descartes, who wrote in his Optics (1637), "'It is the mind which sees, not the eye.'" David Blinder, "In Defense of Pictorial Mimesis," *The Journal of Aesthetics and Art Criticism* 45, no. 1 (Fall 1986): 19–27.

11. Green, "Picasso's Visual Metaphors," 71.

12. Ibid., 71.

13. Ibid., 38.

14. W. G. Sebald, *Austerlitz,* trans. Althea Belle (New York: Random House, 2001), 3.

15. Vladimir Nabokov, *Pale Fire* (New York: Vintage, 1989), 13.

16. Isak Dinesen, *Last Tales* (New York: Vintage, 1975), 99.

17. Ibid., 99.

18. Frank Kermode, *The Sense of an Ending: Studies in the Theory of Fiction* (New York: Oxford University Press, 2000), 39. Kermode draws his category of "the consciously false" from the philosopher

Hans Vaihinger, who argued that fictional "as if" reasoning can be used in mathematical proofs to extract truth from fictional absurdities.

19. Henry James, "The Jolly Corner," *The Turn of the Screw, The Aspern Papers, and Two Stories* (New York: Barnes and Noble Classics, 2003), 280–82.

20. Ibid., 281.

21. Ibid., 290.

The Art-Historical Photograph as Fiction: The Pretense of Objectivity

Ralph Lieberman

By the phrase "photograph as fiction," I do not mean playful images put together in Photoshop but something produced by the camera alone, something more credible and therefore much more dangerous. The title of this essay is not intended to suggest that what follows is an exposé; I do not claim that art history is inherently bogus because at times it is about misleading images more than about the works those images purport to show. The points I raise are part of a larger study of how photography, the enabling medium of the new discipline, shaped art history and limited it to what can be shown by photographs, while at the same time the images demanded by art historians often tended to describe works of art in exaggerated or over-simplified ways.

Both photography and art history emerged during one of the great periods in the history of science, when many discoveries were aided by new or newly improved instruments, such as the spectrograph, which made it possible to see hidden things or to see and understand visible ones better. As dramatic advances captured the attention of an educated public, students of the humanities strove to make their own disciplines scientific and often claimed that they had. And so it came to pass that in those days *Kunstwissenschaft*, an oxymoron, was born.

In 1839, the year photography was introduced, Johann Passavant published his monograph on Raphael, regarded as a pivotal work in the history of art history because it contained the first catalogue raisonné.[1] Passavant was trained as a painter, and most of the illustrations in his book were reproductions of his own drawings of Raphael's works; those that were not were based on drawings by artists he felt represented the works with the degree of objectivity he felt necessary. He insisted that his long training as an artist, and constant, painstaking care to be precise and impartial prevented inaccuracies in his study (figs. 1a and 1b).

Passavant had been introduced to art history in Florence in 1817 by Karl Friedrich von Rumohr, who was regarded by his colleagues and students as instrumental in establishing an advanced type of enquiry. Rumohr wrote that, while it was difficult to avoid subjectivity, it could be done, but it meant rooting out one's personal prejudices; he believed that "the objective standards of a truly scientific method could be reached only by curbing subjectivity: 'Only a mind free of limiting preferences for certain tendencies, certain schools and

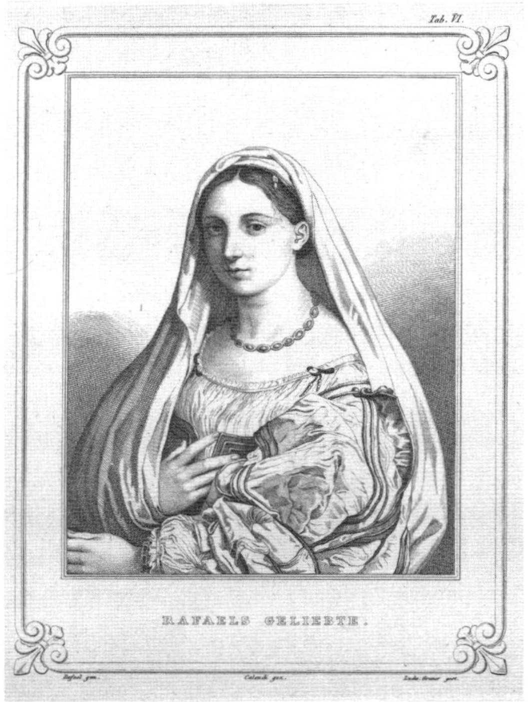

Fig. 1a. Ludwig Grüner (German, 1801–1882) after Giuseppe Calendi (Italian, 19th century), after Raphael (Italian, 1483–1520), *Rafaels Geliebte (Raphael's Beloved)*, 1839. Engraving. Published in Johann David Passavant, *Raffael von Urbino und sein Vater Giovanni Santi* (Leipzig: F. A. Brockhaus, 1839–58), vol. 2, plate 6

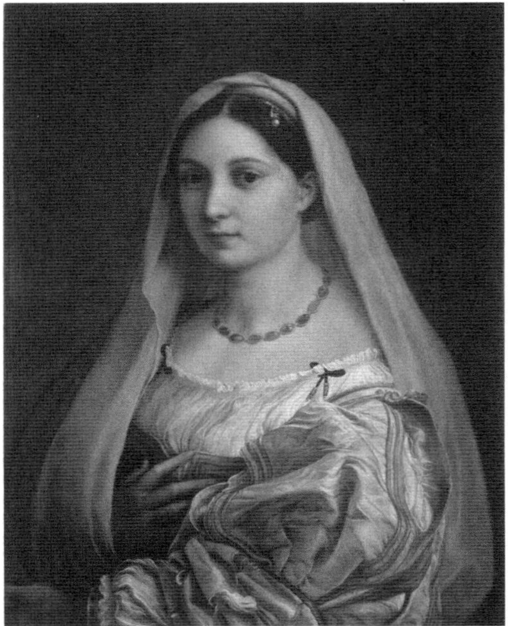

Fig. 1b. Raphael (Italian, 1483–1520), *Veiled Woman*, c. 1513. Oil on canvas, 32 1/2 x 23 1/2 in. (85 x 64 cm). Galleria Palatina, Palazzo Pitti, Florence

artistic conventions can grasp the essence of art.'"[2] One had to be scientific, not aesthetically sensitive; the necessary objectivity was achieved by what has been called "the double reformation of self and sight."[3]

Photography appeared to offer exact, value-free images, and some claimed that it provided illustrations so accurate that with them one could write about or study a work of art as if in front of the piece itself. The claim for the camera was essentially the same as that made for laboratory instruments: it allowed precise observations on which to base objective statements.

In the early days, photographs of paintings were not used for illustrations because the medium was crude when it first appeared, and the light-sensitive material that made it possible was limited and largely color-blind. It darkened most when exposed to blue light, rendering blue areas white in the print. The skies in early photographs of architecture or landscapes are invariably white, which is not necessarily unrealistic, but seeing the Virgin in a white mantle is more problematic. Yellow was darkened and anything red became black. These distortions led people in the early days to use photographs almost exclusively for the study of drawings and prints, claiming that with no color to confound the film those media at least could be accurately represented. As would later be clear, they were merely more credible, but connoisseurship begins with the study of drawings, which is the earliest example of the direction of art history being determined by the character and limits of photography.

Although early on photographs were used for study, they did not fully replace engraved reproductions in publications until the twentieth century. Before then, books and periodicals were illustrated by the work of copyists, some of whom who could make Passavant look remarkably amateurish. However, in the preference for images produced by "objective" means, any handmade image, even a rendering as painstaking as Gaillard's illustration of Michelangelo's *Dusk* (fig. 2), suffered from the a priori assumption that it was necessarily inaccurate to some degree.

Photography was therefore to be the foundation of art history, and as photochemical technology advanced, early images were dismissed as defective and misleading, while more recent ones were celebrated for their exactness. In 1893 Bernard Berenson, whose work depended more on photographs than that of anyone up to his time, described those made with the new isochromatic film. Claiming that the modern study of art had been changed most by the railroad, which allowed people to go see things easily, and photography, which brought things to the viewer, he singled out Passavant's work on Raphael, written before

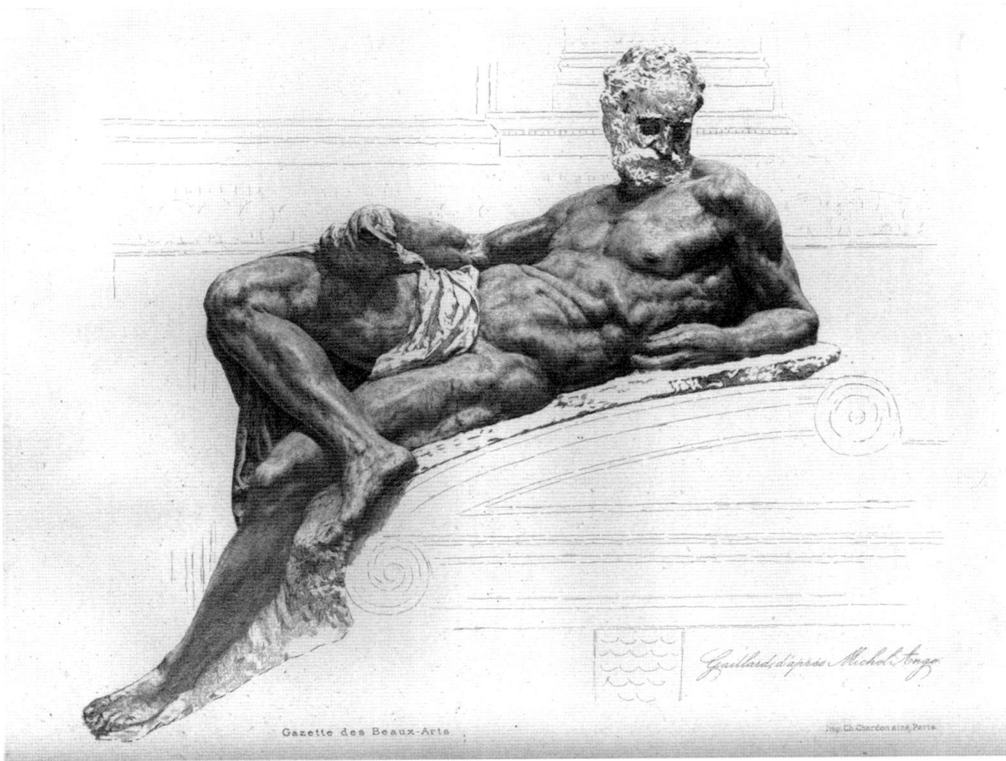

Fig. 2. Claude-Ferdinand Gaillard (German, 1834–1887), *Dusk (after Michelangelo)*, 1876. Engraving on chine, 7 x 9 ½ in. (18 x 24 cm). Published in *Gazette des beaux-arts* 13 (1 January 1876), pp. 102–3

the development of either, as “therefore so unsound that . . . it no longer has any value.”[4] Regarding his own more up-to-date method, he wrote:

> Of the writer on art today, we all expect not only that intimate acquaintance with his subject which modern means of conveyance have made possible, but also that patient comparison of a given work with all the other works by the same master which photography has rendered easy. And when the continuous study of originals is supplemented by isochromatic photographs, such comparison attains almost the accuracy of the physical sciences.[5]

Berenson’s claim that at last photographs finally made the study of art scientific (“really accurate connoisseurship” is “so new a science that it has as yet scarcely found its way into general recognition")[6] was based on new photosensitive material, but the faith in camera-made images is the old one; the underlying assumptions about their accuracy and objectivity were still not being questioned openly or systematically.[7]

The lack of skepticism about photographs reveals the degree to which art historians practice their craft in a fundamentally non-scientific way. A scientist is engaged in a constant struggle with recalcitrant devices—experimental physicists spend most of their time trying to determine which of their findings are false readings from faulty instruments—and analysis of those tools is part of their basic training, for they often design and build their own apparatus from the ground up, and understand it completely. Art historians, by contrast, are not usually taught anything about cameras or lenses or the nature of the images they produce; I have met some who were unaware that image contrast is the photographer's choice and can be altered to achieve a better effect. The problem with the camera is not that it tells lies but that it commits perjury, swearing to its big lies by means of small truths. It will not simplify a complex form from fatigue or incompetence, and it renders textures with stunning clarity, so we are often seduced by such evidence of accuracy into believing everything else it shows.

While some art historians have learned from bitter experience not to take photographs literally, many still tend to do so, sometimes with comic results. In the early eighteenth century, the church of Santa Maria in Cosmedin, Rome, was given a Baroque facade (fig. 3a). In the 1890s that front was removed and one thought to imitate the original reconstructed (fig. 3b). From a photograph of the church made before that restoration, the bell tower was eliminated, most likely because someone thought it did not go well with the Baroque facade (fig. 3c). That campanile is one of the most important Romanesque monuments in the city, but when a prominent medievalist saw the photograph of the church without it, he concluded that the original had been torn down when the Baroque facade was put on, and the campanile there now is a copy put back up in the nineteenth century when the earlier facade was restored. So strong was the acceptance of the picture without the tower as authoritative that it trumped the scholar's better judgment. He would have been far less likely to be deceived by a typographical error in a published date than by a doctored image, because art historians are conditioned by their training to question dates, but not photographs.[8]

The appearance or absence of a large bell tower is a crude example of the snares photographs set for us; less crude is the difference between how visitors first

Figs. 3a–c. Three photographs of Santa Maria in Cosmedin, Rome. *Left:* a nineteenth century view documenting the Baroque facade and Romanesque campanile. *Bottom:* a recent photograph showing the restored medieval-style facade. *Right:* an altered version of the photograph at top left, illustrating what the "prominent medievalist" might have seen and mistaken for a document of the campanile's destruction

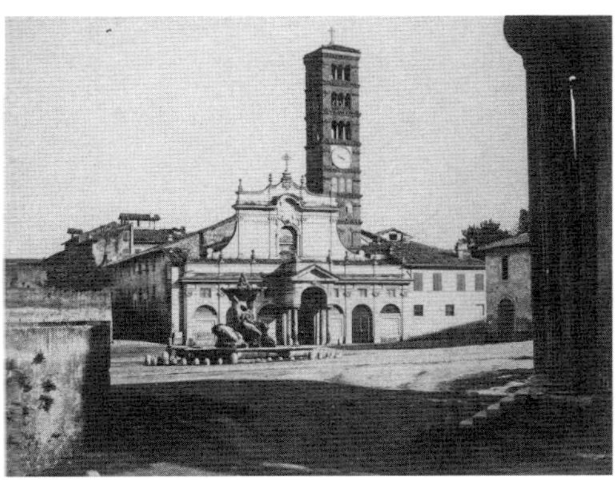

Fig. 3a. A. De Bonis, (French, active 1850–80), Santa Maria in Cosmedin, Rome, 1860–65. Albumen print from a glass negative. Private collection

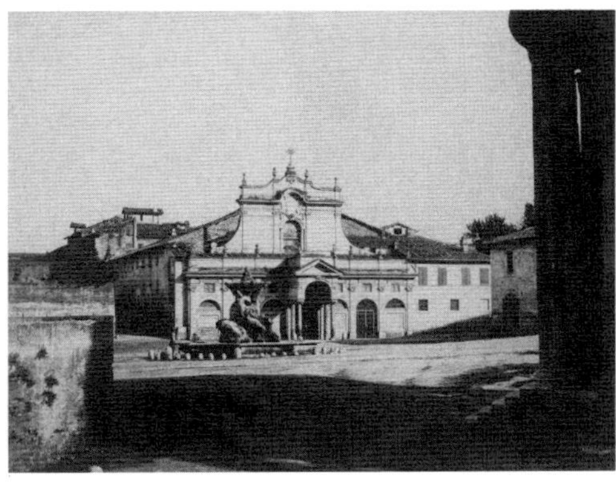

Fig. 3c. Santa Maria in Cosmedin, Rome (altered version of fig. 3a by the author)

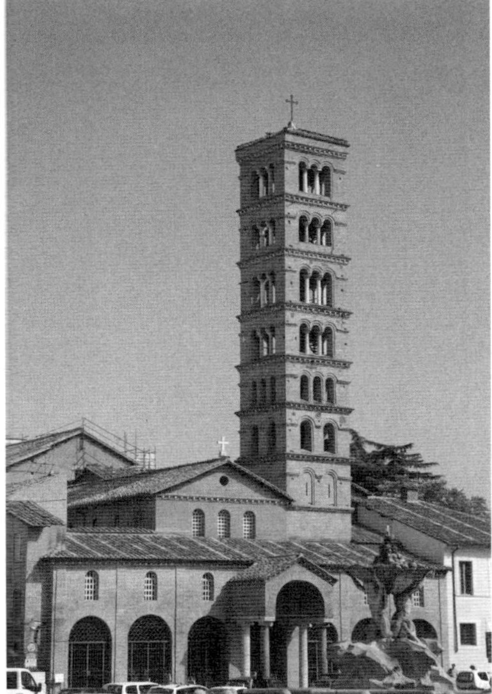

Fig. 3b. Santa Maria in Cosmedin, Rome. Michele Falzone/AWL Images/Getty Images

Figs. 4a and b. Two views of The Frederick C. Robie House in Chicago, Illinois (1908–10), designed by Frank Lloyd Wright, photographed in 2011 (*top*) and in 1973 (*bottom*)

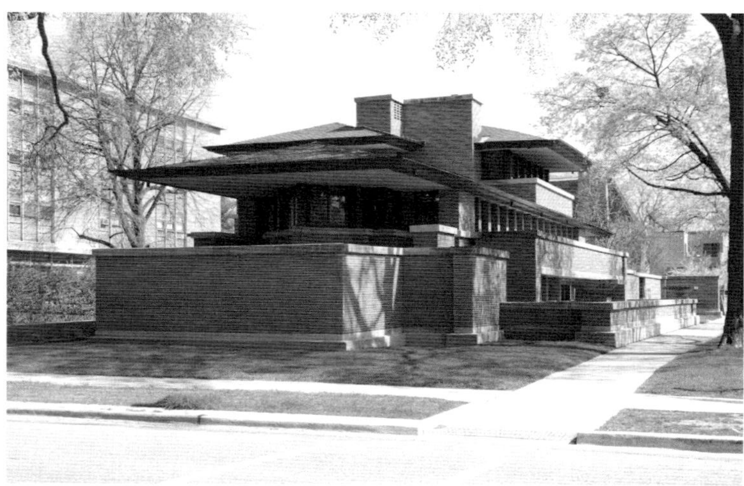

Fig. 4a. Frank Lloyd Wright (American, 1867–1959), The Frederick C. Robie House, 5757 South Woodlawn Avenue, Chicago, Illinois, constructed 1908–10. Photographed 25 March 2011. © 2012 Frank Lloyd Wright Foundation / Artists Rights Society (ARS), New York. Raymond Boyd / Michael Ochs Archives / Getty Images

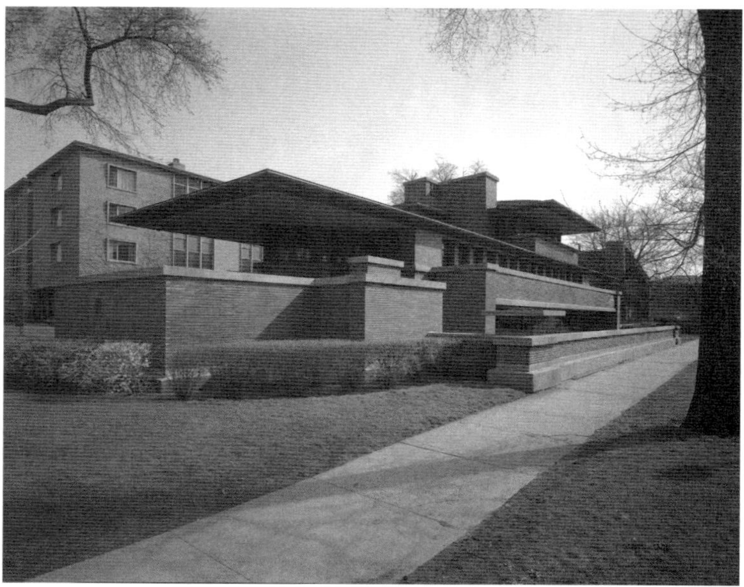

Fig. 4b. Frank Lloyd Wright, The Frederick C. Robie House, 5757 South Woodlawn Avenue, Chicago, Illinois, constructed 1908–10. Photographed 1973. Chicago History Museum, HB-19312-C. © 2012 Frank Lloyd Wright Foundation / Artists Rights Society (ARS), New York

see Frank Lloyd Wright's Robie House—which can seem compact and drawn in on itself (fig. 4a)—and what one sees in the familiar images that celebrate and thereby exaggerate the cantilevered roofs (fig. 4b).

A much more subtle trap is set by pictures of a small statue of a saint in the collection at the Villa I Tatti in Florence. The slender, elongated body and swaying stance (fig. 5a) are features that art historians seize upon as characteristics of the piece, yet a picture made from farther away, but at the same angle (fig. 5b), reveals them to be fictions of the photograph. Photographs do not show things as they look, but how they can be made to look.

Figs. 5a and b. Two views of a statue of an apostle (Florentine School, c. 1410–20) in the Berenson Art Collection, Villa I Tatti, Harvard University Center for Italian Renaissance Studies, Florence (photographs by the author)

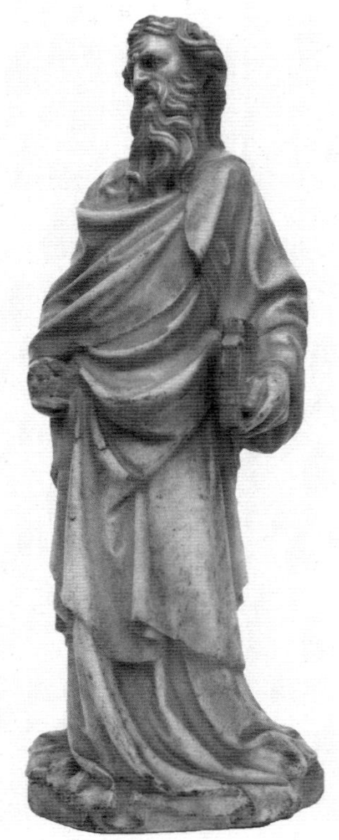

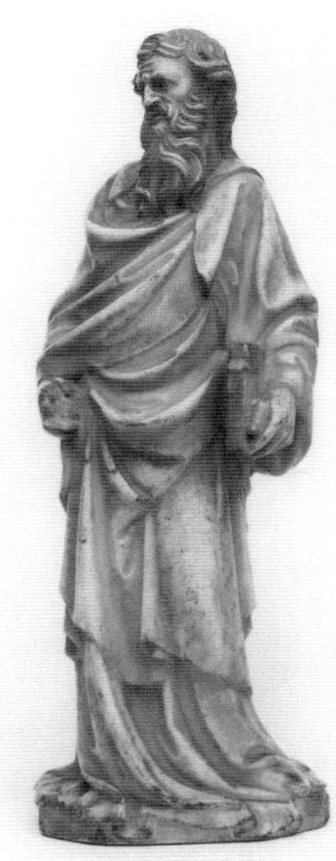

Figs. 6a and b. Two photographs of Westminster Abbey, London, taken with natural lighting (*left*) and using long exposure (*right*)

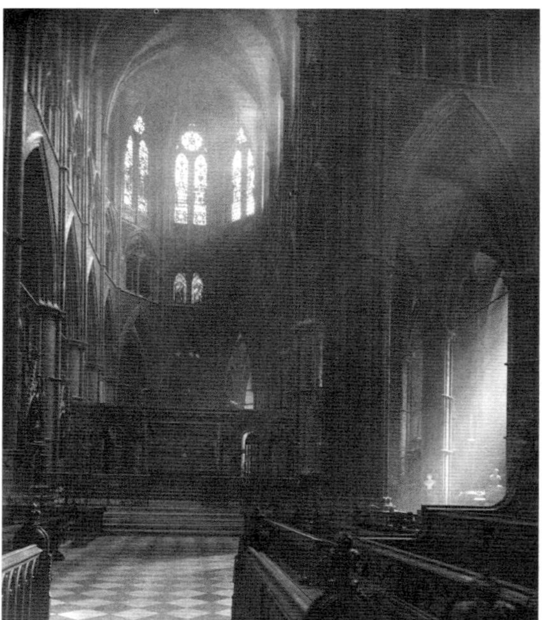

Fig. 6a. Frederick Evans (English, 1853–1943), *Westminster Abbey: Apse from Choir*, 1911. Platinum print, image: 9 5/16 x 7 1/2 in. (23.7 x 19.1 cm); mount: 22 1/8 x 15 1/8 in. (56.2 x 38.4 cm). Philadelphia Museum of Art. Purchased with the Lola Downin Peck Fund, 1969-35-3

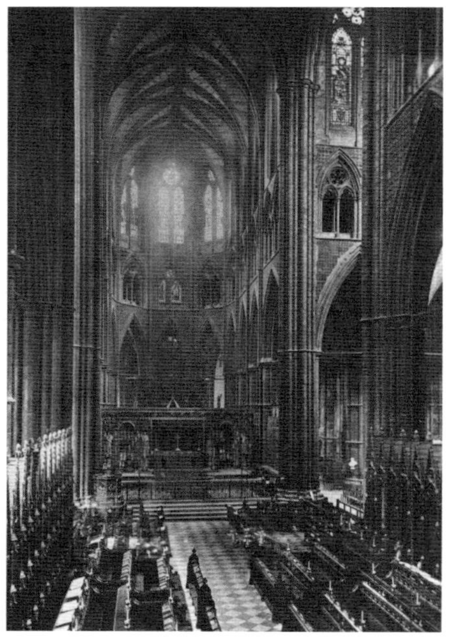

Fig. 6b. Artist unknown, The nave, choir, and east window of Westminster Abbey. London, 1915

Regardless of the fact that it is produced by apparently objective means, a photograph is a picture, and we are heirs to a long tradition of dealing with and writing about pictures. The notion that a photograph seduces us by selective accuracy into accepting all of what it shows is close to what Sydney Freedberg wrote about Mannerist paintings:

> The high Maniera image is . . . stylized and purposely artificial, yet it conveys its own kind of intense convincingness. The fine and insistent technique . . . and the care taken with often seemingly indifferent detail, sharply affirm all but the substance of reality. Fragments of an unreal whole may be given with the precision and the plastic emphasis of trompe l'oeil. The existence of the whole, essentially abstracting as it may be, is asserted by the extreme truth of fragments of it; we are baited with the small verity to swallow the whole poetic lie.[9]

Freedberg's sensitivity to the character of Maniera painting may not have been formed by his experience and analysis of camera images but his words are perfectly applicable to both.

What art historians want in photographs is objective information, and they are drawn to surface detail, the camera's strongest suit, but information about worked surfaces is often acquired at a high cost, and the images that show it are often at variance with our experience. Frederick Evans's best pictures are unrivalled evocations of Gothic interiors (fig. 6a), yet his photographs have found no place in books on medieval architecture. The pictures one does see tell us a great deal about what is there, but next to nothing about what it is like to be there. Long exposure raises the level of apparent interior illumination to the point at which all the shadow areas are lit brightly enough to show full detail in every surface (fig. 6b). All mystery is eradicated in the nearly surreal uniformity of light, and we see the church as if it had no stained glass and no roof. That last is no mere figure of speech; some of the pictures of Reims cathedral published in books on Gothic architecture show the walls as bright as they appear in pictures of the building made after it had been shelled in World War I and the vaults destroyed so that it was open to the sun (figs. 7a and 7b). Much is obscured in a Gothic church, as every visitor knows and as Evans makes clear. It is paradoxical that tourist photographs made with point-and-shoot cameras or cell phones and posted online are often closer to our experience of medieval buildings than the exacting images made by architectural photographers to enable detailed study of them.

Evans shows us the effect of the architecture, but we can find no information to help us understand the means by which that effect is accomplished. In an art-historically acceptable view of the same church, we understand the means, but we don't get their point. Comparing the Evans photograph and one from a book on Gothic architecture would seem to suggest that images are regarded as informative in direct proportion to their unpleasantness. It should not be surprising that beautiful photographs are less enthusiastically embraced by art historians than merely informative ones if we recall that since Rumohr's time art historians have regarded it as important to suppress their aesthetic responses to seductive works. While doing so may have allowed for the development of the discipline, it did not satisfy everyone. Max Friedländer lamented it, writing in the 1930s, that "a professional art scholar finds it hard to regard works of art, the objects of his study, with enjoyment. Without enjoyment there is no understanding of works of art. This lack I have often observed in colleagues. Genuine love of art is found more in dilettantes and collectors who, as a relaxation from their professions,

Figs. 7a and b. Two photographs of Reims Cathedral, taken shortly after the bombardments of WWI destroyed the vaulted ceilings (*left*) and after restoration (*right*)

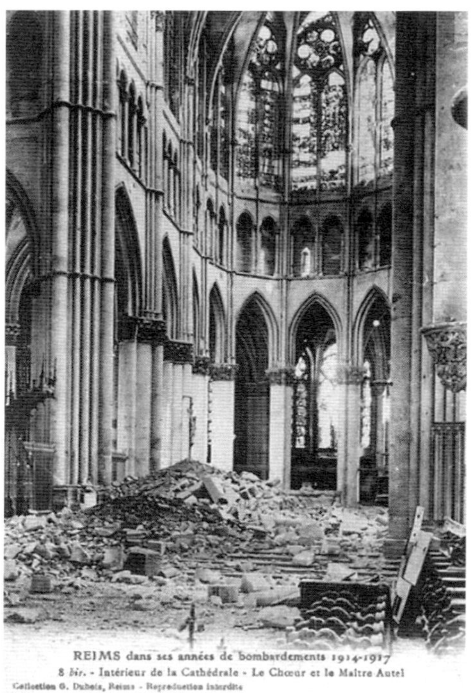

Fig. 7a. Reims Cathedral during years of bombardment, 1914–17. Interior of the cathedral: the choir and the high altar, c. 1917

Fig. 7b. Reims Cathedral: central nave toward the apse, c. 2000

occupy themselves with art in their leisure hours."[10] If the detachment Friedländer decried strikes us as Spartan when applied to things intended to produce aesthetic responses, it should be pointed out that objectivity, like all other forms of moral virtue, requires asceticism.[11]

The real problem with art-historically useful images of medieval churches, however, is not that they are less appealing than pictures by Evans but that they distort the history they were made to illustrate. This becomes particularly clear when we view a sequence of them in chronological order. Anyone who has taken an art history survey course knows that there was a steady development from solid, thick-walled Romanesque churches with small nave windows to the glazed cages of the high and late Gothic, and that the difference was most apparent in the interior light. Pictures that show all church interiors equally bright obliterate the point of the changes; the desire for information results in evidence that then has to be thought or taught away in order not to obscure the development. I have always wanted to make a series of pictures that accurately shows the relative brightness of medieval church interiors, but I suspect few architectural historians would care about them if I did.

With sculpture, too, we often find that a concern to know everything about the object results in photographs that are wrong from every point of view. A photograph of Gian Lorenzo Bernini's *Beata Ludovica Albertoni* shows that someone wanted to know what was in the deeply cut drapery folds, so the piece was lit from the front, destroying its effect completely (fig. 8a). The figure is placed in a chapel that Bernini himself designed with care, with the illumination contrived in a remarkably effective manner. Another photograph (fig. 8b) shows the sculpture as it was meant to be seen and reveals the finely wrought passage from foreground shadow to highlighted figure. Some people who have seen this image, which is my own, concluded from it that I am a gifted photographer, but I only pushed the button, Bernini did the rest; I just kept out of his way.

The unreflective quest for information can destroy not only the aesthetic effect of a sculpture but its meaning as well. The natural light in the Medici Chapel comes from high above the tombs; the downturned face of Michelangelo's *Night* is in shadow. As a result, she is often photographed lit from straight on or, even worse, from below, so that we may see her features. But she is Night, and her face ought to be largely obscured by darkness. The hidden face of Night is an ancient image of which Michelangelo, a poet himself, was surely aware; he knew exactly what he was doing. In our quest for information, we deeply distort the meaning of the work and reduce our appreciation of it through the fiction that if we see everything the artist did we will understand the work better. That Michelangelo did not intend us to see into shadows is made clear by the way the gorgeous velvety line under the torso—like a sinuous charcoal trace in three dimensions—nearly disappears in any but the chapel's natural light.

A consideration of the art-historical photograph as fiction must also confront the fundamental issue of picture selection. The photographs of the Farm Securities Administration, once held to be the essence of documentary objectivity, are now recognized as having been carefully selected for their political effect in the New Deal process of giving a national problem a human face. That ought to have made art historians sensitive to the raveled sleeve of photography's reputation, but it has not; students of art often take argument for illustration and even the fiction of objectivity evaporates.

Figs. 8a and b. Two photographs of *Blessed Ludovica Albertoni* (1674) by Gian Lorenzo Bernini (Italian, 1598–1680), San Francesco a Ripa, Rome, taken with frontal lighting (*top*; photograph by Gianni Dagli Orti) and natural lighting (*bottom*; photograph by the author)

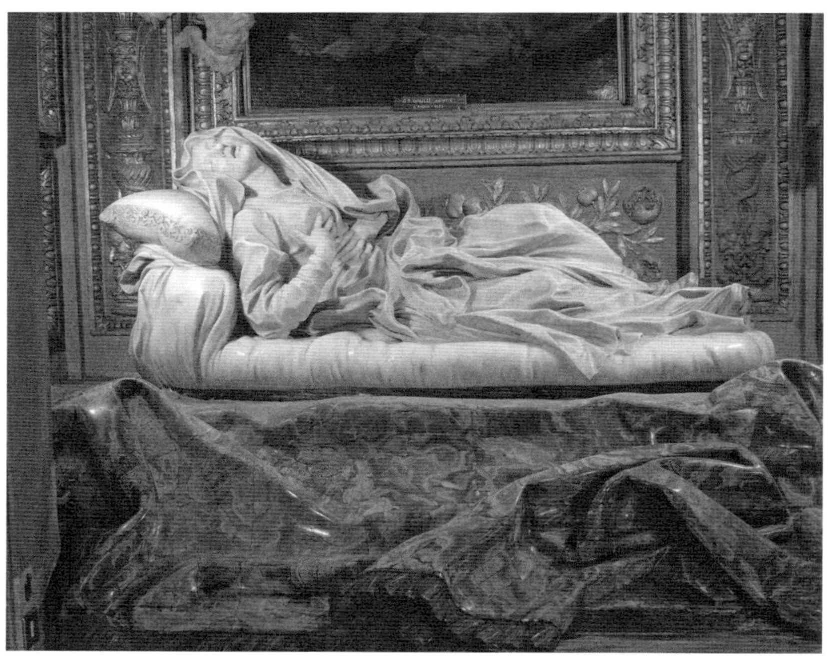

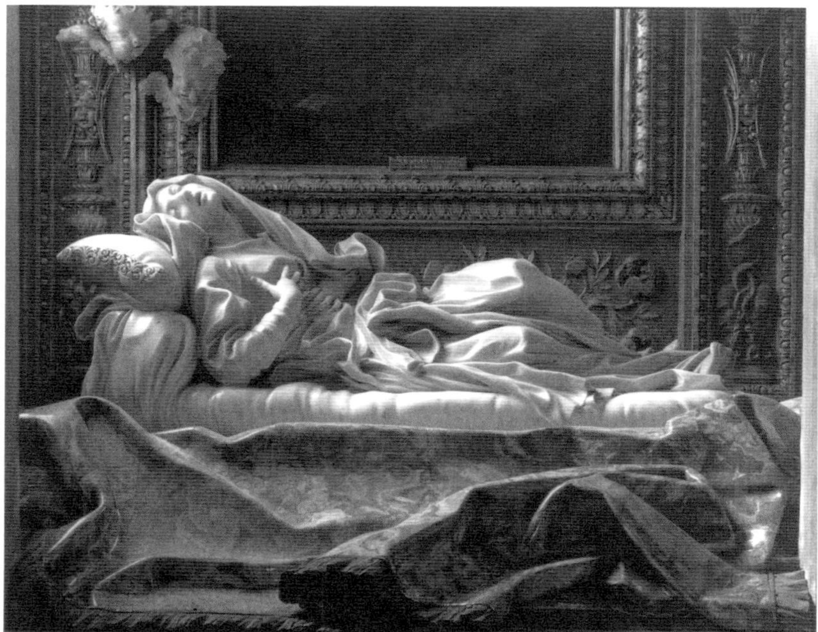

Fig. 9. Page nineteen from John Pope-Hennessy, *Donatello Sculptor* (New York: Abbeville Press, 1993), featuring photographs of (*at bottom, from left to right*): Bernardo Ciuffagni (Italian, 1381–1458), *St. Matthew* (c. 1410–15), Niccolò di Pietro Lamberti (Italian, c. 1375–1451), *St. Mark* (c. 1408–15), and Nanni di Banco (Italian, c. 1380/85–1421), *St. Luke* (c. 1408–15), Museo dell'Opera del Duomo, Florence (photographs top and bottom right by Takashi Okamura)

the buttresses of the Cathedral, the base of Donatello's *David* is likely to have done so too.

Figs. 5–7 One surviving statue satisfies these three conditions. Originally on the Campanile and now in the Museo dell'Opera del Duomo, it shows a figure that can reasonably be regarded as the Prophet David.[20] Its lips are parted, as though in song, and its head is slightly turned. Whereas Nanni di Banco's *Isaiah* is supported by folds of cloak reaching to the ground, here the dress terminates in front above the ankles and both feet are exposed. The dress hangs forward of the legs, and the folds at its front edge are treated with deceptive naturalism. The right knee is bent in a way that suggests movement, and the dress, especially the knotted belt, is carved with exceptional skill. The right forearm is raised, and is attached by a marble bridge to the shoulder. The whole surface is seriously abraded, and the tips of the fingers of the right hand are missing, but the veining on the hands is rendered realistically. There are no parallels for the inspired head in other statues carved for the Duomo, but in the half-length silver figures made by Brunelleschi for the Pistoia altar the same emotional repertory is employed. The third condition also is fulfilled, in that the base of the figure is pentagonal.

There are, moreover, in the Museo dell'Opera del Duomo, two small prophets, which were installed in 1431 over the east entrance to the Campanile. One of these,

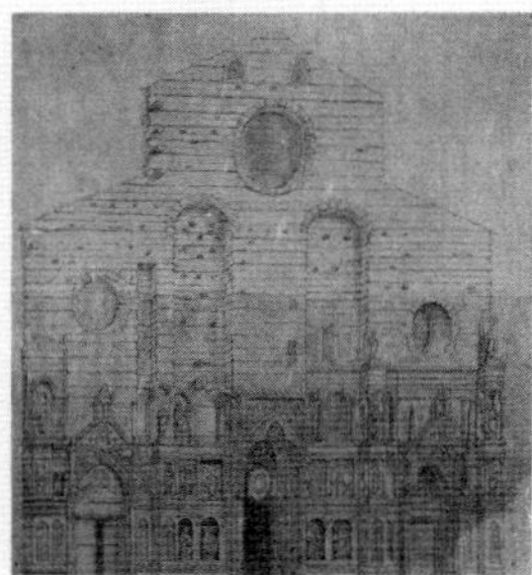

FIGURE 8.
Poccetti, *Facade of the Duomo in Florence* (1587). Pen on paper. Museo dell'Opera del Duomo, Florence.

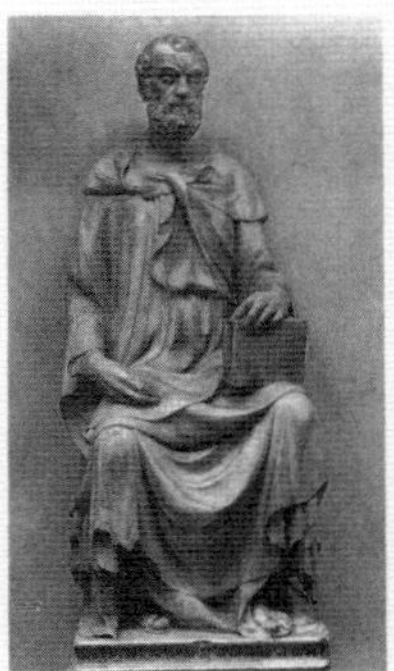

FIGURE 9.
Bernardo Ciuffagni, *St. Matthew.* Marble, H. 224 cm (88⅛ in.). Museo dell'Opera del Duomo, Florence.

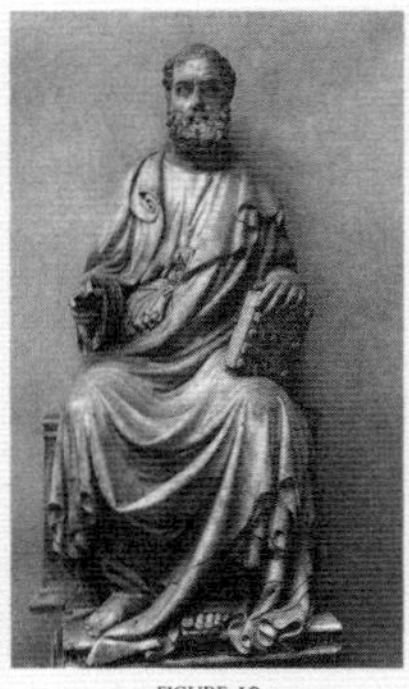

FIGURE 10.
Niccolo di Pietro Lamberti, *St. Mark.* Marble, H. 215 cm (84⅝ in.). Museo dell'Opera del Duomo, Florence.

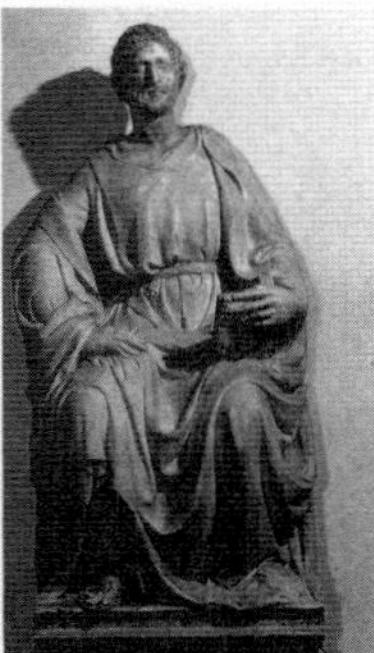

FIGURE 11.
Nanni di Banco, *St. Luke.* Marble, H. 207.5 cm (81⅝ in.). Museo dell'Opera del Duomo, Florence.

19

On page nineteen of John Pope-Hennessy's *Donatello Sculptor*[12] are images of three evangelists carved for the facade of Florence's cathedral by Bernardo Ciuffagni, Niccolò di Pietro Lamberti, and Nanni di Banco (fig. 9). The fourth, by Donatello, is the subject of several large color pictures on nearby pages. It is widely agreed that the two great marble sculptors of early fifteenth-century Florence were Donatello and Nanni, and that their evangelists for the cathedral make clear how weak and old-fashioned is the work of the other two.

Here we seem to have the pictures to prove it, but a moment's closer look reveals that the Ciuffagni and Lamberti evangelists were photographed in light that makes what are in fact three-dimensional forms look shallow, fussy, and irrelevant. In the picture of Nanni's Luke, the light is nothing like what we see in the other two pictures, as is clear from the long shadow of the head above the saint's right shoulder. This stronger raking light emphasizes the bold heft of the drapery, clarifies the volumes of the figure, and, in general, serves to make the piece look more successful than either of the others.

Whether this trio resulted from an intentional effort to deceive or from a misguided effort to convince by dubious rhetorical means, what seem differences in quality would not have been so clear had all the figures been lit the same way. In matched photographs made in natural light in the cathedral museum (fig. 10 a–d), the differences among the works appear much less dramatic, and while the Nanni and Donatello saints may still strike us as the better two, the others are by no means as brittle and nasty as Pope-Hennessy's pictures suggest.

On page 19 the accepted view of the relative quality of the figures led to the selection of photographic "evidence" that reconfirms it. If this is science, it's cold fusion. It is clear once again that what makes a photograph of a work of art "good" turns out to have little to do with the accuracy of the image. For Pope-Hennessy, any pictures that make the Ciuffagni and Lamberti saints look weak are correct, valid, and "good," as they are in furtherance of his views; anything that makes them look better than mediocre would be regarded as flattering and thus inaccurate. On the other hand, any picture that does not show off the strength of the Nanni is bad. A photo of Saint Luke in the same light as the others would not make it look better, as he thought it should, and so was not selected.

The images that Pope-Hennessy chose for the book make life a lot simpler. With pictures like mine, it is necessary to do some careful analysis to support the standard view of their relative quality. That takes time and effort, and the money to provide more than one picture of each figure, all of which can be saved by the use of images that permit even the myopic to get the point in a moment. So, it could be argued, the Pope-Hennessy pictures do not mislead, so much as clarify, and, as they are, after all, in the service of the truth, their use, like the exaggerations permitted in sermons, may be accepted as legitimate means to lead us to the "right" conclusion. I have already acknowledged that I am slightly cynical about how people would respond to a series of photographs accurately

Fig. 10. Photographs of statues of four evangelists from the Florence Cathedral, taken with even lighting. *From left to right:* Donatello (Italian, c. 1386–1466), *St. John* (c. 1409–15), Bernardo Ciuffagni, *St. Matthew* (c. 1410–15), Niccolò di Pietro Lamberti, *St. Mark* (c. 1408–15), and Nanni di Banco, *St. Luke* (c. 1408–15), Museo dell'Opera del Duomo, Florence (photographs by the author)

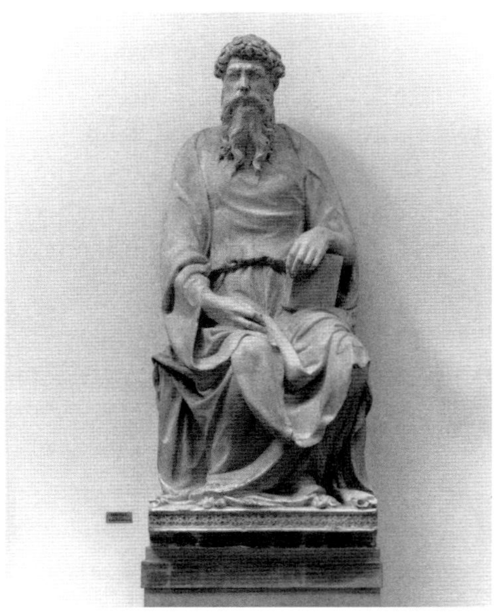

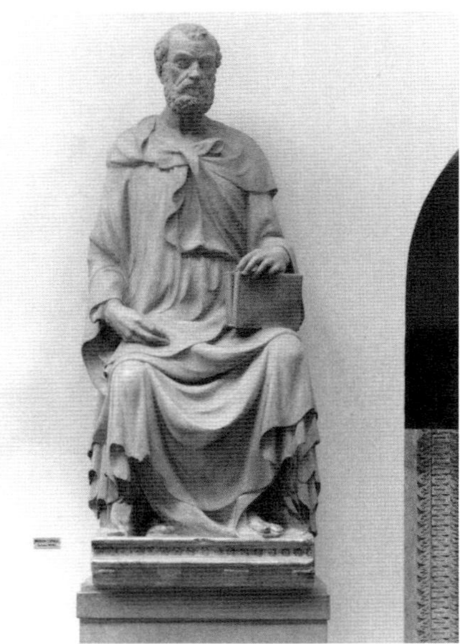

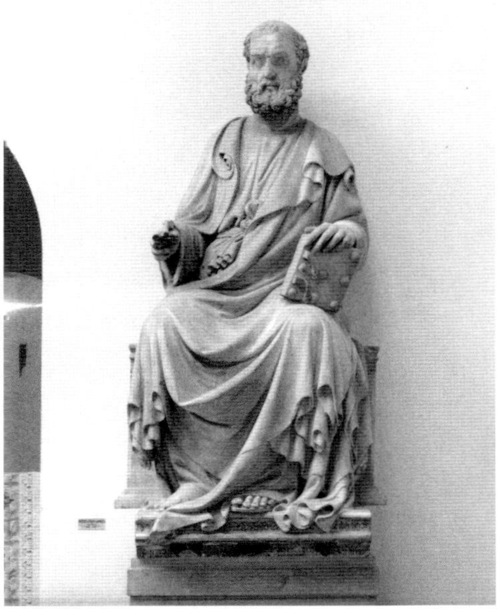

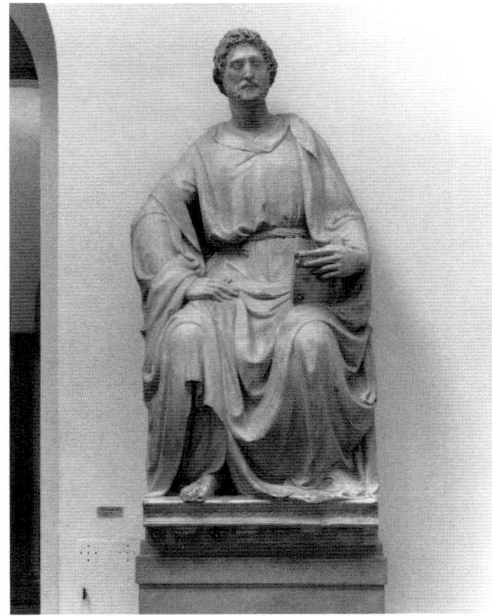

showing the relative brightness of church interiors; that view was based on my experience of responses to the evangelist pictures, which ranged from a mild "that's interesting" to a somewhat indignant "you made them all look the same!" The last comment revealed that I'd at least made the point that the four sculptures are more alike than different, and that dramatic contrasts that appear in the carefully selected photographs are largely fictional.

If there is any sort of fiction to which an art-historical photograph can be most accurately likened, it would be the *roman à thèse*: a propagandistic work of imaginative literature that seeks to shape attitudes. Examples are books like Benjamin Disraeli's *Sibyl, or the Two Nations*, published in 1845, which sought to bring to the attention of the English reading public the dire condition of the exploited working poor. Another obvious example is Harriet Beecher Stowe's *Uncle Tom's Cabin*. In the *roman à thèse*, exaggerations, distortions, and heightened contrasts are permitted to make a case more compelling, which is also true of the pictures in the Pope-Hennessy book.

If photographs can be selected for their fictional content, they can be made in ways that have little bearing on reality, and none on experience. Clarence Kennedy is not as well known as he should be, but his photographs of sculpture are astonishing. A trained art historian who wrote his PhD thesis on the role of light in Greek sculpture, he began to make photographs because he did not like the ones he saw. He developed new ways of lighting sculpture, both in museums and in the studio. His pictures could make sculpture look far more beautiful than it was, and he was hired by Joseph Duveen to photograph whatever pieces the shrewd dealer had for sale. When Duveen sold a terracotta bust, now at Harvard, the optimistic claim that it was a portrait of Philippe Le Beau by Michel Colombe was supported by ravishing Kennedy photographs (fig. 11a); on his own in the Fogg Art Museum's catalogue (fig. 11b), without Kennedy behind the camera to determine his appearance, the sitter is now listed as an anonymous Fleming by an unknown sculptor and dated between 1510 and 1550.[13]

In his studio, Kennedy lit his subjects with great care. We see into every depth, and the light, which seems to come from all directions at once, is totally controlled. This was not possible in the field, so when working in a church Kennedy carried a battery-powered motorcycle headlamp and lit his subject by constantly moving a beam of light over it. With long experience he became very good, if necessarily a bit inconsistent, at getting the light even, and while his

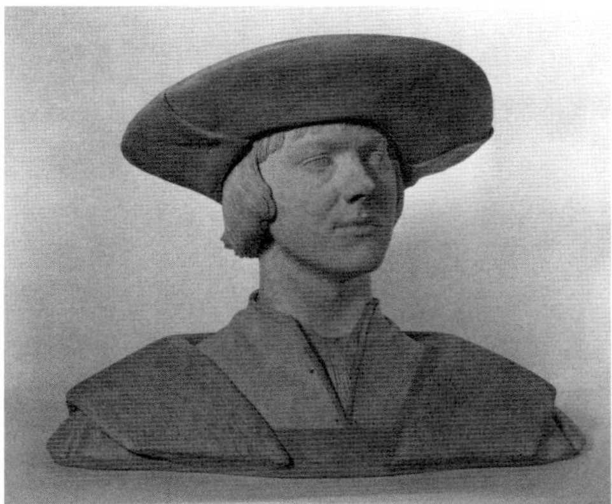

Fig. 11a. Clarence Kennedy (American, 1892–1972), *Terracotta Bust of "Philippe le Beau" by Michel Colombe (c. 1510–50)*, c. 1930. Photograph. Published in *Certain of the Sculptures from the Collection of M. Gustave Dreyfus, Paris, which was acquired in its entirety from the executors of his estate in MDCCCXXX by Sir Joseph Duveen, Bart.* (Florence: Privately printed, 1930)

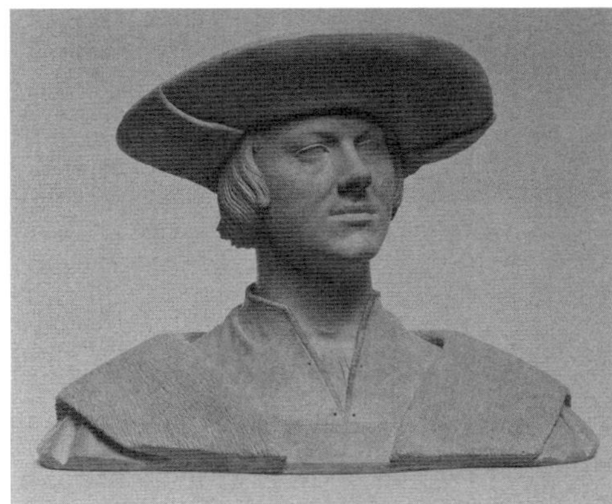

Fig. 11b. Unknown artist (Netherlandish, 16th century), *Portrait Bust of Man*, c. 1510–50. Terracotta, 17 3/16 × 21 1/2 × 14 7/8 in. (43.6 × 54.6 × 37.8 cm). Harvard Art Museums/Fogg Museum, Gift of David Rockefeller in memory of his mother Abby Aldrich Rockefeller, 1981.188

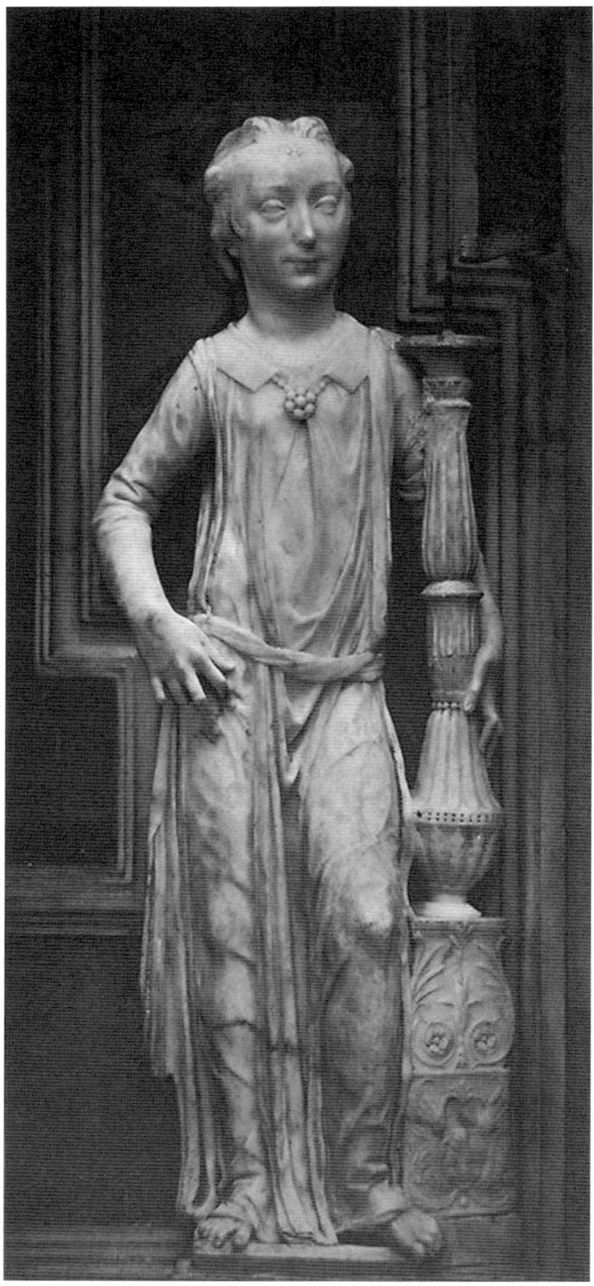

Fig. 12. Clarence Kennedy, *Candle-Bearing Figure from the Tabernacle of the Sacrament by Desiderio da Settignano and Assistants*, c. 1929. Photograph. Published in *Studies in the History and Criticism of Sculpture*, vol. 5 (1929)

images are always compelling, there is an oddly unreal quality to many of them (fig. 12) that is hard to define. Here the figure seems detached from its context by the light concentrated preferentially on it.

The technique of a moving light source takes advantage of the capacity of film to accumulate light, or, as it were, to remember it. Had we been in the church when Kennedy was working, we would have seen a small patch of bright light moving steadily over a sculpture, but it would have been impossible to get a clear sense of the figure; we would never have seen it even remotely like the way we see it in the resulting photograph. Kennedy's pictures, although grounded in reality and often quite convincing, show us things as they are never experienced in the real world, which could serve as a definition of fiction.

1. Johann Passavant, *Raffael von Urbino und sein Vater Giovanni Santi*, 3 vols. (Leipzig: F. A. Brockhaus, 1839–58); see also Udo Kultermann, *The History of Art History* (New York: Abaris Books, 1993), esp. 83–84, 87–89.

2. Karl Friedrich von Rumohr, as quoted in Kultermann, *History of Art History*, 89

3. Lorraine Daston and Peter Galison, *Objectivity* (New York: Zone Books, 2007), 122.

4. Bernard Berenson, "Isochromatic Photography and Venetian Pictures," *The Nation* 57, no. 1480 (November 9, 1893): 346. The article offers several perceptive remarks about studying works of art from photographs and why the medium had, until then, represented Tuscan painting, with its emphasis on line, much better than Venetian.

5. Ibid.

6. Ibid.

7. In fairness, it must be acknowledged that in the passage quoted above (see note 5), Berenson was talking about making comparisons of paintings with a number of photographs, but it is nonetheless the case that he appears never to have given much thought to the fact that images must be made under exacting and probably unobtainable laboratory conditions that completely eliminate every variable but style for any photographic comparison even remotely to approach the "scientific."

8. I owe this amusing anecdote to William Tronzo, who would not reveal the identity of the quaintly deluded scholar.

9. Sydney J. Freedberg, *Painting in Italy: 1500–1600*, 3rd ed. (New Haven, Conn., and London: Yale University Press, 1993), 422.

10. Max J. Friedländer, *Reminiscences and Reflections*, ed. Rudolf M. Heilbrunn (Greenwich, Conn.: New York Graphic Society, 1969), 46.

11. Daston and Galison, *Objectivity*, 122.

12. John Pope-Hennessy, *Donatello Sculptor* (New York: Abbeville Press, 1993).

13. "*Portrait Bust of a Man*, c. 1510–50 (1981.188)," Harvard Art Museums online collection database, http://www.harvardartmuseums.org/art/227922

PART THREE

ARTISTS, STORIES, OBJECTS

"The Reality Bodily before Us": Picturing the *Arabian Nights*

Marina Warner

> These mute and sometimes inanimate beings rise up before me with such a plenitude, such a presence of love that my joyful eye finds nothing dead anywhere . . . mute things speak to me.
>
> —Hugo von Hofmannsthal, "Letter," 1902, in *The Lord Chandos Letter and Other Writings*

In the book known in English as the *Arabian Nights* or *Tales of a Thousand and One Nights*,[1] things are made to talk in ways that disturb distinctions between animate and inanimate; they become, to use Lorraine Daston's categories, both *eidola* and evidence.[2] Things are also made visible in the numerous illustrated editions of the book that followed its first appearance in print in Antoine Galland's translation into French in 1704. Among the many classes of things that appear in the stories, jars and vessels dominate; they include Aladdin's wonderful lamp (the most familiar and best-loved example) and the copper bottle that the fisherman in the opening story finds in his nets.[3] When the fisherman breaks the seal and opens the bottle, he releases a huge and terrifying *afrit*, whom he later dupes to spiral back into the bottle in the celebrated scene of trickster tricked, or biter bit. The lamp and the copper bottle endow their owners with wealth and power; they are goods and they bring goods, although one is a dirty old lamp like a million others and the other mere barnacled jetsam. Ordinary things, banal household objects and instruments such as these, offer a key metaphor to two of the fictive strands that have run through art-historical responses to the culture from which the *Arabian Nights* originate.

The genie of the lamp is a jinni, a member of the numberless intermediary between the gods and humans, neither an angel nor a devil in the Christian sense, though possessing some capacities and characteristics that resemble both. Made of "the fiery wind" or "shimmering flame," according to the Qur'an (Sura 15 and Sura 55), some of the jinn disobeyed the true God and were punished by Solomon for their impiety, imprisoned in flasks and bottles and cast to the depths of the sea. But others saw the light, and they attend Solomon, carrying him in state through the air on his carpet-covered throne.

Jinn come in several different varieties; called *marid* or *afrit* in the Qur'an, they increase in species and denomination in the apocrypha and related folklore and mystical literature. They form a large class of *daimones*, pervading the world, sometimes visibly, but mostly invisibly. Toward the start of the *Nights*, for example, a traveling merchant chucks a date pit to the ground and finds he has inadvertently killed the son of a jinni. The bereaved father erupts in rage, towering to the sky and determined on vengeance—and in this way triggers another cycle of ransom tales (fig. 1).

Jinn give a particular flavor to the *1001 Nights*, acting as the dazzling catalysts of the action and the chief mobile vehicles of the plots, as they ferry the protagonists from one side of the world to another or between this realm and others. They can do good; they also bring harm. They can fly, they can dive to the depths of the sea, they can whisk up a palace overnight and make it disappear as quickly. They are, above all, hidden inside things, sometimes as guardians—their presence charges talismans and amulets, magic automata and weapons; they ground their fiery bodies in humdrum matter, to adapt Alexander Nemerov's metaphors of lightness and gravity.[4]

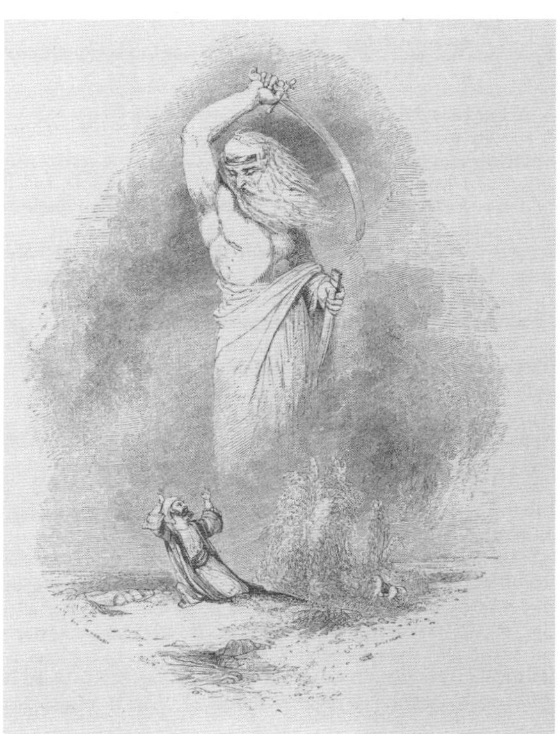

Fig. 1. "Having eaten the date, he threw aside the stone, and immediately there appeared before him an Afrite, of enormous height, who, holding a drawn sword in his hand, approached him and said, Rise, that I may kill thee, as thou hast killed my son." *The Merchant and the Genie*, wood engraving by S. Williams, after William Harvey (English, 1796–1866), from *The Thousand and One Nights*, edited and translated by Edward W. Lane (London: John Murray, 1850)

They also keep things—sometimes living things—hidden inside other things, like the beautiful human wife whom a colossal jinni keeps locked in a glass box in the story of the two brothers, part of the frame story of the *Nights*. When the jinni falls aleep, she slips the lock and practices her seductions on passing strangers—the Sultan Shahryar and his brother Shahzeman, the king of the Indies, are her ninety-ninth and one hundredth conquests—and she has a century of rings as proof. The storyteller is able to disregard problems of size and plausibility: the genie is a giant, but she can lay his head in her lap and he can keep her in a box. A visual artist has more trouble than the storyteller with such logistics; in Albert Letchford's illustration (fig. 2), the glass box is a Snow White-style coffin within a stouter exterior casing that enables her master to carry his "wife" safely.[5] Letchford's illustrations create a moody, sometimes phantasmic, Symbolist atmosphere, but at Burton's urging he added local color in a contradictory mode of verisimilitude. His work on the *Nights* consequently offers a clear example of the way the tales involve all manner of vessels—jars, bottles, caskets, and flasks—from which spring the protagonists, adversaries, and helpers of the plots—in this case the embodiment of irresistible female loveliness, figured here as an Oriental inversion of Susannah and the Elders, since she is actively soliciting the two kings.

The society to whose belief system the jinn belong flourished through the making and marketing of things: Baghdad was the greatest city in the world at the time when the stories in the *Nights* were forming (the earliest extant manuscript is now thought to date from the fourteenth century, and the collection reflects the wealth and industry of the Abbasids); Baghdad and Basra were rich artisanal and mercantile centers of manufacturing, trading all manner of goods by land and sea. The culture that arose from this extensive trade gave birth to the original collection of *Alf layla wa layla* stories; more stories and embellishments were layered in later dates, especially in Egypt and its capital Cairo during the Mamluk period.

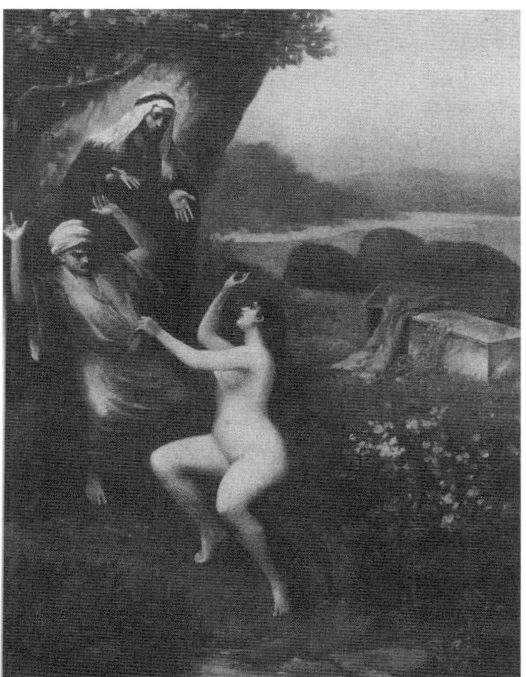

Fig. 2. The captive wife of a jinni solicits the two kings while he sleeps. The artist has borrowed the iconography of Susannah and the Elders, but inverted the meaning. *The Story of King Shahryar and His Brother*, after Albert Letchford (English, 1866–1905), from *A Series of Seventy Original Illustrations to Captain Sir R. F. Burton's "Arabian Nights"* (London: H. S. Nichols Ltd., 1897)

The things emanating from the culture did not only hold the jinn of Islamic cosmology; figuratively, they came to embody, for visitors and explorers, scholars and strangers, the essence of the society where they were made and its expertise and riches. The lamp, the flask, the casket: if they could be opened they might yield something that would lead to greater understanding; they might impart their makers' knowledge. Daston comments, "As seeds around which an elaborate crystal can suddenly congeal, things in a supersaturated cultural solution can crystallize ways of thinking, feeling, and acting. These thickenings of significance are one way that things can be made to talk."[6]

Even when Orientalist antiquarians and collectors and travelers and artists were communicating a vicarious experience of their exotic and unfamiliar subjects, and drawing attention to the luxury and gorgeousness of the East, they also revealed their inquisitiveness about the exact means of wealth production and military effectiveness in the Ottoman empire.[7] They were examining the success of a formidable rival—often an enemy. So, rather surprisingly, technology as well as tulips, engines as well as damasks attracted the attention of early witnesses. Utensils and contrivances, every kind of manufacture from tools to bibelots were made visible and bore witness to the society in which they circulated as useful or enjoyable articles. When the Arabic of the travelers was nonexistent or so scholarly as to prevent easy communication with the locals, things became the chief media through which information and sympathy traveled between strangers.

Edward Said's famous polemic against the Orientalists saw this hunger for knowledge primarily as a quest for possession, control, and power. But his valuable critique can be modulated to yield further meanings that the exchange between East and West also generated.[8] The Orientalists—writers, artists, linguists, philosophers—who observed and documented, sectioned and measured the things of the East found themselves confronting a phenomenon that they recognized as a sign of their own changing relationship to things. Although these encounters and exchanges were taking place in modern times—Napoleon's scientific magnum opus, *Description de l'Égypte*, was produced after 1798 and published between 1809 and 1828—concepts that evoke the power of things in the traffic and markets of modernity are often captured by a lexicon forged in Baghdad and Basra, Shiraz and Cairo centuries earlier: to other imported terms, such as "amulet" and "fetish," additional terms, such as "genie" and "talisman," were adopted around this time into French, English, and other European languages. The new terminology was needed, and the vocabulary imported, because related terms (for example, "relic") had a Christian function, while the modern auratic character of goods as dramatized in the *Nights* existed outside a Christian frame of reference.

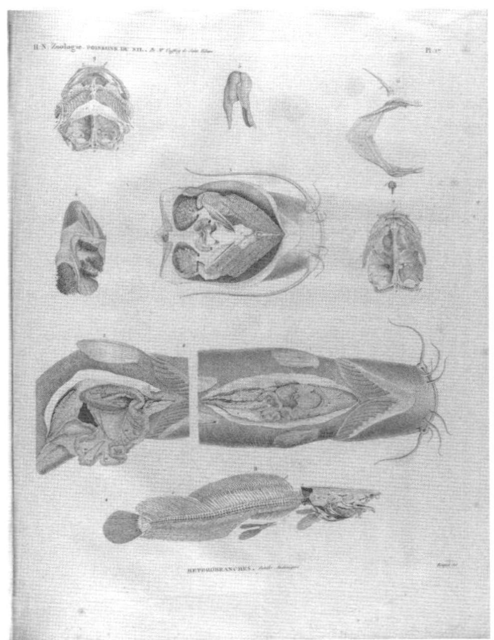

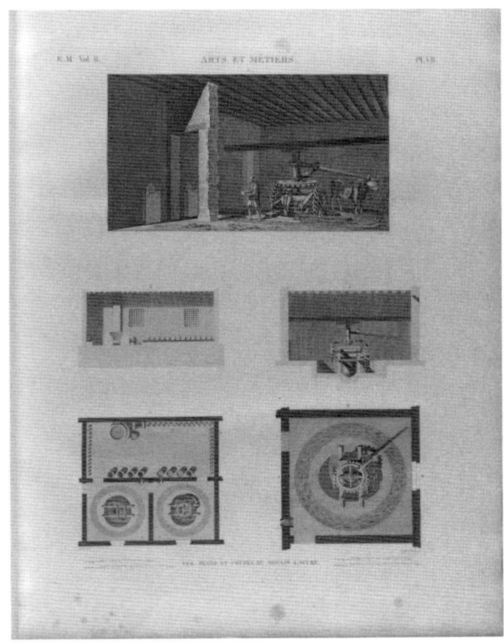

Figs. 3a and 3b. The savants dissect the fauna of the Nile, including the air-breathing catfish, or *Heterobranchus technologiyas*, part of the imperial encyclopedic enterprise. *Heterobranches. Détails Anatomiques*, engraving by Louis Bouquet (French, 1765–1814), after Étienne Geoffroy de Saint-Hilaire (French, 1772–1844), from *Description de l'Égypte*, vol. 9, *Histoire Naturelle I*, plate 17. The expedition turned its attention to contemporary technology and applied forensic skills to the inner workings of a sugar mill, powered by a blindfolded ox, drawn by the expedition's leading engineer, François-Charles Cécile (French, 1766–1840), and engraved by Mme de St Morien, one of several women artists involved in the lavish publication. *Vues, Plans et Coupes du Moulin à Sucre*, from *Description de l'Égypte*, vol. 8, *État moderne II*, plate 7. General Collection, Beinecke Rare Book and Manuscript Library, Yale University

When artists and technical illustrators, seeking to picture the Middle East, looked at the things made there, they were working in a spirit of mercantile enterprise, on the one hand, and within a desire to enrich the art-historical corpus of knowledge, on the other. But they were also communicating a fresh sensitivity to the presence of the marvelous in the banal—the genie in the lamp. Forms of attention that explorers and travelers had previously focused on flora and fauna, minerals and their properties, as well as other aspects of the natural cosmos, were extended to the built environment and the world of goods—machines, implements, lamps, carpets, flasks, caskets, and the various paraphernalia that is so often enchanted in the stories of the *Arabian Nights*. These artists *sounded* such things as they made their observations; they tried to hear what they were saying. Take the image of the Nile fish (*Heterobranchus*) from the volumes on natural history in *Description de l'Égypte* (fig. 3a), for example, and compare it to the dissection of the mechanism of a linseed oil press, or the multiple analyses of a sugar mill's engineering (fig. 3b) as recorded in minutely absorbed detail in the closing volume of plates, *État moderne*: the images reveal how the artists were investigating their subjects in comparable fashion, whether addressing a living creature or a machine.[9] Both are anatomized, their exteriors opened to expose and lay bare their innards; the limits of the visible breached by the artist's inquiry. Like the automata, kinetic devices, and other charged things in the stories, the objects in the plates suggest activity, not inertia. Consequently, rather than identifying the analogy through a statement that reifies those living creatures, it may be fruitful to think of these inert things being ascribed animist powers.

This vitality of things, as dramatized in the *Arabian Nights* and refracted in *Description*, affects a second wave of crosscurrents flowing between East and West, especially regarding the reading and reception of Oriental fiction. By the nineteenth century, when the *Nights* came to be illustrated in ever more popular, often magnificent, editions, the documentary records made by earlier travelers and scientific observers profoundly influenced the way artists envision the stories. The fairy tales, with their fantastic characters and complex and wonder-filled plots, are pictured by means of veracious set-dressing, with numerous objects introduced strategically to enhance the persuasiveness of a fantastic scene. The effect is rationalizing: the stories' wild implausibilities and supernatural cast of characters are tamed and ordered in images furnished with historical props and managed with verismo care. For example, Mercury Ali's transformation into a bear, in the illustration of this story by Albert Letchford, takes place in a credible nineteenth-century Cairene interior (fig. 4).

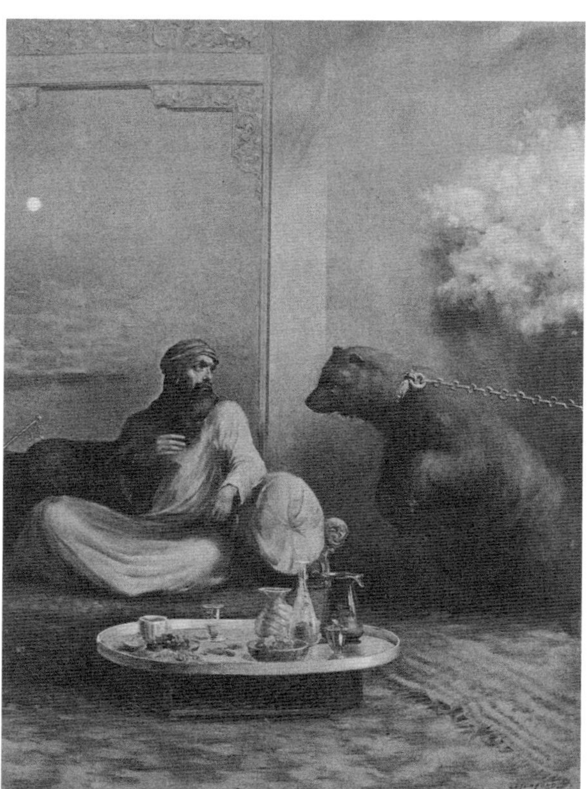

Fig. 4. *Mercury Ali's Transformation into a Bear*, after Albert Letchford, from *A Series of Seventy Original Illustrations to Captain Sir R. F. Burton's "Arabian Nights"* (London: H.S. Nichols Ltd., 1897)

Antoine Galland's translation of the *Nights* into French in 1704 was the first print appearance of the book in any language, and its influence went very deep. Many of the widely read translations into other languages that followed were based on Galland's version even when claiming to be taken directly from the Arabic. In the *Avertissement*, or Notice to the Reader, Galland begins by drawing attention to the unsurpassed inventiveness of the Arabs in the arts of the wonder tale.[10] Although the composition of the stories took place several centuries before the translations, he swiftly progresses to propose another reason for reading the stories:

> They should also give pleasure through the customs and the manners of the Orientals [they depict], the ceremonies of their religion, pagan as well as Muslim; and these things are better represented here than in those authors who have written of them and in the accounts of travelers. All the Orientals, Persians, Tartars, and Indians can be distinguished here, and appear just as they are, from the sovereigns to the people of the lowest condition. And so, without having suffered the weariness of going to look for these peoples in their country, the reader will have the pleasure here of seeing them act and hearing them speak.[11]

With this framing device, directing the reader toward edifying armchair traveling, Galland set the rhetorical ground for reading the *Nights*. Mary Wortley Montagu's letters from Turkey, from her visit to the Sublime Porte in 1716–18, were written soon after the first appearance of the *Nights* in English, which she also imitated in her fiction.[12] Calling on the great ladies of the Ottoman court, Wortley Montagu claims a sisterhood of aristocracy, and rhapsodizes about the luxury of their apartments and the splendor of their jewels, their dress fabrics, porcelain, and glassware. She writes to her sister, Lady Mar:

> Now do I fancy that you imagine I have entertained you all this while with a relation that has, at least, received many embellishments from my hand. This is but too like, says you, the Arabian tales; these embroidered napkins, and a jewel as large as a turkey's egg! You forget, dear sister, those very tales were writ by an author of this country and, excepting the enchantments, are a real representation of the manners here.[13]

The comparison becomes a refrain: Edward W. Lane (1801–1876), the first English translator to render the full cycle of the stories from the original Arabic, also insists that the book gives a faithful picture of life in the contemporary Levant.

The view is predominantly museological: the tales of the *1001 Nights* become a catalogue of beautiful and picturesque elements selected for their preciousness and splendor. It is an approach that has become entrenched in conservation policy, and grows from a combination of antiquarian hope and aesthetic desire, filled with a longing to step into the same river not merely twice but again and again. It flattens history onto an unchanging and static horizon; the perspective of history disappears along with its differences and its texture. Galland's idea of presenting the *Nights* as a kind of Baedeker to the Middle East of his time is tantamount to urging a contemporary setting out for Italy to read Dante, or pressing a copy of Macbeth on someone interested in the Highlands. Dante and Shakespeare would afford much pleasure and knowledge; there would be similarities of topography, culture, customs, and language—but within limits. This approach is also ideological, as critics have trenchantly observed: it presents the Levant as unchanging, a fossil rather than a living organism. But, if anything, nostalgia enhanced the craze for everything Oriental. The past could be faithfully retrieved by recording the present.

It was in the midst of this enthusiasm that Napoleon set out for Egypt in 1798. The future Emperor belonged to a generation who had grown up with Orientalizing fever: readers—French and English—had been devouring not only the stories themselves but also a spate of Oriental tales played on the stage, sung, and dramatized.[14] This aspect of the Egyptomania that seized Europe has not been sufficiently acknowledged.[15] Insistent themes included unimaginable sumptuousness, ferocious tyranny, and meltingly amorous beauties. Works of imagination that had mined these leitmotivs flourished as vigorously as the Enlightenment's pursuit of its scientific interests—Napoleon was a new Alexander, a new Augustus, but he was also Harun al-Rashid, the wise and enigmatic ruler of the *Nights.*

From the opening frontispiece, *Description* throws the emphasis on elegiac retrospection, and evokes the magnificence of ancient Egypt through its ruins. Many critics have disparaged the book for showing more interest in stones than in living people, but the aspersion, however justified, can be looked at differently. When artists attempted to render the culture visible, they had recourse to a category of evidence for those customs and manners, rites and organization of the Orientals: their things. The frontispiece of the first edition came out when

Napoleon had become "Emperor of the French," as was proclaimed on the title page; for the second edition, after the defeat of Napoleon at Waterloo, he disappeared from view and was replaced with the now-famous frontispiece, in color, juxtaposing monuments and sculptures, rubble and weapons, artifacts and other eloquent goods. By 1829 his glory had long dimmed, kings had come and gone, and Napoleon's name had vanished from the pages of his commission.

The publication was a princely enterprise in more ways than one. By the end, hundreds of artists and engravers had been engaged by the Institut d'Égypte to work on the materials accumulated by the expedition and to support the research of the large team of savants—scientists and scholars. The first "Imperial" edition includes plates illustrating the antiquities and monuments of Pharaonic Egypt and the wonders of the natural world, which have become familiar from numerous later editions and single framed prints.[16] But the two imposing closing volumes of the *Modern State* are not nearly as well known; they are what the French call "Mammut" format, and the English call "elephant folios"; taking them out at the British Library caused quite a stir as they required a special table to lie on (I had to conquer my own large expanse of territory to look at them).

Description de l'Égypte does not adopt Galland's ahistorical angle of view altogether, however. In the large section at the end devoted to the "État moderne," the current condition of Egypt, it tells a very different story; one that sprang numerous surprises on the makers of this vast picture album, this atlas of a world of marvelous otherness. The plates are organized in sections under headings such as "Arts et Métiers" (Arts and Trades), followed by "Costumes et Portraits"; these clusters of images make *Description* a self-conscious successor of the *Encyclopédie*, as they unfold the culture of contemporary, Mamluk Egypt in all its variety and industriousness. With assiduous and close attention, the artists made an inventory of the techniques, inventions, trades, crafts, products, and people of the country the French had just overrun. They did not merely pay lip service to the culture they encountered or put on a false show of respect to the people living in the ruins of the civilization the Europeans revered and coveted. The records that show irrigation and sprinkling methods, threshing and shucking machines, drills and knife grinders (fig. 5), and manifold other forms of technology are acts of epistemological penetration: cool, analytical, and wondering, and often eliciting genuinely admiring comment. They reveal ways Egyptians made vinegar and distilled wine from dates, how they forged iron and blew glass, wove mats and carpets, and every stage involved in preparing Egypt's crops, linen, cotton, and rice. It is nevertheless

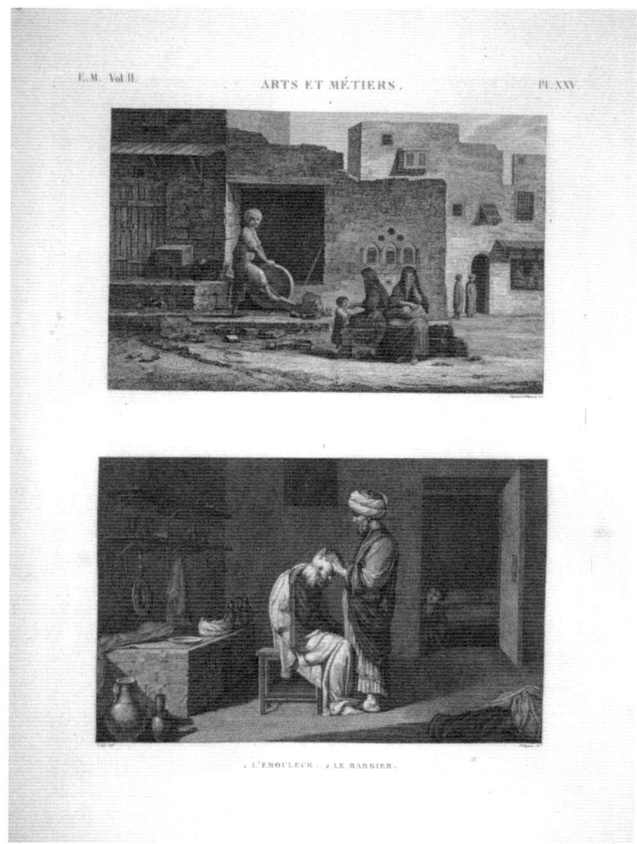

Fig. 5. From drawings by Nicolas-Jacques Conté (French, 1755–1805), street scenes showing the expedition's curiosity about trade skills: the use of feet to turn the grindstone of a knife sharpening machine excited special comment; the attentions of a barber, below, were also the subject of careful observation. *L'Émouleur* (*top*) and *Le Barbier* (*bottom*), engraved by Legrand and Voisard (*top*) and J-L. Delignon (French, 1755–c. 1804) (*bottom*), after Nicolas-Jacques Conté, from *Description de l'Égypte*, vol. 8, *État moderne II*, plate 25

telling that the arrangement of sections runs from Arts and Trades to Customs and Portraits, in that order. This accentuates the importance of costumes and their social significance, denoting rank and occupation, religion and degree of education: in the absence of speaking subjects, it is the creations and apparel that are eloquent instead (fig. 6).

Although all this information reaches the reader at several removes, the plates do not lose their force on the printed page. Engravers often worked from the drawings made in situ and followed notes taken by engineers, architects, surveyors, and painters who were deployed in the field by the emperor. For example, the studies anatomizing the structure of a waterwheel with hollow felloes for irrigation purposes were drawn by F.C. Cécile, one of the architects involved in the expedition, and given to a certain Mme de St Morien to engrave. The latter, whose skills are especially fine, was involved on some of the other plates, such as one delineating the structures of a rice-whitening machine, a winnow, a flour mill, a ploughshare, and a sugar mill (see fig. 3b).

The handsome pages of *Description* do include some individuals, but usually as figures in traditional costume books; only a handful of actual portraits appear. The tremendous assembly of activities and skills portrayed encompasses many of the professions that figure in favorite stories in the *Arabian Nights*: tan-

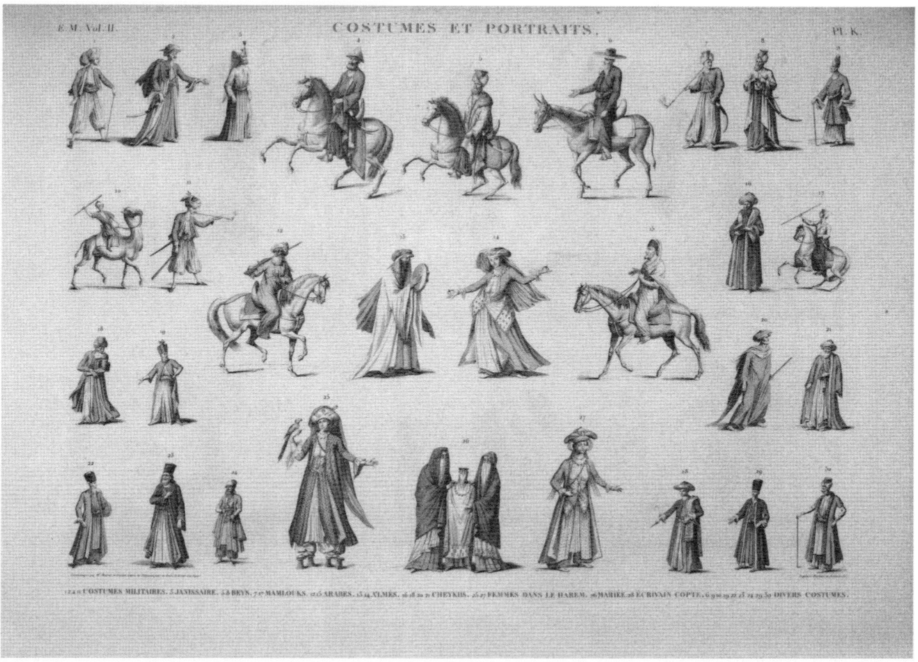

Fig. 6. The illustrated inventory of the modern state of Egypt included a section on costumes and portraits, including this plate containing thirty vignettes of different ranks and occupations. A bride (bottom row, center) is held up between two attendants. Page of costumes, engraving by Jean Duplessis-Bertaux (French, 1750–1818), and Audoin after Mr. Marcel (after originals drawn by a Copt in Cairo), from *Description de l'Égypte* vol. 8, *État moderne II*, plate K

ners and barbers, belt weavers and water carriers, dervishes and attendants at the baths, porters and traders, embroiderers and felt makers (fig. 7); *almehs*, the celebrated professional dancing girls (fig. 8), and wandering holy men. But these occupy only a very small portion of the whole, and the magnificent sequence of images concludes with crowded pages of things. Every kind of thing used by modern Egyptians is represented: cradles and tents; turbans and lutes; locks and lathes; every kind of tool; pens and paper; astrolabes and measuring devices; carpets and bath towels; daggers and helmets; and saddles, carpet bags, rugs, baskets, and narguiles or hookahs. The commentary finds much to praise in the ingenuity and range of these tools and instruments.[17] Finally, an entire, enthralling page of vessels seems to wish to parade every possible manifestation of the container in Oriental manufacturing—flasks and bottles, vases, caskets and phials, basins and ewers, jars and pots (fig. 9)[18]—showcasing the shapes, spouts, ornaments, delicacy, and variety of materials. The artist, working at the behest of the committee

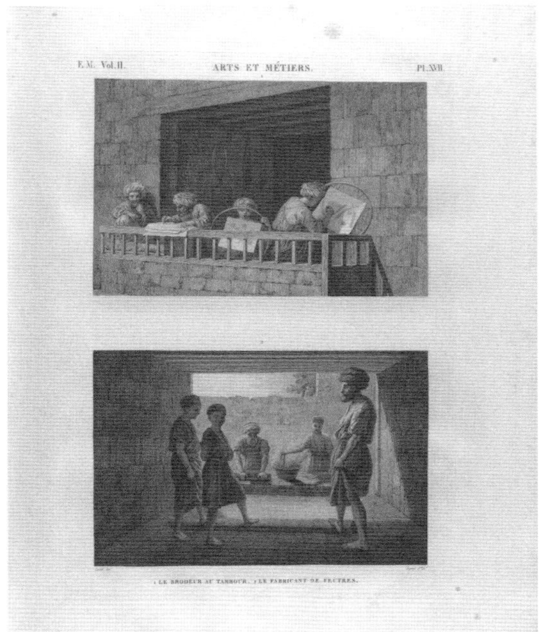

Fig. 7. The many craftspeople of modern Egypt drew the close attention of the *Description*'s artists, who were led by Nicolas-Jacques Conté (also a balloonist and inventor of the modern pencil). Embroiderers working on frames, above, and feltmakers, below. *Le Brodeur au Tambour* (*top*) and *Le Fabricant de Feutres* (*bottom*), engraving by F. R. Ingouf (French, 1747–1812), after Nicolas-Jacques Conté, from *Description de l'Égypte*, vol. 8, *État moderne II*, plate 17. General Collection, Beinecke Rare Book and Manuscript Library, Yale University

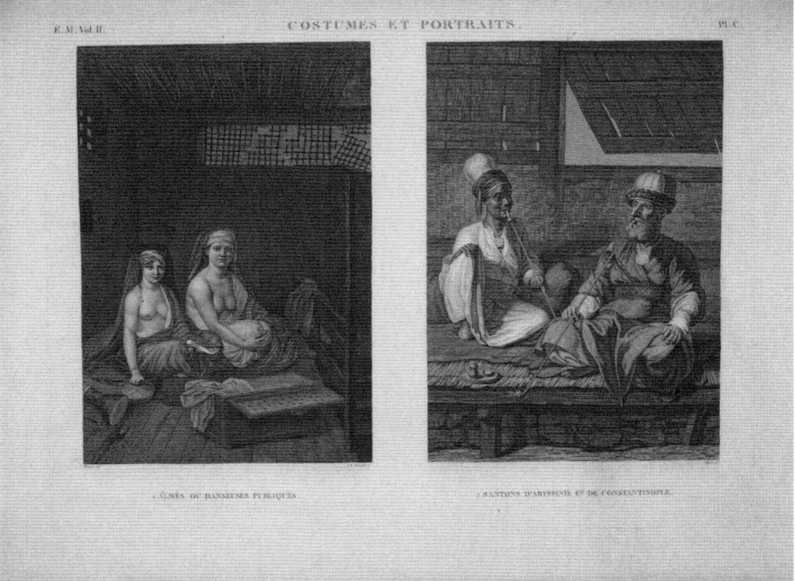

Fig. 8. Unusual portraits portray the professions of modern Egypt in characteristc settings: *almehs*, or dancing girls, with their drum and costume and the hamper. *A'lmés ou danseuses publiques* (*left*) and *Santons d'Abyssinie et de Constantinople* (*right*), engraving by J. B. Massard (French, 1775–1843) (*left*), and Maurice Blot (French, 1753–1818) (*right*), after André Dutertre (French, 1753–1842), from *Description de l'Égypte*, vol. 8, *État moderne II*, plate C. General Collection, Beinecke Rare Book and Manuscript Library, Yale University

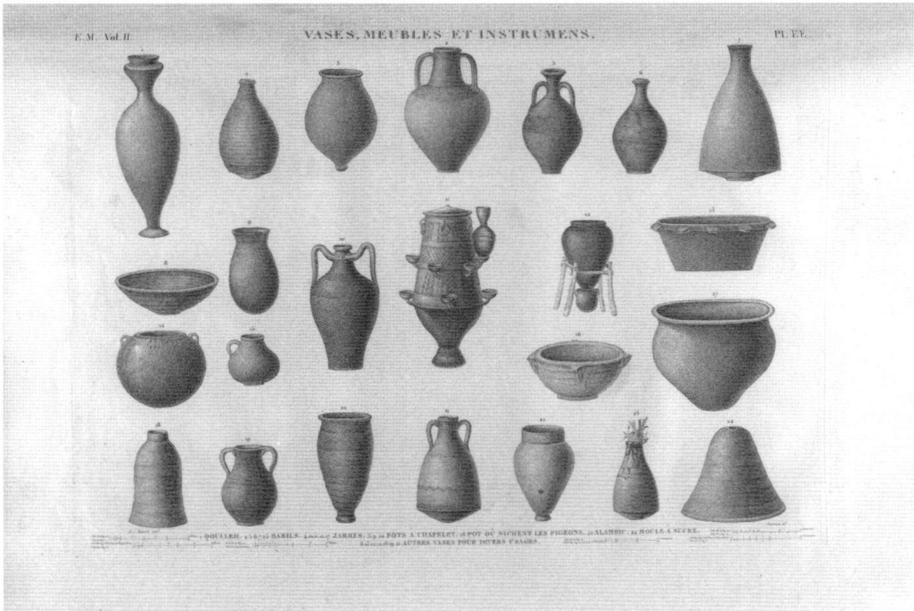

Fig. 9. The meticulous assembly of ewers, bowls, pots, and jugs speaks eloquently of the connection to antiquity in their forms and of the functional aesthetics of modernity. Page of vessels, engraving by J. F. Cazenave (French, 18th century), after H. J. Redouté (French, 1766–1852), from *Description de l'Égypte*, vol. 8, *État moderne II*, plate EE. General Collection, Beinecke Rare Book and Manuscript Library, Yale University

and the Institut d'Égypte, sought to illustrate specific examples of artifacts, but to quest after totality; so many vessels testify to a longing to inventory everything, not to miss out on a single vessel. However, the ambition to record objectively topples from an excess of desire.

"The City of Brass" is a beautiful story in the *Arabian Nights* that tells of a great prince's quest for a lost civilization in the desert.[19] In some versions, Solomon is the prince, in others it is Alexander, but in the *Nights* it is the historic Ummayad Sultan of Damascus, Abdelmelik. The tale is a variant on the medieval Ubi Sunt tradition of threnody; it is cadenced throughout by outbursts of extravagant lamenting.

The protagonists have been sent by the sultan in Damascus to North Africa to find the vessels in which Solomon has imprisoned the rebel jinn. After years of long and arduous journeying, the party reach the fabled lost City of Brass and manage to penetrate the enchantments that preserve it against intruders. Inside, they discover the markets, palaces, and streets are frozen, with the corpses still at the tasks they were undertaking when death struck. It is a vision that warns against vanity, arrogance, and hubris, but it also sings the splendor of that past and turns it into art, effigy, and monument; a hymn and an ode. The dead queen's mummy lies on a bier heaped with jewels; when a looter lays his hands on them, the statues around her lop off his head. They are not quite inanimate: they are things, but they are active. "The City of Brass" is a fiction about wealth and luxury and their penalties, but the gaze of the story is not turned only to the past. As in *Description de l'Égypte*, the story's image of the past transmits a picture of the present: the riches of Baghdad, Shiraz, and other great cities flourishing when the story was first told are captured in the performance of grief for the destroyed cultures of the heroes' predecessors, but this monumental lament for the vanished civilizations of the past reflects flatteringly on the present. *Description de l'Égypte* also opens with an elegiac tone: it too is the story of a princely expedition, and Napoleon also met defeat. Is *Description* likewise a memorial inventory of a City of Brass?

Following *Description*'s encyclopedic attempts at revelation, artists around the world, from Norway to Japan, imagined Shahrazad and the dramatis personae in the stories in terms set by information of the sort displayed on the plates. Edward W. Lane, one of the crucial hinges in this history of transmission, receives a furious lashing from Edward Said; Said is correct in stating that such scholars forged the Orient for the imaginations of Europeans.[20] And yet, if the entanglement is unpicked with more sympathy, some other qualities emerge.

Lane is one of the clearest examples of a charmed encounter with the East. He was an early reader and critic of *Description*, and as a young man was fired up by the Egyptomania that followed the exhibition in London of Belzoni's antiquities, and set out almost immediately to discover Egypt for himself and rectify the French view. In 1829 he landed in Egypt, quickly became fluent in Arabic, and began working on a book that he called *The Description of Egypt*.[21] This project suffered many vicissitudes and never appeared in his lifetime, but in 1836 he published part of it, his richly detailed and loving *Account of the Customs and Manners of the Modern Egyptians*, which had another clear, defiant echo of its French predecessor in the title.[22]

Lane was a great nephew of the artist Thomas Gainsborough, and had trained as an apprentice engraver; his book on modern Egypt is profusely illustrated from his sketchbooks of his travels in Egypt. He sought out many of the scenes and subjects of the French *Description*, but with significantly less emphasis on technology, expertise, labor, and trades, and far more inquisitiveness about domestic arrangements. Using a camera lucida, he made many excellent studies of interior and exterior architecture. He was especially fascinated by women's customs, though as they were forbidden to view by a male and a foreigner like himself, he co-opted his sister, Sophia Lane Poole, to investigate. The result was her book, *The Englishwoman in Egypt*, written in the form of letters after a short stay in the country, in conscious emulation of Mary Wortley Montagu.[23]

Customs and Manners was soon followed by Lane's astonishing translation of the *Nights* (1839–41), which he had been working on concurrently. In three volumes, purified of bawdiness and salaciousness, violence and eroticism, Lane's version, illustrated with six hundred woodcuts, is the one I read, in my great-grandmother's copy from 1850. I still enjoy the stories in this version. Lane's book is wonderfully capacious, and includes scores of tales that are still unfamiliar; he also included all the lyric poetry that Galland had removed. Most valuable of all, Lane organized an astonishing album of engravings by William Harvey and other mid-Victorian artists who worked from his detailed sketches and notes and were kept fully instructed in the furnishings, scenery, and daily utensils of the times: very fine renderings of mosque lanterns, mule saddles, decorative wall interlace tiling, and so forth punctuate the stories with a lively rhythm, giving an endless supply of triggers for the reader's mind-pictures.[24] Lane provided Harvey with the necessary materials for imagining the scenes: Lane's own copious sketches and notes, the celebrated and popular album of Cairo by his friend and colleague Robert Hay, and many original views by other traveling artists of his acquaintance.[25] The list of illustrations in the book conscientiously names all the engravers who transferred Harvey's images to steel plates for the publication, but surprisingly does not include Lane or his brother Richard among the artists. Some of the vignettes and scenes are brought across from both the planned *Description* and from *Modern Egyptians.*

Like Galland, Lane advocated reading the *Nights* as true reports of life in the Middle East in his time, praising "the fullness and fidelity with which they describe the character, manners, and customs of the Arabs. . . . They bring," the critic continued trustingly, "the reality bodily before us."[26] The drawbacks of this approach can be felt in the placement of certain illustrations: a fine depiction of the great Mosque in Cairo accompanies the climax of "The City of Brass," when the travelers finally enter the desolate place, which is guarded by jinn and where everyone is frozen in time yet some of the objects live.[27]

The explorer and adventurer Captain Sir Richard Burton followed Lane in translating the *Nights*, largely because Lane's piety and politeness infuriated

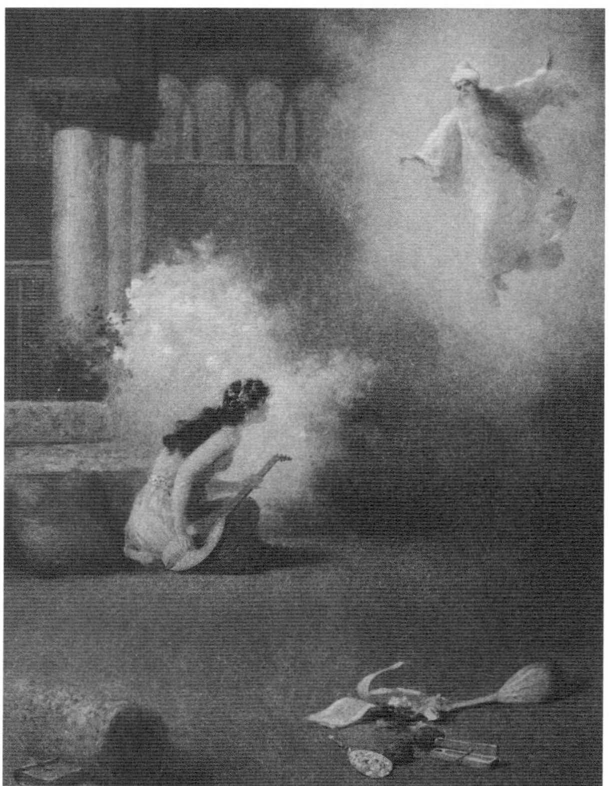

Fig. 10. Strategically arranged book, instruments, pencil case, and jug in an imagined palatial Eastern interior provide authority for the apparition of the jinni to his captive. *Damsel, Tohfat al'Kalib, in "The Tale of Sayf al-Muluk and Badi'at al-Jamal,"* after Albert Letchford, from *A Series of Seventy Original Illustrations to Captain Sir R. F. Burton's "Arabian Nights"* (London: H.S. Nichols Ltd., 1897)

him; he worked from Galland combined with the Arabic in a spirit of full contradiction to the prevailing prudery of Victorian Britain. Burton expanded and embellished with further attention to illuminating the customs of the Arabs, which he also documented with glee and a fair deal of invention, projection, and transference. His friend Albert Letchford's paintings, later engraved for publication, stage the *Nights* in recognizable landscapes and cities of the Levant in the nineteenth century, which he sometimes combined with the scenery around Naples, where he was living; they naturalize the jinn and other supernatural aspects of the *Nights* in vivid realistic interiors, furnished with objects from daily use in Cairo, where Letchford did his chief observing and collecting; these objects are treated with absorbed attention and lovingly illuminated to give them presence. His illustration to "The Tale of Sayf al-Muluk and Badi'at al-Jamal" carefully arranges a still life beside the imprisoned "Damsel," Tohfat al-Kalib, including a lute, an incense burner, a mirror, and books on the floor (fig. 10).[28]

Letchford is taking his cue from Burton, who provided voluminous footnotes commenting on the customs and values of Arab civilization as revealed by the *Nights*; his is an ethnographical or collector's approach, and the things he is introducing into his illustrations are frequently containers: vessels, flasks, bottles, and boxes, placed in such a way as to hint at their contents. Their presence makes a statement about latency and promises disclosure. Almost certainly, the images say, there is more to be found inside or beneath the surface (Hugo von

Hofmannstahl, an Oriental enthusiast, put the question to himself, "Depth must be hidden—where?" and answered, "On the surface").[29]

It is significant that many features of the "Modern State" that Napoleon's team of engineers had investigated with curiosity and admiration were overlooked by Lane and Harvey and by Burton and Letchford. By eliminating references in the images to technology, devices, trades, and machines, the pictures could then capture more evocatively—more enchantingly, it was supposed—the environment of the protagonists of the *Nights*: the city of Baghdad under Harun el Rashid.

Such selections and omissions are doubly misleading: first, many of the irrigation techniques and other devices represented in Napoleon's *Description* are in fact very ancient, as ancient as writing and astronomy. But the presence of such technology would have spoiled the atmosphere of the *Nights*, the mystery and timelessness (you can have water bottles, but not water wheels). Secondly, the stories in such illustrations are taking place in the contemporary Levant, in modern day Cairo or Damascus. Egypt in the mid-nineteenth century might exhibit a perennial picturesque, but it was not the selfsame place it had been when the hero of the story of Hasan of Basra touched down in Alexandria on the back of a jinni.

While many European languages apply the same word, "Storia," "Histoire," to history and to story, as has been often pointed out, in artists' treatments of Egypt and the *Arabian Nights* the rich interplay between fiction and history raises powerful images that invite a way of looking and understanding the Levant that has become indelible.

By the end of the nineteenth century, when Aby Warburg was rethinking the methods of art history through his ethnographical encounters, the animist view of things, which had been so disparaged at the conscious level in Enlightenment and later epistemology, was gaining respectability and recognition, especially in relation to the purposes of art and art history. As Philippe-Alain Michaud comments in his book, *Aby Warburg and the Image in Motion*, Warburg laid new emphasis on the processes by which meaning was imbued into a thing, on "the ensemble of procedures—no longer technical or formal, but symbolic—by which the subject depicted came to inhabit an image."[30]

There are no more fervent collectors of Orientalist art of the nineteenth century than the present citizens of the old Ottoman empire and its neighbors, especially in the Emirates, who appear to receive with delight the fantastic reportage or documented fantasies of European visitors and travelers. Walter Denny

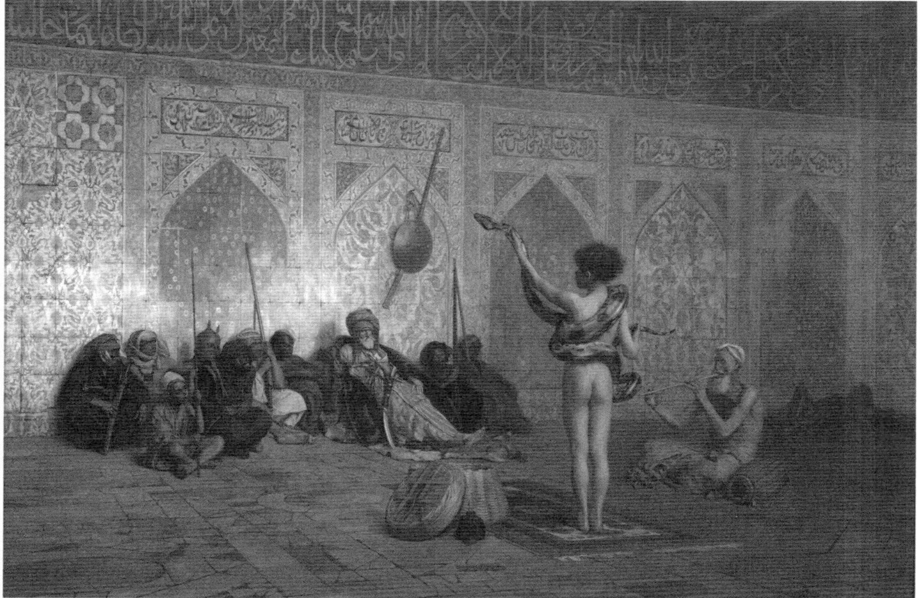

Fig. 11. The artist mixed and matched elements of disparate origins, but his queasy Orientalist fantasy unexpectedly provides accurate records of tiles from the "Golden Way" and of inscriptions in the Topkapi palace. Jean-Léon Gérôme (French, 1824–1904), *The Snake Charmer*, c. 1879. Oil on canvas, 32 3/8 x 47 5/8 in. (82.2 x 121 cm). Sterling and Francine Clark Art Institute, Williamstown, Massachusetts, 1955.51

commented, in 1993, "the painstaking attention to detail manifested by some Orientalist painters, whose motives from this 'realism' were often highly complex, occasionally turns out to have interesting implications both for the history of art and the history of taste, especially when works of Islamic art and architecture themselves form the subject of Orientalist paintings and prints."[31] *The Snake Charmer* by Gérôme (fig. 11), in the Sterling and Francine Clark Art Institute collection, presents a supreme example of this conjunction of the fictive and the accurate: the artist has fantasticated a scene of queasy lubriciousness, but given it a backdrop of scrupulously authentic Iznik tiles from the harem in the Topkapi Palace, melded with equally accurate inscriptions from another courtyard and created at a different date.[32] Through such bricolage, the facts of history and the inventions of fiction fuse and react, both as a consequence of the stories' wildfire success for their early readers in Europe and as the supplement that gives validity to the supernatural fantasies in the stories. The *Arabian Nights*'s enchanted landscape had opened a vision of a charged universe of inanimate, mysterious, and eloquent artifacts.

This title is taken from *Dublin Review* 8 (February 1840): 127, as quoted in Leila Ahmed, *Edward W. Lane: A study of his life and works and of British ideas of the Middle East in the nineteenth century* (London and New York: Longman and Librairie du Liban, 1978), 145.

1. The latter is closer to the Arabic title, *Alf layla wa layla*, and to the French *Mille et une nuit(s)*, the title of Antoine Galland's French translation, which was first rendered in English as *The Arabian Nights' Entertainments.*

2. Lorraine Daston, "Introduction," *Things That Talk*, ed. Lorraine Daston (New York: Zone Books, 2004); see also Lorraine Daston and Peter Galison, *Objectivity* (New York: Zone Books, 2007). See also Bill Brown, "Thing Theory," *Critical Inquiry* 28, no. 1 (Fall 2001).

3. "The Fisherman and the 'ifrit," *The Arabian Nights: Tales of 1001 Nights*, trans. Malcolm C. Lyons with Ursula Lyons, 3 vols. (London: Penguin, 2008), 1:19–24; "Histoire du Pêcheur," no. 3, *Les mille et une Nuit: contes arabes*, trans. Antoine Galland, ed. J. P. Sermain, 3 vols. (1704; repr., Paris: GF Flammarion, 2004), 1:8–27, 65–112; "Le Pêcheur et le Démon," *Les mille et une Nuits*, trans. and ed. Jamel Eddine Bencheikh and André Miquel, 3 vols. (Paris: Gallimard, 2005), 1:29–64; "The Story of the Fisherman and the Demon," *The Arabian Nights*, trans. Husain Haddawy, vol. 1, no. 8–10 (New York: W.W. Norton, 1990), 30–35; "Story of the Fisherman," *The Arabian Nights' Entertainments*, trans. and ed. Edward W. Lane, 3 vols. (London: John Murray, 1850), 1:32–71; "The Story of the Fisherman," no. 3, *Arabian Nights' Entertainments*, ed. Robert L. Mack (c. 1706; repr., Oxford: Oxford University Press, 1998), 8–27, 30–65.

4. See Alexander Nemerov, "Weightless History: Faulkner, Bourke-White, and Eisenstaedt," in this volume.

5. Albert Letchford, *A Series of Seventy Original Illustrations to Captain Sir R. F. Burton's "Arabian Nights"* (privately printed, 1897), The Arcadian Library, London. See Robert Irwin, *The Arabian Nights: A Companion* (1994; repr., London and New York: Tauris Parke, 2004, 2011), 102–3. See Robert Irwin, *Visions of the Jinn* (London and Oxford: Oxford University Press / The Arcadian Library, 2011), 101–3.

6. Daston, "Speechless," in Daston, *Things That Talk*, 20.

7. See Ernst Jonas Bencard, Erik Fischer, and Mikael Bogh Rasmussen, *Melchior Lorck*, 4 (5) vols. (Copenhagen: Royal Library / Vandkunsten Publishers, 2009); see also Marina Warner, "View of a View," *London Review of Books* 32, no. 10 (May 27, 2010): 15–17; Marina Warner, *Stranger Magic: Charmed States and the Arabian Nights* (London: Chatto and Windus, 2011), 167–75.

8. Said himself admired the perspective of Raymond Schwab, *The Oriental Renaissance: Europe's Rediscovery of India and the East, 1680 to 1880* (New York: Columbia University Press, 1987).

9. *Arts et Métiers*, plates 1, 3, 7, in *Description de l'Égypte: ou Recueil des observations et des recherches qui ont été faites en Égypte pendant l'expédition de l'armée française*, vol. 2, *État moderne*, ed. E. F. Jomard, preface by M. Fourier, publié par les ordres de Sa Majesté l'empereur Napoléon le Grand Paris (Imprimérie impériale, 1809–28).

10. "Si les Contes de cette espèce sont agréables et divertissants par le merveilleux qui y règne d'ordinaire, ceux-ci doivent l'emporter en cela sur tous ceux qui ont paru, puisqu'ils sont remplis d'évènements qui surprennent et attachent l'esprit, et qui font voir de combien les Arabes surpassent les autres nations en cette sorte de composition." Galland, "Avertissement," in *Les mille et une Nuit*, 1:21–22.

11. "Ils doivent plaire encore par les coutumes et les moeurs des Orientaux, par les cérémonies de leur religion, tant païenne que mahométane; et ces choses y sont mieux marquées que dans les auteurs qui en ont écrit et que dans les relations des voyageurs. Tous les Orientaux, Persans, Tartares et Indiens, s'y font distinguer, et paraissent tels qu'ils sont, depuis les souverains jusqu'aux personnes de la plus basse condition. Ainsi, sans avoir essuyé la fatigue d'aller chercher ces peoples dans leurs pays, le lecteur aura ici le plaisir de les voir agir et de les entendre parler. On a pris soin de conserver leurs caractères, de ne pas s'éloigner de leurs expressions et de leurs sentiments, et l'on ne s'est écarté du texte que quand la bienséance n'a pas permis de s'y attacher. Le traducteur se flatte que les personnes qui entendent l'arabe, et qui voudront prendre la peine de confronter l'original avec la copie, conviendront qu'il a fait voir les Arabes aux Français, avec toute la circonspection que demandait la délicatesse de notre langue et de notre temps. Pour peu même que ceux qui liront ces Contes soient disposés à profiter des exemples de vertus et de vices qu'ils y trouveront, ils en pourront tirer un avantage qu'on ne tire point de la lecture des autres Contes, qui sont plus propres à corrompre les moeurs qu'à les corriger." Ibid.

12. Malcolm Jack and Anita Desai, eds., *The Turkish Embassy Letters* (London: Virago, 1994); also published as Mary Wortley Montagu, *Letters from the Levant, During the Embassy to Constantinople, 1716–18*, ed. J.A. St. John (London: J. Rickerby, 1838).

13. Mary Wortley Montagu, "Letter to Lady Mar, 10 March 1718," in *Turkish Embassy Letters*, 118.

14. For insightful studies of the expedition, see Yves Laissus, *L'Égypte, une aventure savante: Avec Bonaparte, Kléber, Menou*, 1798–1801 (Paris: Fayard, 1998); and Darcy Grimaldo Grigsby, *Extremities: Painting Empire in Post-Revolutionary France* (New Haven, Conn.: Yale University Press, 2002).

15. For a most entertaining history of further consequences of the craze for Egypt, see Roger Luckhurst, *The Mummy's Curse: A New Cultural History* (Oxford: Oxford University Press, 2012).

16. These can be seen in a splendid digitized and interactive website recently created by the Library of Alexandria, the modern Bibliotheca Alexandrina, rebuilt since the last time it burned down. See http://descegy.bibalex.org/ (accessed August 11, 2010).

17. For example, the knife grinder's use of his feet to turn the stone excites particular admiration. *État moderne*, vol. 2, note to plate 25, in *Description de l'Égypte*.

18. Ibid., plate EE.

19. "The City of Brass," *Arabian Nights*, trans. Lane (1850), 2:518–46; "La Ville de Cuivre," *Les mille et une Nuits* (2005), 2:553–81; "The Story of the City of Brass," *Arabian Nights' Entertainments*, 3:1–37.

20. Edward Said, *Orientalism: Western Conceptions of the Orient* (1978: repr., London: Penguin, 1995), passim; on Lane, 159–66.
21. Jason Thompson, "Edward William Lane's 'Description of Egypt,'" *International Journal of Middle East Studies* 28, no. 4 (November 1996): 565–83.
22. Edward W. Lane, *Account of the Customs and Manners of the Modern Egyptians* (1836: London: J.M. Dent, 1908).
23. Sophia Lane Poole, *The Englishwoman in Egypt: Letters from Cairo* (London: C. Knight, 1844).
24. William Harvey was the favorite student of the pioneer book illustrator Thomas Bewick. See Jenny Uglow, *Nature's Engraver: A Life of Thomas Bewick* (London: Faber, 2006), 345–50.
25. Leila Ahmed, *Edward W. Lane: A study of his life and works and of British ideas of the Middle East in the nineteenth century* (London and New York: Longman and Librairie du Liban, 1978), 144.
26. *Dublin Review* 8 (February 1840): 127, quoted in Ahmed, *Edward W. Lane*, 145.
27. Captioned, even more misleadingly, *The Palace of Kosh, son of Sheddad*, eng. by "Miss Williams" after William Harvey, *Arabian Nights' Entertainments*, ed. and trans. Lane (1850), 3:7.
28. "The Tale of Sayf al-Muluk and Badi'at al-Jamal," *Les mille et une Nuits*, trans. and ed. Bencheikh and Miquel, (2005), 3:94–148; Lane, *Arabian Nights' Entertainments*, ed. Mack, 3:95–145.
29. Von Hofmannsthal, "Letter."
30. Philippe-Alain Michaud, *Aby Warburg and the Image in Motion* (New York: Zone Books, 2004), 32.
31. Walter B. Denny, "Quotations In and Out of Context: Ottoman Turkish Art and European Orientalist Painting," *Muqarnas*, vol. 10, *Essays in Honour of Oleg Grabar* (Cambridge, Mass.: MIT Press 1993), 219–23.
32. Ibid, figs. 1, 3–4, 220–22.

The Ekphrastic O

Cole Swensen

Ekphrasis is a subset of art writing distinguished by a particular deployment of the poetic. Like much art writing, it is engaged with the line between representation and experience; it is also often engaged with reinforcing that line and the framing that keeps art separate from the world in order to allow it usefully to comment on it. There's been an explosion of ekphrastic poetry in the past twenty years. Much of it, surprisingly, takes an opposite tack, determined instead to disturb and erode that line. In looking at how that disturbance operates, it seems that moving the location of truth allows the line between representation and experience to move too, heading ever inward to entangle with the subjectivity of both writer and reader, and doing so in ways that do not disturb the integrity and sovereignty of the work of art.

In that it deals with a sovereign entity, ekphrasis is a form of documentary poetry. It is this reality that problematizes its relationship to truth. Whereas fiction advertises its invented nature, flaunting its untruthfulness, and nonfiction flaunts its veracity, poetry has a much less settled position because its truth is based in its own haecceity, its own *is-ness.* Similarly, truth itself is usually a mimetic relationship created by how faithful one thing is to another—an account to a series of events, a description to an object—but in poetry, truth can function differently, not by mimesis but (like poetry itself) by haecceity. Ekphrasis that makes use of this possibility can engage art in particular and complex ways.

I have chosen three versions of a single story to illustrate this point, all of which operate on a continuum that allows us to examine the relationship between representation and experience as mediated by the location of truth. The story is that of Giotto's O, made canonical by Giorgio Vasari, the sixteenth-century biographer. Vasari is the starting point of this continuum. His version strives for a factual truth, representing historical events in the most accurate way possible, given the limitations of language. His purpose is history, not creativity (even if the two can never be separated). A much more recent rendition by the contemporary French writer Jean Frémon will be the second point. His version is not concerned with the distinction between history and creativity; he not only assumes history to be a creative act but even assumes that history is not an end in itself, but an occasion for further creativity. History for Frémon is never the site of truth, guaranteed by the fact of its having already occurred in the past; instead the assumption is that truth can only exist in the present. This assumption shifts us from the realm of factual truth to that of sensual truth. The third example is a poem by the New York poet Tom Healy, which moves further from the historic and the factual and deeper into the particular and the subjective, putting the emphasis on the interpretive, positing the site of truth in the mind of the perceiver, and so arriving at an emotional truth.

Refracting any one story through these three different lenses would reveal underlying assumptions about truth in our culture, but the story of Giotto's O is particularly appropriate, for it distills and presents the dream of perfect representation and underscores that this ideal can only be achieved with the abstract because representation is in fact an abstraction's only existence. In turn, it reminds us that any attempted representation of the actual is doomed (even where a perfect reproduction does seem to exist, which is only possible with manufactured things, it is always a second instance, thus fundamentally different). This is true also of truth as a representational system: it can never achieve perfection; the truth of something can never match the actual something, and in this case there is no partial exception because, by virtue of its being immaterial, there is necessarily nothing that shares truth's material. Truth is necessarily unique, which makes it fail as a representational system. However, if it can instead attain presentation, it can succeed.

Vasari's O

> The Pope was planning to have some paintings made in St. Peter's. This courtier, on his way to see Giotto and to find out what other masters of painting and mosaic there were in Florence, spoke with many masters in Sienna, and then, having received some drawings from them, he came to Florence. And one morning going into the workshop of Giotto, who was at his labours, he showed him the mind of the Pope, and at last asked him to give him a little drawing to send to his Holiness. Giotto, who was a man of courteous manners, immediately took a sheet of paper, and with a pen dipped in red, fixing his arm firmly against his side to make a compass of it, with a turn of his hand he made a circle so perfect that it was a marvel to see it. Having done it, he turned smiling to the courtier and said, "Here is the draw-

> ing." But he, thinking he was being laughed at, asked, "Am I to have no other drawing than this?" "This is enough and too much," replied Giotto, "send it with the others and see if it will be understood." The messenger, seeing that he could get nothing else, departed ill pleased, not doubting that he had been made a fool of. However, sending the other drawings to the Pope with the names of those who had made them, he sent also Giotto's, relating how he had made the circle without moving his arm and without compasses, which when the Pope and many of his courtiers understood, they saw that Giotto must surpass greatly all the other painters of his time. This thing being told, there arose from it a proverb which is still used about men of coarse clay, "You are rounder than the O of Giotto," which proverb is not only good because of the occasion from which it sprang, but also still more for its significance, which consists in its ambiguity, *tondo*, "round," meaning in Tuscany not only a perfect circle, but also slowness and heaviness of mind.[1]

This account presents itself as "true"—an accurate representation of events as they occurred—and, in order to convince us, uses language that is relatively clear and direct. There is no figurative language, and there are very few adjectives and adverbs. There is no play of sound or rhythm or any heightening of the material qualities of the words that might distract us from their meaning. In addition, there are no images for image's sake; the only imagery used is that necessary to advance the story. Considered as a whole, it has a very low level of poeticity, which I'm defining here as anything that deviates from or obstructs the ideal one-to-one relationship between sign and referent. All aspects of the language used here are designed to channel us toward the narrative truth, which is Vasari's goal. This is no accident; it is not even a matter of Vasari's or the translators' particular style. It is a matter of the bias in Western culture that equates truth with clarity and directness; a bias that puts truth and aesthetics at opposite ends of a spectrum: the more poetic a text seems to be, the less it is presumed to be true. We witnessed this on a national scale during the 2004 elections, in which John Kerry was presumed by many to be less than truthful because his speech was rhetorically elaborate and used sound and rhythm to give it grace, while George Bush, because he spoke in short, simple sentences, was presumed to be telling the truth, to be honest. This amounts to a dangerous conflation on the part of the hearer of understanding and veracity: If I understand it, it must be true; if I do not understand it, it must be a lie. Much nonfiction, whether on the subject of art or not, conforms to this bias, striving for a streamlined, unambiguous surface.

Frémon's O

Below is another account of the same story that has a different aim and therefore takes a very different approach. For one, it has a much higher level of poeticity, mostly manifest through imagery, though also through immediacy. Jean Frémon, unlike Vasari, is primarily interested in putting us there, on the spot, which he does through sensual information. We might say that, while Vasari's account achieves a factual truth, a connection to the world as known, Frémon's achieves a sensual one, a connection to the world as experienced. This version, the second stage on the continuum, provides more details, a closer focus, and material that appeals to a variety of senses.

> Stefano, emissary of the pope, sang as he walked along, and from the hills of Oltrarno, the coo-coo replied. Primula brightened the path through the oaks bustling with starlings, and a litter of young black boar scattered into the undergrowth. The abbot Stefano sang.
>
> On his way back from Siena, he had crossed San Donato, stopping to fill his gourd at the fountain of Tavarnelle, and passed the night in San Casciano at the Order of Friars Minor. In the morning, he'd passed through Galluzo to buy a loaf of bread and some sweet onions. And now he'd arrived—from the top of the hill, he could already see the Arno down in the valley and the towers of Florence beyond.
>
> Under his arm, he carried a large roll of drawings by the best painters in Siena. Ugolino had given him a journey of the magi, Martini, a baptism of Christ, and Lorenzetti, an annunciation, to mention only the most illustrious, while their students had outdone themselves to show how well they'd help their masters if the latter were chosen.
>
> For the pope had come up with a project: frescoes for Saint Peter's in Rome, frescoes that would enlighten the conscience through image, that would render faith irrefutable. He'd asked the abbot Stefano to visit all the studios in Tuscany in search of the very best. Mediocrity simply does not convince, said the pope. While his secret wish was to bend genius to his will.

Stefano stopped at the top of the hill; the sun had disappeared behind the ridgeline, and night was beginning to fall. He tucked his roll into the fork of an olive tree to protect it from the morning dew, and, spreading his cloak out on the ground, sat down to eat his bread and onions, drink the Tavarnelle water, say his prayers, and go to sleep.

In his dreams, he saw the most beautiful frescoes imaginable. He no longer distinguished the golden halos from sunsets or the coats of the soldiers sleeping at the foot of the cross from simple rocks. The crucified body hung among the trees, and Gabriel, lily in hand, was more real than any image ever could have made him. He saw the monk Francis preaching to the birds gathered in a circle at his feet; he saw the night of the magi, and the luminous star above them.

In the morning, Stefano, having slept in a fresco, woke up in a fresco. Cypresses, silhouetted, stood cut out against the sky, and three larks argued over the crumbs of the Galluzo loaf. His back was stiff. He picked up his coat. Was it he or his painted shadow that then descended the hill with a rickety step toward the bridge that crossed the Arno? Night had not yet entirely left him; exhaustion held him in a lightly luminous fever. He was headed toward the studio of Ambrogiotto di Bondone, student of Cimabue, whose reputation had begun to spread beyond the borders of Tuscany.

It was said that Giotto, always a clown, had once painted a fly on the nose of a portrait that Cimabue was working on. The master, returning to his painting and simply thinking that the fly had been attracted by the egg in the tempera, tried several times to brush it away before he realized the trick.

Lifting the bronze lion-head and letting it fall, the abbot knocked at the painter's door. Giotto di Bondone did not take off his hat. He was an ugly man, and generally disagreeable. Stefano explained the great plans of the papacy, emphasizing the honor of the invitation, and then spoke highly of the Sienese painters' enthusiasm. Giotto said nothing.

Leaving the abbot on the threshold, he took a sheet of paper out of a trunk, dipped his brush in red and, with a single movement of his wrist, traced a perfect circle without taking his elbow from his side. He then handed the drawing to the abbot saying, "There you are."

> Stefano, thinking this a joke, replied, "Great halo, but it's missing a saint." Then he added, "Do you think that this can compete with the work of the heirs to the great Byzantine style? Here in this roll, I have a journey of the magi, all three of them with their horses, their donkeys laden with gifts, the star guiding them. I have a baptism of Christ; he's up to his waist in water, and the painter has rendered it so clear that you can see the holy virility between the Savior's legs, and I have an annunciation that shows the Virgin, terrorized by the appearance of the archangel, clutching at a column for support. Their details grasp it all—doctrine, tradition, and nascent innovation. Who do you think you are to scorn such an opportunity?"
>
> "I mean no scorn," said Giotto, laying his drawing on top of the kings, the baptism, and the archangel. "Show this to the one who sent you, and tell him what you have seen."
>
> So Stefano, though with great misgivings, did.
>
> Yet when they saw the audacity of that perfect circle and heard how it had been drawn, the pope and his advisors knew instantly that Giotto surpassed all the Sienese. They called him to Rome, covered him with gold, and commissioned him to do five scenes from the life of Christ for the ceiling of Saint Peter's. People came from all over Italy to admire them.
>
> "Rounder than Giotto's O" became the term for a dullard who could be easily duped, and the Tuscan dialect uses the same phrase to indicate both a circle and a closed mind.[2]

In many ways this is the same story, but there are significant differences. One that we miss here, because this is a translation from the French, is the web of subtle sound relationships and rhythms that animate the original. Partly this occurs because there are many fewer word endings in French, which means that it is much easier to get accidental rhymes and off-rhymes, but mostly these sounds and rhythms are a product of the writer's attention to the surface of his text as an aesthetic object. While Vasari's goal is to impart information to increase our knowledge of Giotto's life and character, Frémon's purpose is to create an art object that will incite an experience; his version is not told for our edification, it is told for our delectation. While Vasari, like many writers of nonfiction, wants us to look right through the language to a supposedly freestanding truth, Frémon draws attention to the constructed nature of his tale with his confusion between the internal and external frescoes, finally asking, "Was it he or his painted shadow that then descended the hill?"

Another difference announces itself with the first word: the courtier is named—anonymity has been replaced by specificity. The power of the proper name is always sharply focused—it pries things open; it calls things into presence. Frémon uses it lavishly. Not only is the main character named but so are the rivers, the towns, and, in particular, the things that nourish Stefano, which become, in turn, their own proper names: the water from the fountain at Tavarnelle becomes "the Tavarnelle water"; the bread from Galluzo becomes "the Galluzo loaf." This makes the proper name into an anchor and then into a responsibility; it is a particularity from which we cannot turn. We, as readers, are called to witness, which is a passive act that makes observance into social and political activism; only the extreme particularity of the proper noun can make that call.

These proper names, like most of Frémon's differences, are completely invented. But what if one or more of them just happened to be, coincidentally, true? What if the name of the man sent out on this mission by the pope in the early 1300s just happened to have been Stefano? Would it be or have been the same Stefano? And by that, would we mean the same person, or the same word? It is there that the incommensurability is sealed, for Vasari's unnamed emissary was a person and Frémon's Stefano is a word. The person is dead and has passed from truth into non-truth. The fact of his life is true, but he is not. Whereas Frémon's word can never, in itself, be false. Fremon's tale is using the proper noun to bring us constantly back to materiality.

Most of the differences between Vasari's version and Frémon's are, like the proper nouns, details. Detail is the site of first fragility; it's where truth, understood as the particularity of any given thing, is the most vulnerable, whether we are considering a sculpture buried for hundreds or thousands of years or a story retold over generations. To invent detail is, on the one hand, to brazenly disregard truth, but on the other, it is to create a mechanism by which we can again access the particularity of the given thing. Such details focus our eye and imagination in intimate relation to events and objects described; we become immersed in them, and the margins, the frame that keeps this event of art separate from the larger world, begin to fade. This fictional tale is heading into ekphrastic territory as it attempts to swallow us in experience and make us forget the line between experience and representation.

That said, by giving us the story obliquely, Frémon's version reinvigorates the very margin that he so usefully erased. For most of his piece, our attention is directed away from the principal point of the story, and we concentrate instead on the emissary and the vivid, evocative details of his journey, such as his sleeping on the ground and his meal of bread and onions. There is something in this obliqueness itself that is essential to art, to its way of increasing "truthiness"—a notion that recalls Viktor Shklovsky's comment that "art exists to make one feel things, to make the stone again *stony*." In a similar way, it can also make truth more *truthy*, heightening the accessibility of its particularity. Shklovsky went on to say that "The purpose of art is to impart the sensation of things as they are perceived and not as they are known."[3] By concentrating on the margin, by seeing obliquely out of the corner of the eye, the habits of seeing are disrupted and we are more likely to see without the veil of expectation and preconception. From the margins, we see the center more vividly.

Futhermore, in Frémon's version, the scene is enacted; we are not told so much as shown. This is largely achieved through imagery. Throughout we are given vivid pictures of the countryside with its various plants and animals, and he piles on extra images by describing the religious scenes that the Sienese painters have submitted, all the while using rich, charged verbs: laden, terrorized, clutched, grasp. We're invited not only to see but also to feel, hear, taste, smell, and touch. We feel the hard ground when he lies down to sleep and the stretch in our arm when he places the roll in the crotch of the tree. But it's not just the sensual engagement occasioned by these moves that we feel, it is also the slight, but uncanny, oddity of the details he imparts—we would never today think of sleeping on a cloak on the ground in anything other than dire extremity, and we would never have to keep drawings on parchment safe from dew with no resources (such as a plastic tube) to aid us. These details, while not only appealing to the kinetic and the tactile, also take us back into another time by engaging the body's imagination as well as the mind's. Frémon gets us to span time, to mentally place our bodies in two times simultaneously. For Frémon, history is not an account of what occurred, it is the radically different experience of the body in the world from one age to another.

This is the core of the difference between the two vignettes: Vasari is trying for history, while Frémon is trying for a story. Frémon's story does not reverberate into the larger narrative of human events as does Vasari's—which emanates outward to find a relative relationship to the hundreds of other anecdotes that he tells and from which it derives its importance—but rather it exists on its own and for its own sake. In this sense, it has been decontextualized; its framing has been radically changed, and as such, it puts pressure on the very issue of framing, always an active site in a work of art.

Healy's O

All these differences come together to begin a break with the model of truth as mimesis, and in its stead they create an experience that is not *like* another experience but that *is* another experience. This is even more true of the next stop on the continuum, which takes us further from the verifiable accuracies of the story and deeper into poeticity, shifting the site of truth increasingly inward. If Vasari strives for factual truth, and Frémon for sensual truth, Tom Healy aims for emotional truth; a connection with the world not as it is known or as it is experienced but as it is responded to. Thus his is a truth whose root is deeply embedded in the reader.

> "The View From Here"
>
> Giotto drew a perfect circle
> with one quick
> turn of coal.
>
> the shape
> of astonishment,
> forever's empty frame,
>
> a coin on the tongue,
> how our eyes never are.
> but relax, love,
>
> into this world we're finding
> and the perfect hurt
> of how it turns.[4]

The differences here are considerable. This poem in no way provides a true account of events; its perspective on the story is oblique to say the least, something that is announced in the first line. In fact, this is not a story at all, and has no interest in being one. Instead, it goes straight through the story to the work of art itself and begins there. Yet even that has been importantly changed. The resulting circle is no longer in red ink but black coal, which makes even starker this essential gesture to which the entire tale has been reduced—starker, but also more indelible, more momentous. Giotto is here not as a historical figure but as an instance of the emptiness of perfection and the possibility of emptiness itself. This instance and this possibility have implications not for the development of art but for a truth of a universal nature. Here language itself is attempting to constitute truth, not report it and not reenact it. Truisms are just this sort of truth, and they are often stated in aphoristic language that strives toward memorability through the kind of concision we see here, as well as through foregrounding the material, even visceral, qualities of language.

By insisting on its materiality, the poem models a haecceitic truth, which evokes, but does not try to represent, the similarly haecceitic truth of the truism. The difference that a high degree of poeticity makes is precisely this move into materiality, which is to say, into its own commensurability with itself and itself alone, refusing representation and insisting on experience. The poem alludes to the mimetic truth of the story only in order to move toward other truths; the truths of the outside, evident world become occasions, portals into more abstract and universal truths that touch on the invisibles and the unsayables, which can only be sensed, but not represented, and thus not communicated in any other way.

The universality of the truth that the poem presents takes it out of time, on the one hand, making its affective field enormous, while on the other hand, the "we" of the lovers is the sole basis of that truth, which restricts its affective field to an intimate invention. This simultaneous expansion and contraction creates a paradox that constitutes one of the piece's modes of poeticity.

Another mode is the reliance on visual imagery: one image replaces another along a metonymic chain of variations on the circular shape. The image as such is unarguable. We cannot prove the shape of astonishment, and we cannot say "true" or "false" to the phrase "a coin on the tongue." It takes the sensual presence of Frémon's version and, by extending it into the abstract, pushes it beyond the reach of the truth test.

Healy's poeticity is also subtly but forcefully present in his close sound relationships. Although he avoids full end-rhymes, the first line begins the poem with the internal rhyme of "perfect circle," which is echoed two lines later in the word "turn." It is the same sound that ends the poem on the "we're/perfect/hurt/turns" series of embedded rhymes. The two middle stanzas are ruled by the off-rhymes of "shape" and "frame" and "tongue" and "love." Sound is subtly holding the poem together from the inside, creating a delicate music that becomes as much the content of the piece as the statements made, and also fundamentally contributes to those statements by forming an equation between "circle" and "hurt" through the sliding adjective "perfect."

Healy, in this poem, is taking ekphrasis in a new direction. He is refusing the traditional model, based upon mimesis, in which the poet looks directly at the work of art and tries to represent it; instead, he is insisting upon the more delicate and difficult truth of presentation by turning the work of art, in this case Giotto's O, into a companion that travels along with him to discover a truism about the world. In this way, the work of art, while remaining an end in itself, simultaneously becomes a lens through which the world is seen in a new perspective. The result is a collaboration in which poem and art operate together to keep the world unfolding.

1. Giorgio Vasari, *The Lives of the Artists*, trans. Julia Conaway Bondanella and Peter Bondanella (Oxford: Oxford University Press, 1991), 235.

2. Jean Frémon, *The Real Life of Shadows*, trans. Cole Swensen (Sausalito, Calif.: Post-Apollo Press, 2009), 1. Reprinted by permission of the publisher.

3. Viktor Shklovsky, *Theory of Prose*, trans. Benjamin Sher (Normal, Ill.: Dalkey Archive Press, 1991), 6.

4. Tom Healy, "The View From Here," in *What the Right Hand Knows* (New York: Four Way Books, 2009), 51. Reprinted by permission of the publisher.

Anecdotes and the Life of Art History

Mark Ledbury

In a book that explores the complexity of art history's relationship with a wide variety of sophisticated literary forms, genres, and tones of voice, it might seem churlish or bathetic to spend time with the anecdote. As Paul Fleming recently put it:

> The reliance on anecdotes in the midst of making a point or, worse still, as argumentation itself seems to mark a certain helplessness, a sign of not knowing what to say next; or of wanting to avoid the heavy lifting required for fine argumentation; or of hoping to reach a wider audience by employing a more accessible, popular medium; or of simply giving in to the seduction of narration.[1]

However, one of the joys and triumphs of New Historicism in the humanities was the revival of serious interest in the anecdotal. The anecdote was a counterweight to the authoritative, dominant, and "joined-up" narratives of History with a capital H in order to puncture a bland fabric with the prick of the mysterious, fragmentary, joyous, violent, and overlooked. Anecdotes thereby enriched or subverted coercive tales of progress and victory by way of the destabilizing frisson of Eros, the salutary shudder of Thanatos, or the resonant, melancholy minor key of resistance.[2]

In the history of art, we have never had to "bring back" the anecdote, champion it, or defend it as an alternative to authoritative or authoritarian narratives, as it has been deeply rooted in art-historical writing since its origins, and remains a powerful and fertile presence in our thinking and writing. Here, I will briefly explore the depth of our debt to the anecdotal, and suggest that we see anecdote not as a last resort but as a profound and effective strategy, one that has constantly provided provocation and nourishment to the discipline.

From the very origins of art-historical accounts, from the fragmentary (but vastly influential) writings of Pliny on ancient artists about whom we know almost nothing else, through Vasari and all Vasari's imitators, histories of artists are saturated with anecdote. It is worth reminding ourselves that even the best known and most foundational of art-historical narratives is an anecdote:

> There is a story, too, that at a later period, Zeuxis having painted a child carrying grapes, the birds came to peck at them; upon which, with a similar degree of candour, he expressed himself vexed with his work, and exclaimed—"I have surely painted the grapes better than the child, for if I had fully succeeded in the last, the birds would have been in fear of it." Zeuxis executed some figures also in clay, the only works of art that were left behind at Ambracia, when Fulvius Nobilior transported the Muses from that city to Rome. There is at Rome a Helena by Zeuxis, in the Porticos of Philippus, and a Marsyas Bound, in the Temple of Concord there.[3]

Pliny's text is a telling hybrid of "evolutionary" discussion of materials, factual cataloguing of whereabouts, and provenance, but at its heart is the telling anecdote: "there is a story, too." Neither this tale nor any of Pliny's other deeply influential thumbnails fully transcend the status of hearsay, but Pliny is deeply aware, it seems, that chronicling these stories, assembling them, is a precious act given the vicissitudes and non-survival of many artworks and the inevitable fragmentation of true evidence. Anecdote is indispensible to art-historical narrative from the very outset.

If necessity and the challenge of fragmentation and loss was one early driver of art-historical anecdote, then thirst for a truth "beyond the record" was also powerful motivation, as evidenced by another powerful ancient model of anecdote that propels and sustains art-historical narrative. The *Secret History of Justinian* (in Greek ἀνέκδοτα, meaning things unpublished)[4] retained its compulsive attraction for generations of humanists and supplied an authoritative blueprint for the proliferation of "off the record" chronicles of great men (and women) in similar levels of unverifiable or salacious detail.[5] The *Secret History* has some claim to be the foundational text of the history of anecdote,[6] but was of particular use to art history, demonstrating the appeal of a nonofficial history with its salty truths not fit for the official record.

No wonder, then, that Vasari—who, in compiling his *Lives of the Artists*, availed himself of so many models—drew heavily at the Procopian well. Though

"Giotto's O" remains his most talked-about anecdote (witty, pithy, beautiful as it is), I would here point to a different Vasarian tale, the "capture" passage of the elegant, entirely undocumented life of Filippo Lippi as exemplary: the layer cake of anecdotes of enslavements and escapes that sets up life is a beautifully concise and delicately erotic paean to the impossibility of confining artistic temperament.[7] In Vasari's *Lives*, it is clear that the informal, secret history model was a deliberate, constant copresence in the text with more scrupulously documented assertions. The comingling of registers was so entertainingly established by Vasari that it remained a staple of the *Lives* model and thus of most authoritative art-historical accounts for centuries.[8]

The familiar narrative of the history of our discipline, though, insists that the antiquarian waves of the seventeenth and eighteenth centuries marked the beginning of the professionalization of institutions and discourses of history and a new model of art history that began to marginalize the anecdote and prepared the way for the fully "academic" histories of the nineteenth and twentieth centuries.[9] But the evidence that this new model ever dominated or replaced the anecdotal strain at this late eighteenth-century moment of the "origin of art history" is contradictory, to say the least. We can gauge the continuing currency of the anecdotal model by way of two exemplary eighteenth-century enterprises, one justly celebrated, the other more obscure.

If Denis Diderot cannot precisely be called the originating voice of art criticism, he has a claim to be among the first writers to prove that the genre could be rich, polemical, and philosophical, and he certainly extended its length and reach and directed its attention to the currents of contemporary art.[10] What interests me here, though, is the anecdotal strain that permeates all his most complex writing, especially on the great Salons of 1765 and 1767. Responding to works in ways that knit together a range of anecdotes of all varieties, Diderot did not just recount stories of artists but punctuated and sometimes framed his expositions and his philosophical arguments with an astonishing variety of anecdotal material not always directly to do with the artists themselves but more loosely aimed at ensuring that the tone of his criticism remained resolutely earthy, conversational, and accessible, even in its most philosophical flights.

One of the most celebrated examples of this occurs in the Salon of 1767, as Diderot tries to explain why some impressive sketches do not flesh out into equally distinguished finished paintings:

> Buffon and the President de Brosses are not young any more—but they were once . . . when they were young, they sat down to drink early, and carried on a long time—they loved good wine, and they drank a lot of it. They loved women, and when they were drunk they used to frequent ladies of pleasure. One day, while with the ladies in the relaxed undress of the house of pleasure, The President, who was hardly taller than a dwarf, revealed to them a member of such astonishing, prodigious, and unexpected proportions that they all let out cries of admiration. However, after admiring it for a long time, they began to think about it a little—one of them, having taken a few silent turns around this marvellous little President, said to him: "that's all very well, all very nice, no doubt about it: but where's the arse to keep it pumping?" So, my friend, if someone presents you with a sketch for a comedy or tragedy, take your turn around the man, and ask, like our prostitute friend, "Where is the arse to keep it pumping?" do the same for an outline of a novel or speech—of a painted sketch—ask "where's the arse to keep it pumping?". . . (ou est le cul?) A sketch is perhaps only so appealing to us because it is indeterminate, and leaves to our imagination the pleasure of seeing in it what we will.[11]

That Diderot should use this story to explain the need for the promise of a sketch to be delivered within the complex frame of the finished work is both amusing and economical. Here anecdote no longer simply serves to flesh out a career or a life but is raised to the status of metaphor and vehicle for philosophical and aesthetic thought. Diderot and his companions (including Buffon) had been exploring just such idiomatic communication of complex philosophical truths as central to their encyclopedic project. We should recognize, however, that the particular origin of art criticism in the pamphlets and manuscript correspondence of the eighteenth century encouraged an approach that was simultaneously anecdotal and philosophical in complex ways that prefigure, to an extent, the more self-consciously anecdotal maneuvers of someone such as Hans Blumenberg.[12]

My other example from this moment is Pierre Jean-Baptiste Nougaret and Nicolas Thomas Leprince's vast compendium, *Anecdotes des beaux-arts* (Anecdotes of the Fine Arts).[13] Published between 1776 and 1780, *Anecdotes* was the brainchild of Nougaret, one of the more active peddlers of informal histories, salacious narratives, and, importantly, the author of a "secret history" of the Reign of Louis XVI, which he began at the same time as the *Anecdotes* in a moment of extraordinary, if now rather forgotten, literary productivity.[14] His coauthor, Leprince, was more serious-minded, and the author in 1782 of a much more "authoritative" history of the King's library.[15] Nougaret was a chronicler of the theater world, and a veritable Stekhanov in the scandal mines of Robert Darnton's pre-Revolutionary Grub Street—extraordinarily lively as a chronicler, gossip, and pornographer by turns.[16] The *Anecdotes* are exemplary of what might be called "unauthorized" versions of art history in the age of Winckelmann.

The preface begins with a universalizing statement of its scope, "a history of every true art from antiquity until now," and the authors jauntily explain that theirs is a condensed and collected summa of the knowledge too often kept in inaccessible volumes. What immediately becomes clear upon further reading is that the enterprise is quirky yet deeply informed, with Pliny and ancient authorities, Vasari, and contemporary connoisseurial and antiquarian accounts cited frequently. Nougaret and Leprince's lengthy preface aims to be both anecdotal and universal, combining a history of materials (with thumbnail sketches of the origin of drawing, painting, mosaic, glass painting, painted ceramics, encaustic, and other forms) and a history of reception, deception, and illusion with a wonderfully humorous passage on paintings with miraculous effects and a fairly extended discussion of anamorphosis—and even an excursus on the power of nature to create painting-like images. To an extent this is the history of painterly wonder, but there is clearly burlesque in the mix here, too. The passages on encaustic painting (62–65) rapidly become a lively and funny mock-dissertation on the origin of the cheese omelet (67–68). This art history is a delightful parody of po-faced antiquarianism, but it is also highly "contemporary," informed by the flood of new journalistic accounts (and its references are as often to recent journal and newspaper debate as to ancient texts). However, the longer sections on the history of the academy, for example, draw on the authority of manuscript accounts and privileged knowledge (in the time-honored traditions of secret histories), while the panorama of painting in Britain and Spain takes a witty, conversational tone as it accounts for the growth of auction houses and picture galleries. The history is fully if sketchily global; we are given digests of history in China, Georgia, India, and Russia. This history of the wonders, strangenesses, and extremes of painting is, intentionally or not, anti-Winckelmann, aimed at creating simultaneous and diverse panoramas rather than a hierarchized and canonical narrative. It joyously plunders a wide range of literary genres from "respectable" histories to travel narratives, novels, and scandal sheets, and throughout the text, as befits the genre, we have citations of poems, anecdotes, and stories, and the authors are clearly alert to the pace and rhythm of their account—indeed, the tone of the text is constantly sliding between familiar, scholarly, and parodic registers. For example, as we come to the complexities of the portrait and its role we are plunged into an elegantly intertextual discussion of the relationship between art and its viewers.

Vasari's *Lives* is plundered wholesale for the sections that discuss "modern" artists, but even here, for example in the condensed biography of Filippo Lippi that takes its outline from Vasari, but condenses it into a story of desire and captivity worthy of any secret history (266–69), there is an intensification of the anecdotal stream of Vasari's founding narrative, one which highlights the picaresque, the extraordinary, and the sexually vivid—as we might expect from one of the undoubted stars of Darnton's Grub Street. In a sense, it is precisely the mixing of antiquarian history, Vasarian biography, and contemporary scandal sheets in the hopper of pre-Revolutionary hackery that are the special hallmarks of the anecdotal art history that Nougaret and Leprince's work exemplifies.

Nor is the *Anecdotes* without cultural-political resonance. Nougaret and Leprince are clearly convinced of a public role for art as a bellwether of social well-being and have a particular and insistent focus in their anecdotal reconstructions of artists' lives on the details of the tensions between popes, patrons, and artists (for example, in the Michelangelo entry and the Leonardo entry, and especially in the Titian entry in which Titian's trials trying to get paid by the monarchs of Spain are the finale of the piece, juxtaposed with a burlesque anecdote about Titian's late marriage to a fifteen-year-old). A central narrative thread is the artist's struggle with inadequate or uncomprehending monarchs, popes, or patrons. Beyond the obvious implied criticism of current conditions in France, this might be seen as a rejoinder to both the Winckelmann narrative of perfect accord between social norms and artistic standards and to the stories of heroic patronage told through not just Italian but French official histories.

Another "fork" of anecdotal art history emerges in the multiplying memoir literature, especially that of the early nineteenth century, dedicated to artists.[17] This branch, too, has remained vital to art history, though often seen as unreliable or subprime. An example of this anecdotal genre—not a vast fresco but an illumination of one individual artist, recently deceased—can be found in the work of artist, raconteur, biographer, and eccentric James Northcote, specifically his

Memoirs of Sir Joshua Reynolds.[18] Though his tone is often irritating, Northcote's particular skill is to immerse us into the grain of artistic conversation and opinion, reconstructing some remarkable (and only occasionally banal) verbal correspondences and meetings of ideas as a way of both sketching the character of his subject and giving us privileged studio and friendship discourse. Patently derived from the blueprint of Boswell's 1791 *Life of Samuel Johnson,* this was one of the first thoroughgoing "conversational" lives of a single artist in English.[19] Northcote, an artist himself and deeply involved in the British literary scene through his friendships with Hazlitt and others, might be regarded as an early example of the modern artist as anecdotalist monographer, helping to intensify the anecdotal gaze onto a single person and thus spread this increasingly popular and influential mode of art-historical writing. The spice in his account of Reynolds, his teacher and friend for many years, is all in the anecdote; what Northcote achieves is a kind of panorama of conversations in which Reynolds is simultaneously object and participant. Thus the monograph, that staple of art-historical business for two hundred years (whose growth in volume and "seriousness" has been beautifully charted recently by Gabriele Guercio), is at its origins profoundly colored by the anecdotal, insider voice and the unverifiable but illuminating conversation.[20] It is instructive that when Northcote, at the end of his life, tried his hand at more "authoritative," less anecdotal forms of art-historical narrative in his biography of Titian, the effort falls flat.[21]

I have so far argued that powerful eighteenth- and nineteenth-century models of critical, art-historical, and biographical writing are sustained and enriched by anecdote used freely and joyously. One could also claim that the anecdotal reaches a kind of ecstasy in the work of some of the great writers and teachers of the nineteenth century. Take, for example, John Ruskin's *Modern Painters*—not necessarily the first work one thinks of as anecdotal, though parts of it rely for their power on a confessional tone of spiritual autobiography that becomes vital to his argument. In the poetic passage that opens "Of Truth and Colour," in order to make one of his most fundamental points about the lack of fit between representations of nature and the complexities of its color, he moves out of his close encounters with the turgid browns and greens of a Gaspard Dughet in the National Gallery and takes us to an entirely unverifiable, but marvelously beautiful, place:

> Not long ago I was slowly descending this very bit of carriage road, the first turn after you leave Albano . . . it had been wild weather when I left Rome, and all across the Campagna the clouds were sweeping in sulphurous blue, with a clap of thunder or two, and breaking gleams of sun along the Claudian aqueduct lighting up the infinity of its arches like the bridge of chaos. But as I climbed the long slope of the Alban mount, Albano, and graceful darkness of its ilex grove, rose against pure streaks of alternate blue and amber. The Upper sky gradually flushing through the last fragments of rain-cloud in deep palpitating azure, half ether and half dew. The Noonday sun came slanting down the rocky slopes of la Riccia, and their masses of entangled and tall foliage whose autumnal tints were mixed with the wet verdure of a thousand ever-greens, were penetrated with it as with rain. I cannot call it colour–it was conflagration. Purple, and crimson, and scarlet, like the curtains of God's tabernacle, the rejoicing trees sank into the valley in showers of light, each separate leaf quivering with buoyant and burning life.[22]

Poised somewhere between the prose-poem and the anecdote, this is Ruskin's vehicle for proving the "truth" of color and setting up his critique of the rendering of landscape in shades of brown. We cannot know or verify his presence on that "very carriage road," but Ruskin wants us to believe that this autobiographical tale is absolutely true and that his own lived experience and perception is the basis for an entire philosophical argument about color. Here the contrast between the lifelessness of a painting and the rich material and spiritual experience related in the anecdote is part of the art-historical argument.

There are those who will argue, of course, that Ruskin is a dead end, and that the central waves of art-historical discourse that have formed the discipline as we know it now—be they positivism, formalism, iconography, or the powerful and central narrative of liberation from the anecdote that defines modernism—might be seen to be determinedly anti-anecdotal. There is some truth to this claim, but even here we do not have to look too far even into these traditions to see how irrepressible is the anecdotal impulse in art history. Wölfflin's *Principles of Art History* opens with an anecdote;[23] so too, one might argue, does Panofsky's *Studies in Iconology*.[24] As for modernist formalists, even Roger Fry, in one of his most illuminating formalist forays into Seurat, cannot resist giving us a little pseudo-anecdotal miniature to distinguish Seurat's work from that of Toulouse-Lautrec.[25] Anecdote prevails in the histories of schools and groupings that constituted the avant-garde, especially as artists began to construct their own histories, and as these histories have increasingly entered the mainstream of art-historical discourse. Around Picasso, and many other artists, has grown the same forest of "telling anecdotes," told and retold. One example among many is particularly telling:

> In occupied Paris, a Gestapo officer who had barged his way into Picasso's apartment pointed at a photo of the mural *Guernica*, asking: "Did you do that?" "No," Picasso replied, "you did," his wit fizzing with the anger that animates the piece.[26]

As Lindsay Kaplan has recently discussed, there is no factual basis or documentation to this anecdote, but it has gained the status of exemplary truth of heroic modernist artistic resistance to brutal authoritarian ideology, and it has the pithy balance and symmetrical beauty of the vintage anecdote.[27] Somehow it resists all our attempts at debunking, all our caution, positivism, and need to check our facts—it has that quality of exemplary and courageous speech in an antique tradition combined with the telling wit that gave Vasari, and later Northcote, such readability.

Thus, when conceptual artists began, like historians, to mine the riches of the anecdotal archives in a deliberate attempt to break the stranglehold of a modernist narrative, their gestures toward anecdotalism were not so much radically new as a rediscovery of the richness of the anecdotal vein in art history. Ian Burn, the great Australian conceptual artist, wrote in his provocative and anti-academic essay, "Is Art History any Use to Artists?" (whose conclusion, incidentally, was that "Art History has always been far too important to be simply left up to art historians") the following lines admiring of the anecdotal style of artist-writers of a previous generation:

> Publicly, these rationales frequently took on the form of anecdotal history, with stories shrewdly selected and edited to make the most telling points. Notice how anecdotes function in William Moore's *The Story of Australian Art* (1934) and in lectures by any of the older generations of artists today, as well as many of the younger. Neither the authenticity of the anecdote nor empirical veracity is an issue, for a story without any factual basis may serve to reveal greater "cultural

> truths" than any other account. An anecdote creates its own necessity, truth notwithstanding. . . . The anecdotal persists as one of the most effective forms of communicating a sense of history among artists. Its power derives from the fact that it personalises, conveys an intimacy, and as a rationale, is reinforced by the dominant art teaching practices of learning from examples and role models.[28]

Not to be outdone, conceptual artists in the United States also claimed to be combating the twin evils of academicism and modernism by means of an anecdotal understanding of their history and the history of their moment.

> We had always put those unfairly debased and mongrelized discourses of anecdote and gossip to good use. In the context of our practice, they remained powerful agents for debunking the myth of Modernism as we saw it.[29]

Burn and the Art and Language group, reacting against an "academic" art history, were in fact redeploying resources that had been the staple of art history throughout its long past, a span in which the anti-anecdotal tendency of twentieth-century "professional" discourses may yet come to be seen as a temporary and untenable blip. We must remember that it is the *norm* in our discipline (taken over its *longue durée*) that artists have written art history; not just the Vasaris and the Northcotes, think too of the rich diversity and sheer quirkiness of the foundational texts of art theory and interpretation that emerged from groups of artists teaching and thinking in early art schools, which we now ossify under the name of "academic discourse." As artists increasingly write and rewrite art histories on the Ian Burn model, and as narratives of the history of art proliferate across media and spaces far beyond the control of academia, the anecdote as form is enjoying a new golden moment.

What motivates the profound tendency to the anecdotal in art-historical discourse? As Joel Fineman eloquently put it, the anecdote is:

> The literary form that uniquely lets history happen by virtue of the way it introduces an opening into the teleological, and therefore timeless, narration of beginning, middle, and end. The anecdote produces

> the effect of the real, the occurrence of contingency, by establishing an event as an event within and yet without the framing context of historical successivity.[30]

It may well be because artworks are "within and yet without" framing historical sequence, enjoying their double life as objects both of and out of their moment, that anecdotes seem to proffer ways of establishing the most compelling or plausible accounts of their origin and their resonance. Or, more simply, anecdotes allow us to deal in complex, entertaining, and meaningful ways with the vast contingencies of art making. More starkly, without wishing to end on too melodramatic note, anecdotes are fleeting, precise, desiring, enlivening stories of kith and kin, love and death, struggle and resistance. They might be what inert, "orphan" pictures (in Michael Ann Holly's provocative formulation) want . . . or, more precisely, what we need to create and re-create the family genealogies of these orphan objects in something more than deadening documentary detail.[31] At the very least they offer us the tantalizing fantasy of a privileged and brilliant insight into the consciousness of artistic creation, a fantasy close to the heart of that secret history that our discipline perpetually longs to tell.

1. Paul Fleming, "The Perfect Story: Anecdote and Exemplarity in Linnaeus and Blumenberg," *Thesis Eleven* 104, no. 1 (February 1, 2011): 74.

2. For a methodological reflection on anecdote and New Historicism, see especially Catherine Gallagher and Stephen Greenblatt, *Practicing New Historicism* (Chicago: University of Chicago Press, 2000), 20–74.

3. Pliny the Elder, *The Natural History*, trans. John Bostock (London: Taylor and Francis, 1855), chap. 36, http://www.perseus.tufts.edu.

4. Procopius and Richard Atwater, *Secret History* (Ann Arbor: University of Michigan Press, 1961).

5. For an exploration of humanist meanings of anecdote in historical discourse, see Donald R. Kelley and David Harris Sacks, *The Historical Imagination in Early Modern Britain: History, Rhetoric, and Fiction, 1500–1800* (Cambridge, UK: Cambridge University Press, 1997). See especially Annabel Patterson's concise chronicling of the fortunes of the anecdotal genre in sixteenth- and seventeenth-century Europe in "Foul, his wife, the mayor, and foul's mare: The power of anecdote in Tudor historiography," 179–210.

6. An excellent lexical history of the term *anecdote* is given in *Oxford English Dictionary Online*, s.v. "anecdote, *n*," accessed July 27, 2012, http://www.oed.com/view/Entry/7367?result=1&rskey=Yp3WEh&.

7. Giorgio Vasari, *The Lives of the Artists*, trans. Julia Conaway Bondanella and Peter Bondanella (Oxford: Oxford University Press, 1998), 191–200; on Vasari's rhetoric the surest guide is Paul Barolsky, *Why Mona Lisa Smiles and Other Tales by Vasari* (University Park: Pennsylvania State University Press, 1991). See also Paul Barolsky, *Giotto's Father and the Family of Vasari's Lives* (University Park: Pennsylvania State University Press, 1992).

8. See especially Gabriele Guercio, *Art as Existence: The Artist's Monograph and Its Project* (Cambridge, Mass.: MIT Press, 2009), chaps. 1 and 2.

9. Alex Potts, *Flesh and the Ideal: Winckelmann and the Origins of Art History* (New Haven, Conn.: Yale University Press, 2000); Elisabeth Décultot, *Johann Joachim Winckelmann, Enquête sur la genèse de l'histoire de l'art* (Paris: Presses Universitaires de France, 2000).

10. On Diderot's art criticism, see especially Else Marie Bukdahl, *Diderot, critique d'art* (Copenhagen: Rosenkilde et Bagger, 1980); Musée de la monnaie (France), *Diderot & L'art De Boucher À David: Les Salons, 1759–1781: [exposition] Hôtel De La Monnaie, 5 Octobre 1984–6 Janvier 1985* (Paris: Ministère de la Culture, Editions de la Réunion des Musées nationaux, 1984); Régis Michel and Richard Wrigley, "Diderot and Modernity," *Oxford Art Journal* 8, no. 2 (January 1, 1985): 36–51; Denis Diderot and John Goodman, *Diderot on Art* (New Haven, Conn.: Yale University Press, 1995); Else Marie Bukdahl, Denis Diderot, and Annette Lorenceau, *Salon de 1765* (Paris: Hermann, 1984); Denis Diderot et al., *Salons: salons de 1767 III, Ruines et paysages* (Paris: Hermann, 2008).

11. Diderot et al., *Salons*, "M. de Buffon et M. le président de Brosses ne sont plus jeunes ; mais ils l'ont été. Quand ils étaient jeunes, ils se mettaient à table de bonne heure, et ils y restaient longtemps. Ils aimaient le bon vin, et ils en buvaient beaucoup. Ils aimaient les femmes; et quand ils étaient ivres, ils allaient voir des filles. Un soir donc qu'ils étaient chez des filles, et dans le déshabillé d'un lieu de plaisir, le petit président, qui n'est guère plus grand qu'un Lilliputien, dévoila à leurs yeux un mérite si étonnant, si prodigieux, si inattendu, que toutes en jetèrent un cri d'admiration. Mais quand on a beaucoup admiré, on réfléchit. Une d'entre elles, après avoir fait en silence plusieurs fois le tour du merveilleux petit président, lui dit : «Monsieur, voilà qui est beau, il en faut convenir; mais où est le cul qui poussera cela?» Mon ami, si l'on vous présente un canevas de comédie ou de tragédie, faites quelques tours autour de l'homme; et dites-lui, comme la fille de joie au Président de Brosses: Cela est beau, sans contredit; mais où est le cul? Si c'est un projet de finance, demandez toujours où est le cul? A une ébauche de roman, de harangue, où est le cul? A une esquisse de tableau, où est le cul? L'esquisse ne nous attache peut-être si fort, que parce qu'étant indéterminée, elle laisse plus de liberté à notre imagination, qui y voit tout ce qu'il lui plaît."

12. Hans Blumenberg and Robert Savage, *Paradigms for a Metaphorology* (Ithaca, N.Y.: Cornell University Press, 2010).

13. Pierre Jean-Baptiste Nougaret and Nicolas Thomas Leprince, *Anecdotes des beaux-arts: contenant tout ce que la peinture, la sculpture, la gravure, l'architecture, la littérature, la musique, & c. & la vie des artistes, offrent de plus curieux & de plus piquant, chez tous les peuples du mode, depuis l'origine de ces différens arts, jusqu'à nos jours* . . . (Paris: Chez J.-F. Bastien, 1776).

14. Pierre Jean-Baptiste Nougaret, *Anecdotes du règne de Louis XVI* (5 vols.; Paris: s.n., 1776–91). The first volumes began to appear in 1776, not long into the reign of the young Louis XVI, but the definitive edition in six volumes was only complete in 1791.

15. Nicolas Thomas Leprince, *Essai historique sur la bibliothèque du roi . . . (par Le Prince)* (Paris: Belin, 1782).

16. Robert Darnton, *The Literary Underground of the Old Regime* (Cambridge, Mass.: Harvard University Press, 1982); Darnton, *The Forbidden Best-Sellers of Pre-Revolutionary France* (New York: W. W. Norton, 1995).

17. Guercio, *Art as Existence.*

18. James Northcote, *Memoirs of Sir Joshua Reynolds . . . Comprising original anecdotes, of many distinguished persons, his contemporaries: and a brief analysis of his discourses. To which are added, Varieties on art* (Philadelphia: M. Carey and Son, 1817).

19. James Boswell, *The life of Samuel Johnson, LLD : comprehending an account of his studies and numerous works, in chronological order . . . the whole exhibiting a view of literature and literary men in Great-Britain, for near half a century, during which he flourished* (Dublin: 1792).

20. Guercio, *Art as Existence*, especially 112–47.

21. James Northcote, *The Life of Titian: with anecdotes of the distinguished persons of his time* (London: H. Colburn and R. Bentley, 1830).

22. John Ruskin, *Modern Painters*, ed. David Barrie (1843–60; New York: Knopf, 1987), 69–70.

23. Heinrich Wölfflin, *Principles of Art History: The Problem of the Development of Style in Later Art* (Dover, U.K.: Courier Dover Publications, 1932).

24. Erwin Panofsky, *Studies in Iconology: Humanistic Themes in the Art of the Renaissance* (Boulder, Colo.: Westview Press, 1972).

25. Roger Fry, "Seurat's La Parade," *Burlington Magazine* 55, no. 321 (December 1, 1929): 290.

26. "In praise of . . . Guernica," *Guardian*, http://www.guardian.co.uk/commentisfree/2009/mar/26/pablo-picasso-guernica-spain-war (accessed August 28, 2012).

27. See Lindsay Kaplan, "The Political Artist: Picasso's Wartime Production and Wartime's Production of Picasso," in Leslie Anne Boldt-Irons, Corrado Federici, and Ernesto Virgulti, *Rewriting Texts, Remaking Images: Interdisciplinary Perspectives* (New York: Peter Lang, 2010), 51–62.

28. Ian Burn, "Is Art History any Use to Artists?," in *Dialogue: Writings in Art History* (Sydney: Allen and Unwin, 1991), 3. The conclusion is to be found on page 14.

29. See Michael Corrin, "Inside a New York Art Gang: Selected Documents of Art and Language, New York," in Alexander Alberro and Blake Stimson, *Conceptual Art: A Critical Anthology* (Cambridge, Mass.: MIT Press, 2000), 470–71.

30. See Joel Fineman, "The History of the Anecdote," in Harold Aram Veeser, *The New Historicism* (New York: Routledge, 1989), 49–76.

31. Michael Ann Holly, "The Melancholy Art," *Art Bulletin* 89, no. 1 (March 1, 2007): 7–17; Holly, "The Author Replies," ibid., 40–44.

The Text is Present

Marianna Torgovnick

A landmark display of performance art; a triumph of marketing; an extended parable, or, perhaps better, a cautionary tale about the interpenetration of art history, fiction, and celebrity: ultimately, the 2010 *Marina Abramović* retrospective at the Museum of Modern Art was all three. While deploying multiple fictions by and about the artist, it ended up suggesting the potent difference between the ways artists and art historians use storytelling. In literary studies, debates between poststructuralism and traditional fact-based knowledge flamed up in the twentieth century and burned out by the twenty-first, leaving behind new ways of thinking about "facts" that have turned it into a concept subject to quotation marks.[1] Literature's experience suggests that art history will find many resources in fiction, but that at its core the discipline will need to let fiction go.

Marketing is Present

Before the *Marina Abramović* retrospective, few potential visitors to the Museum of Modern Art knew who she was, and even fewer had a thorough (or even good) knowledge of her work. There was at least one pragmatic reason: Abramović is a performance artist. Performance art has traditionally depended on a specific place and time that can be counted in minutes or hours, rather than in days or months. Usually available to only a limited number of viewers, performance art often takes place outside of galleries and museums, sometimes challenging the naturalness or inevitability of those spaces for art. It can defy the marketplace and eschew the kind of permanence we imagine art to embody and seek.

Normally, museum exhibitions offer only a facsimile of a performance, which can seem like a poor substitute. Retrospectives of Ana Mendieta's work in 2004 at the Whitney Museum of American Art and in 2010 at Galerie Lelong in New York suffered from such limitations.[2] Mendieta, a contemporary of Abramović and similarly invested in deploying the body in site-specific performances, situated her work in natural or (more rarely) urban landscapes, while Abramović based her art firmly in the exhibition space. Any museum or gallery retrospective of Mendieta's work faces graver challenges than those experienced with an Abramović presentation. Perhaps this is because it is impossible to re-create the original, natural environment of the work. Or perhaps this is because Mendieta (who died unexpectedly in 1985) had not planned on preserving her work. For the Mendieta exhibitions, the institutions were only able to display photographs and videos—images that, by today's technological standards, seem both partial and of poor quality—without reproducing any of the works.[3] The visual record was suggestive of Mendieta's work, but only partial and distant; it lacked the visceral power of the original work.[4]

Presenting a retrospective of the work of a performance artist at a major museum raises a number of concerns. Abramović and MoMA solved the problem of how the artist could be "present" simultaneously in multiple works by making her present only in one, the title piece, *The Artist is Present*, on display in the museum's atrium. In the exhibition galleries, Abramović appeared in many photographs and videos, but the live roles once played by the artist herself were reenacted by a number of younger artists hired and trained by Abramović for the occasion. This was an ingenious solution for displaying multiple performances that, to my knowledge, been not been done previously on this scale.

A video featured on the MoMA website and readily available on YouTube provided reviewers and audiences background on the planning and staging of the exhibition. It shows young artists, many of them quite beautiful, arriving by bus to Abramović's upstate New York house, where they undergo training in preparation for the exhibition. To create the monastic effect she wanted, Abramović collected their cell phones, telling them, "You'll be free for three days. Amazing." She monitored their food, policed their bedtimes. She put them through a series of exercises designed to toughen the body and prepare them to be viewed in the nude, for long periods of time, by the general public. She trained them in timing, grace, and stamina. What they needed most of all, she said, was to learn how to radiate "charisma" as a protective aura. "Probably they'll hate me anyway, at least at first," Abramović suggests to the camera, having previously said the same thing to the artists, one of whom re-creates her words within the short video. That the younger artists will hate Abramović is only a fiction. Every gesture, every bit of body language, and the young artists' words themselves suggest not "hatred" but veneration. This use of video to reproduce or market her art is similar to Abramović's own appropriation of new technologies throughout her career, while also contributing to the branding of Marina Abramović as coextensive, to some extent, with performance art.[5]

Perhaps inevitably, the retrospective did create a space for Abramović among the world's best-known contemporary artists. Some seemed dubious, asking: Does her work deserve so much attention and does that attention occlude the work of others? Does her exploitation of the body and flashy gambits (like exchanging places with an Amsterdam prostitute during a gallery opening) serve art, debase it, or assert art's debased quality? What about her extreme exposure of the female body as a site both of power and of vulnerability? Has she really paid her dues in terms of aesthetics, originality, or influence? Fascinating as such questions are, I will necessarily put them aside except to note that the retrospective generated discussion about such matters among professionals and the general public. I suspect that the very question of whether the Abramović exhibition "deserved" the attention it got masks other questions about the status of celebrity in contemporary art more generally, and who deserves it.

Other well-known performance artists, such as Ana Mendieta, whose tragic death was shadowed by accusations of murder, flamed out early. A suicide, a homicide, premature death from accidental causes: these seal celebrity and confer a retrospective aura on an artist's life, making the art most legible through the death, as with James Dean, Jackson Pollack, and Robert Mapplethorpe. Yoko Ono remains extremely well know, but her fame has relied partly on her relationship with John Lennon since they became a couple in the sixties. Cindy Sherman, Nan Goldin, Jenny Holzer, Gerhard Richter, and Damien Hirst are household names in contemporary art, but their faces, let alone their naked bodies, elude us. Abramović, however, has made her art out of her face and body for roughly forty years. She has pursued a consistent and characteristic set of themes. So why does her being crowned by MoMA as a major performance artist seem problematic?

MoMA has always been in the business of sealing reputations, a position it retained even at the end of the twentieth century when the museum did its notable rehangings of the collection just prior to its expansion. From the start, it established Picasso and Matisse as twin pillars of modern painting. Indeed, MoMA has continued to feature Picasso and Matisse in the twenty-first century.[6] Andy Warhol ginned up a publicity machine essential for his reputation that serves him still, decades after his death. Damien Hirst commands great name recognition and large prices for pieces one might have thought unsellable. Georgia O'Keeffe and Cindy Sherman assiduously cultivated their art and their images (in Sherman's case, an image based on deliberate disguise) as brands. This branding might be extended back through antiquity, with the need for patronage having required older forms of marketing too: the elegant manner, attendance at court.

I feel a little tempted—just a little, and then I'll drop it—to suspect that Abramović may seem like an interloper to some for reasons beyond the judgment that her work is edgy and distasteful and even, in some instances, derivative. Abramović is a fashionable woman in her mid-sixties. At least until recently, women were expected to become invisible by that age. She does not have the patina of a Georgia O'Keeffe or a Louise Bourgeois to see her through; performance art not being painting or sculpture, Abramović may never attain the kind of stature they enjoy. Ultimately, though, the salient fact for our purposes here is that, if Abramović was not especially well known before March 2010, many people knew her by the time the MoMA retrospective ended, on May 31, 2010. And many of those who attended the retrospective found her work both moving and unforgettable. The show successfully broke a boundary between performance art and museum exhibition in fascinating and provocative ways. It also tested—or better yet, exposed as always fragile—the boundary between fiction and art history, in part because Abramović's stock-in-trade is generating fictions based on her life, her images of women, and her ideas about women in art.

Narrative is Present

Art history does many things behind the scenes, some of them the subject of papers at the Clark's "Fictions of Art History" conference. Art historians research and catalogue; they identify artists on unsigned or misattributed work; they puzzle out dates; they establish relationships, movements, canonicity, and value; they conserve; they curate; they teach. Perhaps most of all, they reconstruct stories about the past, painstakingly, with the art historian likened several times during the conference, and with aptness, to the detective. Photography proved a special test case, as several talks suggested, because of its ability to present what seems to be the epitome of the real quite deceptively—the set of *Rome*, the television show, rather than Rome itself; a sailor kissing a woman on V-J Day that exudes the nation's joy, but also a covert violence.[7] Art historians do many things, much of it invisible to the general public. But as a discipline, art history reaches the public most often through textbooks, lectures, and exhibitions, with their accompanying taped tours, museum notes, and catalogues. All these public forms of art history require narrative and story, even if only the bare-bones narrative of names, dates, and placement within an exhibition space. The public receives art, then, embedded in concise and highly edited versions of reality usually chosen by curators, but, in the case of the Abramović exhibition, quite pointedly chosen by the artist herself.

Shall we call these versions of reality, these stories, "fictions"? We should consider, but not overstate the case. Narrative and story form the backbone of

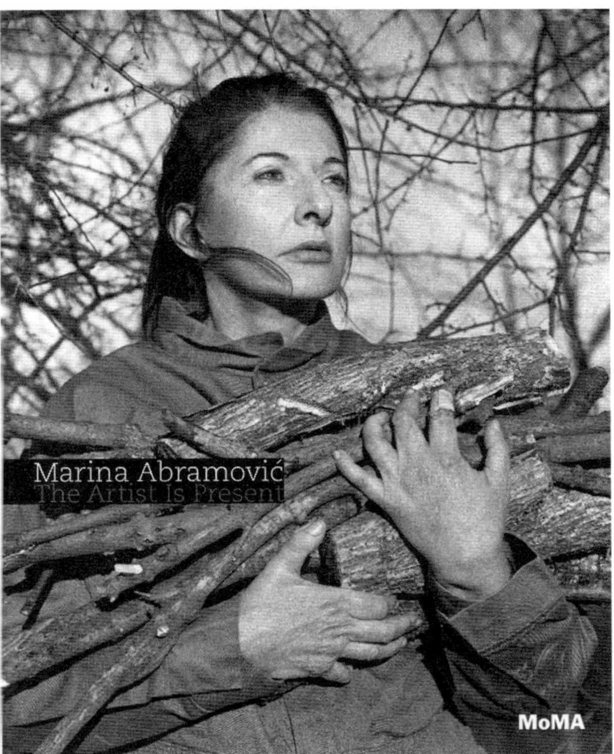

Fig. 1. Front cover of *Marina Abramović: The Artist is Present* (New York: Museum of Modern Art, 2010); featuring Marina Abramović (Serbian, b. 1946), *Portrait with Firewood*, 2009. Black-and-white digital print. © 2012 Marina Abramović. Courtesy Marina Abramović Archives and Sean Kelly Gallery/Artists Rights Society (ARS), New York

nonfiction as well as fiction. It's impossible to relate a series of facts without creating some kind of plot, even if the plot is randomness. Yet we know that not all narratives are fictions. In fact—and this is too often overlooked—narratives range along a *continuum* (a key term and image) all the way from the historical to the utterly concocted. The Abramović retrospective represented a number of points along that continuum, helping us to establish a limit for art history.

As with many highly publicized exhibitions, the narratives generated by *The Artist is Present* began even before viewers entered the gallery. On the front cover of the catalogue to the exhibition, the artist is seen holding sticks, gazing off into the future; online at MoMA, she appears peering at us over flowers (figs. 1 and 2). We can supply the narrative: Abramović as Earth Mother and wise crone. Abramović is, or at least poses as, a lover of nature, associated with the traditional linkage between women and nature. She is a woman who (to riff on an old popular sensation) runs with the wolves. But, as review after review stressed, she is an older woman who, while still attractive and sensual, seems exceptional in being so: if she still runs with the wolves, she no longer menstruates.

Accordingly, the back cover of the catalogue (fig. 3) shows the younger Abramović at one of her landmark performances, *Rhythm 0* (1974), when she offered her exposed body to viewers to decorate, mark, penetrate with an array of items ranging from yarn and Band-Aids to razor blades and knives.[8] Abramović looks beautiful and brave, but also, just a little, wary. A male viewer, his back to us,

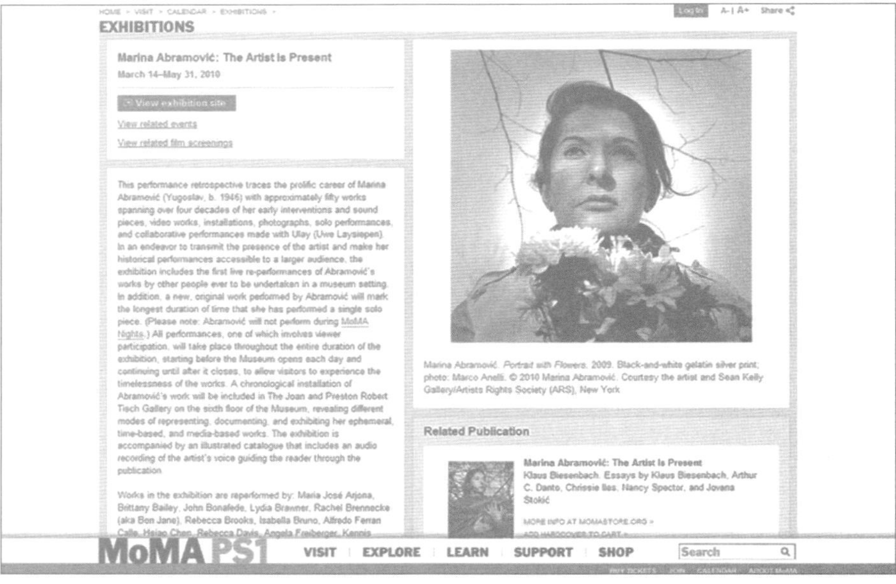

Fig. 2. Screenshot from MoMA.org featuring the publication *Marina Abramović: The Artist is Present* (New York: Museum of Modern Art, 2010); and Marina Abramović, *Portrait with Flowers*, 2009. Black-and-white gelatin silver print. © 2012 Marina Abramović. Courtesy of the Museum of Modern Art, Marina Abramović Archives and Sean Kelly Gallery / Artists Rights Society (ARS), New York

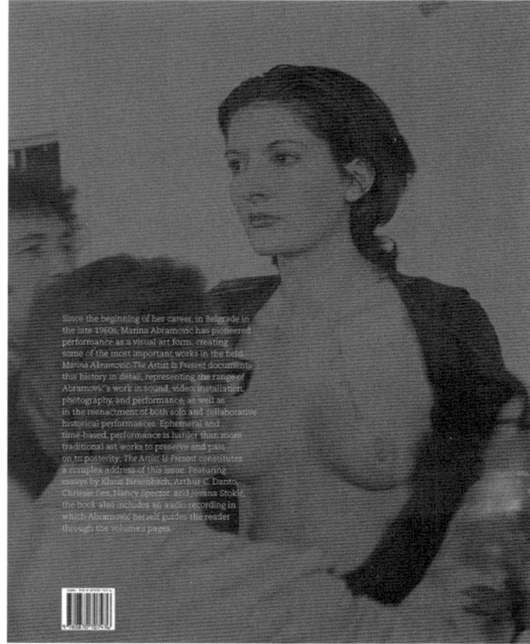

Fig. 3. Back cover of *Marina Abramović: The Artist is Present* (New York: Museum of Modern Art, 2010); featuring Marina Abramović, *Rhythm 0*, 1974. Performance, Studio Morra, Naples, 6 hours. © 2012 Marina Abramović. Courtesy Marina Abramović Archives and Sean Kelly Gallery / Artists Rights Society (ARS), New York

levels his eyes at her breasts. Pulling no punches and making the crone / temptress dichotomy complete, MoMA bathes the black-and-white image in a wash of whorish red.

Virgin and whore; wise crone and temptress: to some extent, the entire exhibition fluctuated, as does Abramović's self presentation, between these archetypal images. Even before the exhibition opened, Abramović and MoMA made us inhabit myth and archetype: elevated fictions so persistent that they approach the level of universal truths, but remain—as so much feminist work since the 1970s has shown us—little more than fictions.

The first reviews tweaked the story or stories that hover between these two archetypes. They consistently placed bodies at the forefront of attention: the artist's body, the bodies of viewers, and the unusually high degree of contact between them. One of the first things potential viewers learned about this show was the presence of a work called *Imponderabilia* (fig. 4). In this work, two artists stand in a doorway, through which viewers must pass in order to see the rest of the exhibit. In the original space, the doorway was narrow and the artists were Abramović and Ulay, her lover. Two naked bodies, one male and one female, framed vertically, might have suggested, to an art-historical eye, Albrecht Dürer's *Adam and Eve* (1504), although the work made a more visceral grab at the viewer's attention. In the original, visitors to the installation had to pass between Abramović and Ulay—there was no other way in—and, given the narrowness of the remaining doorway, had to make a choice of whom to face. Most chose to face their bodies toward the performer opposite them in sex while averting

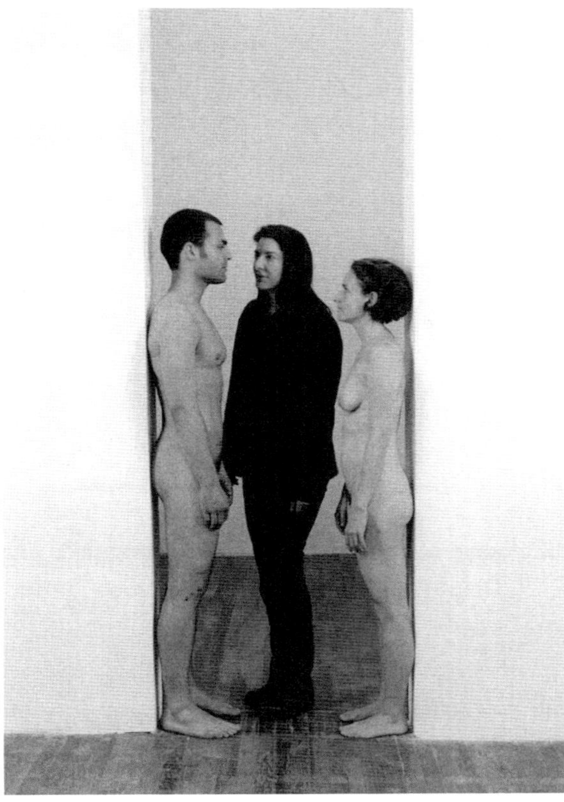

Fig. 4. Marina Abramović, concept photograph for reperformance of *Imponderabilia* (1977), 2010. Reperformers Igor Josifov and Abigail Levine. © 2012 Marina Abramović. Courtesy Marina Abramović Archives and Sean Kelly Gallery / Artists Rights Society (ARS), New York

their eyes, sometimes all the way around to the other performer; in some cases, viewers freely touched the performers.

Imponderabilia was highlighted in reviews, but nonetheless "gutted" at MoMA. The museum provided a second entrance to the room, allowing viewers to bypass the naked bodies. For those who chose to venture between the artists (sometimes two women and sometimes a man and a woman, although not, to my knowledge, ever two men), the doorway was wider. Indeed, a man who ventured to touch one of the artists was ejected by security. *Imponderabilia* suggested many narrations that might accompany the photographs. Had Abramović recorded and charted audience reactions, I imagine it would have been easy for the installation to serve as part psychology experiment as well as all provocation.

Like *Imponderabilia*, the installation *Luminosity* suggests a famous image or series of images in art history: in this case, crucifixion paintings and, perhaps most specifically, Salvador Dalí's *Crucifixion (Corpus Hypercubus)* (1954). A woman "hangs" on a wall, naked, her arms outstretched, her legs dangling, her vulva perched precariously on what looks like a bicycle seat. At first the image appears to be a painting or a photograph, until the woman's arms begin to move.

In this room, the artist and MoMA have arranged a narrative that morphs into a fiction for any viewer attentive to storytelling. At intervals a second woman walks wordlessly to the wall and positions a ladder within the first woman's reach. (I observed only women in this installation on repeated visits, though a male might have performed it too; the change would, I believe, alter its effect.) The woman mounted on the wall descends and dons a laboratory coat held open for her by the new arrival, who then sheds her lab coat and ascends onto the wall. The story might be a deposition narrative; Christ removed from the cross and swaddled by waiting women: a pietà, like Abramović's earlier *Anima Mundi* (1983). It might be something kinkier. In the context of the retrospective, the fiction seems more scientific than religious, prompting such questions as: How long can a woman hold this pose? What amount of blood pressure builds in the vulva? How does that compare to other physiological functions as measured by sexologists such as Masters and Johnson? We think "scientifically" in part because the costuming in this installation echoes with a more overtly narrative piece we will have already seen in the galleries called *Balkan Baroque*, which also features a doctor's coat.

Balkan Baroque is a multi-screen installation. On the left-hand screen, which is elevated, is a large image of Abramović garbed as a warrior and holding a flag while mounted on a horse. This image, like several in the exhibition,

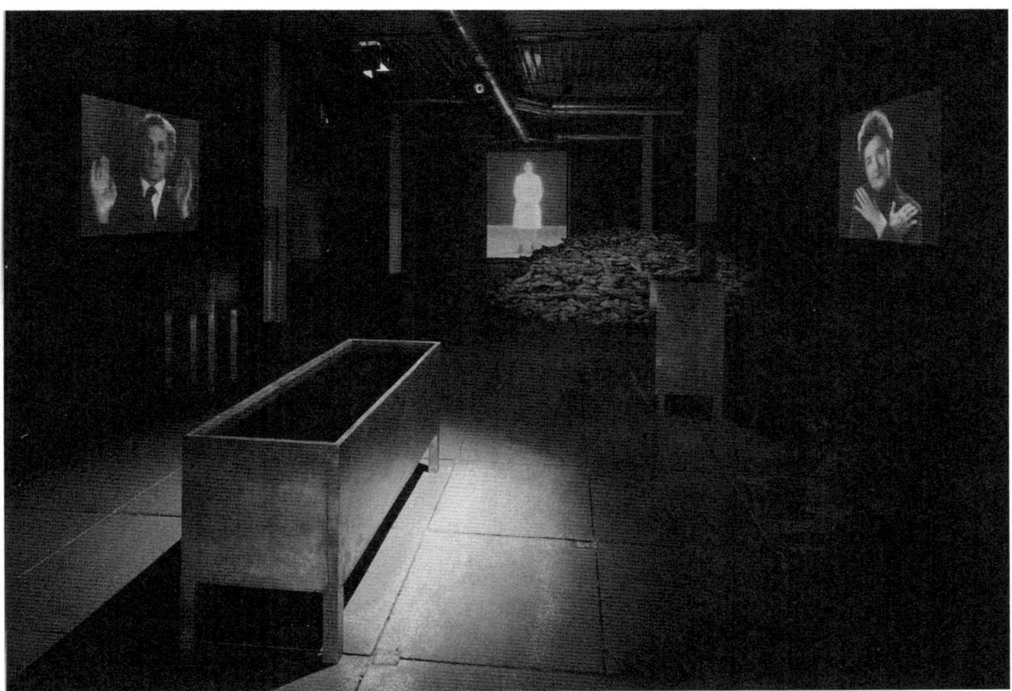

Fig. 5. Marina Abramović, *Balkan Baroque*, 1997. Performance, 4 days, 6 hours. Cow bones, copper containers, water tinted black with ink, bucket, soap, metal brush, dress stained with blood, and three-channel video installation, 4:13 minutes. Venice Biennale XLVII. © 2012 Marina Abramović. Courtesy Marina Abramović Archives and Sean Kelly Gallery/Artists Rights Society (ARS), New York

alludes to Abramović's parents: two hard-fighting and hard-drinking partisans for Yugoslavia. On another screen, Abramović assiduously scrubs the blood from a large pile of cow bones. On the central, largest screen, which confronts the viewer directly, Abramović performs a monologue that turns into a striptease. This video, on continuous loop, features Abramović in a white lab coat, wearing glasses, addressing the audience in heavily accented English (fig. 5):

> I like to tell you story about how we, in Balkans, kill the rats. We take thirty to forty rats from the same family and put them in the cage and give them only water to drink. After a while, their teeth start growing, they get hungry, and they're facing their own suffocation. Naturally they will not kill the members of their own tribe. But, in fear of dying, they kill the weakest one of them. And then another weak one. And then another weak one. Until only the most superior rat is left in the cage.

> Now the rat catcher is continuously giving water to this rat. His teeth start growing. And timing is very important. When the rat catcher sees that there's only half an hour left that he's going to suffocate it, he open cage, takes knife, and pulls both eyes out of his head and let him free. Now the rat is nervous, outraged, panicking. He run into rat holes of his own family and kills every single rat in his way till the strongest and most superior rat to him kills him. This is the way that we in Balkans make Wolf Rat.[9]

Her speech delivered, Abramović removes her white coat to reveal a slinky black dress, from which she pulls a vibrant red scarf. She dances back and forth to what sounds like a Yugoslavian folk song as she waves the scarf above her head, sometimes positioning it prominently across her face.

Clearly this is neither a random nor a neutral set of juxtapositions. What does this series of images mean? How can its meaning become available to the viewer? Two methods for reading fiction must be used. First, viewers must identify patterns among disparate parts: in this case, verbal as well as visual patterns. Second, we must speculate about the relationship between the "How We Make the Wolf Rat in the Balkans" video and the two other videos.

In the central screen, after Abramović's first few utterances, the viewer begins to understand that, despite the artist's medical garb, something more than a scientific experiment about breeding rats is at stake. We begin to read the work ironically. Interestingly, for art-historical purposes, the images vary little while Abramović speaks: only words signal the shift to irony. Verbal patterning occurs in which "weak ones" and especially "weakest ones" become prey for the stronger, and mass prey for the strongest. It's fratricidal; it's murderous. It's all veiled within the language of scientific research and eugenics, as genocide so frequently is in recent history.[10] If the speaker is supposed to be a doctor, she resembles not so much the average doctor, doing no harm, as the Nazi Mengele.

The other screens interact with the more dynamic central image. On horseback, Abramović pays tribute to, but also criticizes, the Yugoslavian state and her parents, who backed it. Scrubbing bones, she laments genocide and, like Lady Macbeth wringing her hands, endlessly tries to wash off the blood. On the center screen, when she strips off her doctor's garb and dances in red and black, she is the temptress of the catalogue's back cover, but also a maenad who celebrates in red and black the frenzy of death.

Ultimately, *Balkan Baroque* provides a commentary on the ethnic cleansing that marked the breakup of the former Yugoslavia, a history Abramović deplores, but for which she does not absolve herself of responsibility. "How We Make the Wolf Rat in the Balkans" can be read as a political parable, a variation on animal fables in which "rats" are political leaders and their followers in the newly divided Balkans. For the viewer to analyze the images in the gallery and understand their meaning actually took less time than was spent breaking them into their verbal components here: the mind assimilates quickly, so accustomed is it to looking for meanings and tracing plots.

Abramović has created other, even more dramatic instances of words and fictions as central to her performance art. In one, presented as twelve panels, she has written out scripts used in performances. Two themes emerge from the psychodrama of the artist's life: the artist being slapped by her mother; the artist walking out and slamming doors. The image of the slap also fuels one of Abramović's better-known works with Ulay, *Light/Dark* (1977), in which the two artists stare into each other's eyes, slapping each other's faces in turn, until one stops. Words, narratives, and the inception of fictions form key elements in much of Abramović's performance art. The core element in the most fully narrative works is the artist's autobiography, "her own private mythology based on family members,"[11] shaped, heightened, and patterned to the point where it becomes impossible to tell, just by looking, what is fact and what is fiction. Here is where we arrive at a crucial point for art history's relationship to the art of fiction.

An artist, especially a performance artist, has unqualified use of narrative, and is free to construct all kinds of fictions. But would it be acceptable for an art historian to take Abramović's autobiographical references as unqualified truth and to write in an article that the formative incident in the artist's life was (as one of the dramatic panels to which I refer above claims) when she gave her baby brother a bath and was slapped by her mother?[12] Such a claim would be based on performance art, which can include outright fictions or fictional embroidery on fact.[13] Within art history, such a claim would remain unsubstantiated unless and until the art historian finds confirmation in letters or diaries or interviews either with the artist or with others. Without outside proof, all the art historian could say with perfect confidence is that Abramović has used and reused the slap and that pattern can be traced in her work to interactions with her mother. In short—and we will return to this point later—the art historian can use the resources of narrative to tell a story, but needs to stop at narrative and not go all the way to invented fiction. The art historian could not adopt what Abramović says about her life in her art without attributing it to Abramović or vetting it with outside sources.

The Artist is Present

The retrospective's title piece was unusually well publicized during the exhibition. Abramović herself sat at the end of a table every hour that the exhibit was open, opposite a chair made available to visitors. Stories about bodily functions proliferated: Was she exercising inhuman control? Was there some kind of a bedpan concealed under her voluminous garb? Whatever the details of the performance, long lines of people, some of whom arrived as early as 6 A.M., waited for a chance to sit opposite the artist. The event became a New York phenomenon. Participants, some of them in tears afterward, described the experience as amazing and cathartic. We can assume that some fictionalized versions of what it means to be Marina Abramović and what it means to sit opposite Marina Abramović circulated freely. Most would have been shaped by the installations, but also, perhaps primarily, by one other piece on the same floor, *Nude with Skeleton* (fig. 6), performed live (I saw it performed by two men) and shown as a video performed by Abramović herself.[14]

Nude with Skeleton features Abramović (or a naked surrogate) lying beneath a fully articulated human skeleton, mouth to mouth, chest to chest, genitals to pelvic bone. Flesh embraces emptiness; bones rise or fall with the artist's breath. The image immediately suggests a memento mori: the ancient practice of monks sleeping in coffins; Hamlet with Yorick's skull. In this work, which seems like a coda for the whole, Abramović represents humans not so much as vulnerable flesh, or even as a Shakespearean "quintessence of dust," but as articulated bones. Like a shaman, the artist manipulates matter, making it lively rather than merely inert.

Shamanic association with bones—which O'Keeffe also instinctively deployed in her art—forms an essential part of Abramović's image and of her power. As the penultimate image in the catalogue, *Carrying the Skeleton* (fig. 7) suggests Abramović's performances are not just about women's bodies.[15] They form an extended meditation on bodily limits and mortality.

The Text is Present

The Abramović retrospective was replete with elements of fictionality and textuality. At several points, and quite self-consciously, the exhibit showed that, rather than

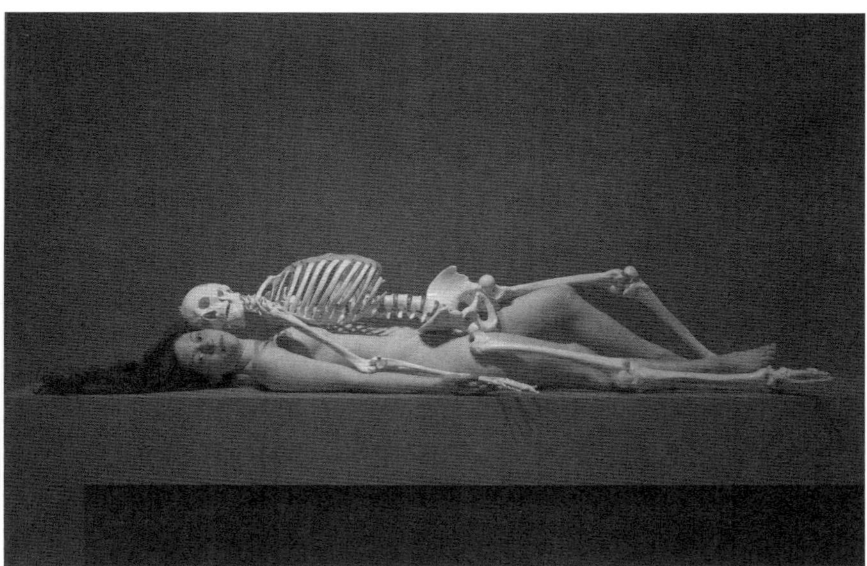

Fig. 6. Marina Abramović, concept photograph for reperformances of *Nude with Skeleton* (2002–5), 2010. © 2012 Marina Abramović. Courtesy Marina Abramović Archives and Sean Kelly Gallery/Artists Rights Society (ARS), New York

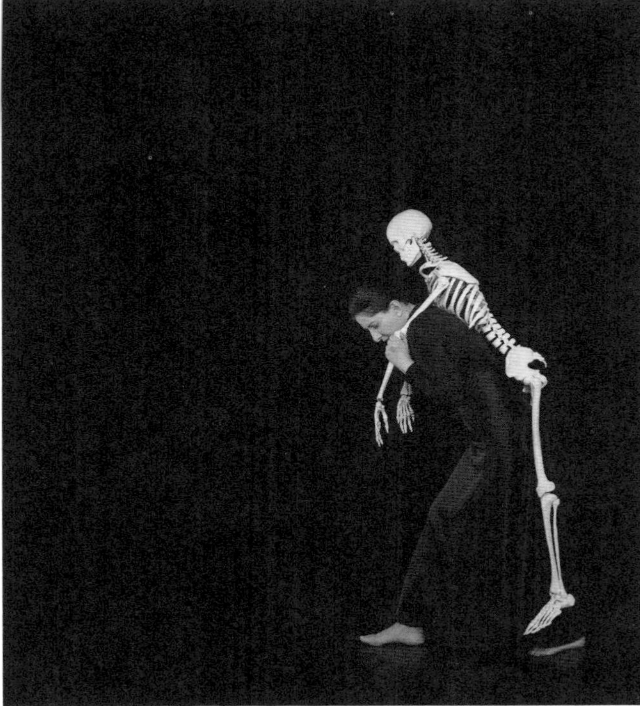

Fig. 7. Marina Abramović, *Carrying the Skeleton*, 2008. Chromogenic print, 81 1/4 x 72 1/4 in. (206.4 x 183.5 cm). © 2012 Marina Abramović. Courtesy Marina Abramović Archives and Sean Kelly Gallery/Artists Rights Society (ARS), New York

being static, art always enters into a narrative transaction with the viewer for which the writing, reception, and interpretation of fiction provides perhaps the surest and supplest model. *The Artist is Present* represents an extreme case of how art can both include its viewers and offer them the pleasure of generating and interpreting fictions. Yet by their very nature—one work hung next to another for a particular reason, sometimes accompanied by written or aural notes—museum and gallery displays offer viewers much the same pleasures. They hang and rehang art to tell different stories. Context, including the exhibit's title or a work's siting in a particular room, makes the same work of art "read" in different ways: it can be a hero or a villain, a star or a supporting player, it can become an example of a larger narrative (Impressionism, Abstract Expressionism, a neutral palette, twentieth-century art), it can represent the acme of the artist's achievement or a passing phase of an artist's career. The same painting (for example, Van Gogh's *Sunflowers*) can limn a biographical history (Van Gogh at Arles) or an art patron's obsession with the painting itself, purchased and hung above his bed.[16] Art history and fiction work hand in hand, and they have far more in common than, at first, meets the eye.

But, at the same time, we intuitively sense a difference, and are right to do so. In their work, and especially their work as curators, art historians often use the techniques of fiction writers: characters (artists, patrons, movements, techniques, historical events), action (specific deeds, causalities, plots), development (beginnings, middles, and ends); in doing so, they suggest meanings. The reader of an art history book or the viewer of an exhibition deploys the same resources in making sense of what is read or seen. But art historians stop short of utter concoction unless some outright parody or theoretical exercise is at stake: I think, for example, of the recent movie *Exit Through the Gift Shop*, which surely suggested certain truths about the contemporary art scene, but also included humorous fabrications.

Understood properly, the techniques of fiction can enrich and enliven art history. They can encourage a range of possibilities within art-historical writing, such as personal writing, which has added new possibilities to literary criticism. But art history as outright fiction? There is a name for that. And the name is not fiction but fraud.

1. In his afterword to *Lolita*, Russian novelist Vladimir Nabokov says that reality is a word that should always be used in quotation marks.

2. *Ana Mendieta: Earth Body, Sculpture and Performance, 1972–1985* at the Whitney Museum of American Art ran from July 1–September 19, 2004; *Ana Mendieta: Documentation and Artwork, 1972–1985* was presented at Galerie Lelong from October 28–December 2010.

3. Spotty documentation characterized early Abramović work, too. However, by the time of her breakup with Ulay—commemorated in a video of them walking toward each other from opposite ends of the Great Wall of China—recordkeeping had become something of a fetish in Abramović's art.

4. Mendieta frequently dealt with burned impressions of the body in the earth or, in one urban installation, of blood seeping from a doorway that was largely ignored by passersby.

5. I say "to some extent" because the museum made no attempt to evaluate Abramović's art in comparison with or in exclusion from other performance artists. Indeed, it featured Yoko Ono's work in close temporal proximity. Ono's early work, like Abramović's, sometimes featured the audience with the artist. In one piece, a possible source for *Rhythm 0*, viewers gradually stripped away the artist's clothing (Ono, *Cut Piece*, 1965). The Ono works displayed at MoMA in July 2010 were, in contrast to Abramović's, disembodied: in *Voice Piece by Soprano*, shrieks periodically roiled through the Museum; another, *Wish Tree*, invited audience participation.

6. In 1999, shortly before closing for expansion and relocating temporarily to Queens, MoMA rehung its galleries four times in four different ways, many selected by younger curators who had been educated during the expansion of the traditional canon to include notions around feminism and poststructuralism. The rehanging revealed the stunning strengths and glaring gaps in MoMA's collection. Notably absent were women artists, represented at MoMA best through photography. Once in Queens and again back in Manhattan, MoMA played to its strengths in Picasso, Matisse, and other artists, such as Monet, Van Gogh, and Cezanne, it has always elevated.

7. The examples come from two papers at the conference, the V-J Day example from Alexander Nemerov's: see "Weightless History: Faulkner, Bourke-White, and Eisenstaedt" in this volume.

8. While part of a larger series called *Rhythm*, this performance also evokes quite strongly *The Story of O*.

9. The transcription is drawn from http://www.youtube.com/watch?v=IE5H8k8VE2M (accessed December 27, 2010), which is the version that was shown at MoMA. Other versions exist in print.

10. Hannah Arendt's *The Origins of Totalitarianism* offers a magisterial treatment of connections between science and genocide in the Nazi cosmography (NY: Harcourt, Brace and Co., 1951).

11. Jovana Stokic, "The Art of Marina Abramović: Leaving the Balkans, Entering the Other Side," in *Marina Abramović: The Artist is Present* (New York: Museum of Modern Art, 2010), 23.

12. The panels to which I refer appeared in the retrospective, but are not included in the catalogue, which provides a more general treatment of Abramović's work.
13. Even within memoir, which is relatively fact-bound compared to performance art, data can become stylized or the writer may include, in all honesty, what later comes to seem like misrepresentations or misunderstandings.
14. The video of *Nude with Skeleton* with Abramović can be found at http://www.youtube.com/watch?v=pno1gCrbeVk.
15. The only images to appear after *Carrying the Skeleton* are of Abramović's face during *The Artist is Present* and a selected group of those who sat opposite her.
16. As noted in *Cezanne to Picasso: Ambroise Vollard, Patron of the Avant-Garde*, (New York: Metropolitan Museum of Art, 2006). Published in conjunction with the exhibition of the same name shown at the Metropolitan Museum of Art, New York, September 14, 2006–January 7, 2007.

Contributors

Paul Barolsky is Commonwealth Professor in the Art History Program at the University of Virginia. His books include *Infinite Jest* (1978), *Michelangelo's Nose* (1990), and *Why Mona Lisa Smiles and Other Tales by Vasari* (1991). His most recent book is *A Brief History of the Artist from God to Picasso* (2011). His research and courses focus on various aspects of Italian Renaissance art and literature.

Thomas Crow is the Rosalie Solow Professor of Modern Art and Associate Provost for the Arts at New York University. He has also served as Director of the Getty Research Institute. He is the author of *Modern Art in the Common Culture* (1996), *The Rise of the Sixties: American and European Art in the Era of Dissent* (1996, 2005), and *Emulation: David, Drouais, and Girodet in the Art of Revolutionary France* (2006). His numerous journal articles include "The Practice of Art History in America" in *Daedalus* (Spring 2006) and his 2012 essay "Endless Summer," which appeared in the 50th anniversary issue of *Artforum*, where he is a contributing editor.

Michael Hatt is Professor in the History of Art at the University of Warwick, having previously been Head of Research at the Yale Center for British Art. He has worked on a range of topics in nineteenth-century British and American art and visual culture and has interests in gender and sexuality and in questions of visual racism. He is coauthor of *Art History: A Critical Introduction to Its Methods* (2006) and coeditor of *The Edwardian Sense: Art, Design, and Performance in Britain, 1901–1910* (2010).

Gloria Kury is Director of Gutenberg Periscope Publishing Ltd., where current titles include Andrew Hemingway, *The Mysticism of Money* (2009) and Darcy Grimaldo Grigsby, *Colossal* (2012). She has taught art history at Vassar College, Yale University, New York University, and the School of Visual Arts. Her scholarship, published in *Art Bulletin* and edited volumes, centers on reflections of diverse sorts, misprisioned texts, and art resistant to interpretation. Her book on Venice is scheduled to appear in winter 2014.

Mark Ledbury is Power Professor of Art History and Visual Culture and Director of the Power Institute at the University of Sydney, and was previously Associate Director of the Research and Academic Program at the Sterling and Francine Clark Art Institute. He is the author of *Greuze and the Boundaries of Genre* (2000), editor of *David after David* (2007), and coeditor of *Rethinking Boucher* (2005). His research interests include the history of French art, particularly of the eighteenth century, and specifically the relationships between theater and visual art as well as genre theory in the Enlightenment.

Ralph Lieberman is an architectural historian and photographer. He is the author of *Renaissance Architecture in Venice 1450–1540* (1982) and articles on the sculpture of Donatello, the architecture and sculpture of Michelangelo, Raphael's *School of Athens*, the Crystal Palace, and the photography of Wright Morris, as well as on the role of photography in the development of modern art history, the subject of his forthcoming book. His photographs are in major art history research library image collections in the United States and Italy, and over nine thousand of his images are on ARTstor. He has taught at Harvard University, Smith College, and Oberlin College and currently teaches at Williams and Amherst Colleges.

Maria H. Loh is a Reader in the Department of History of Art at University College London. Her publications include *Titian Remade: Repetition and the Transformation of Early Modern Italian Art* (2007) and "Early Modern Horror," a special issue of the *Oxford Art Journal* (2011). She was the Willis F. Doney Member (2012–2013) at the Institute for Advanced Study in Princeton, New Jersey, where she completed her second book, *Still Lives: Death, Desire, and the Portrait of the Old Master* (forthcoming). Loh's research interests include ghost stories and the pathos of portraiture; repetition, desire, and the double in art and film; her next project is on the representation of pregravitational skies in art.

Alexander Nemerov is the Carl and Marilynn Thoma Provostial Professor in the Arts and Humanities at Stanford University. His most recent books are *Acting in the Night: Macbeth and the Places of the Civil War* (2010) and *Wartime Kiss: Visions of the Moment in the 1940s* (2012). His research interests include American visual culture from the eighteenth to the mid-twentieth century, focusing on painting, sculpture, photography, and film.

Joanna Scott is the author of eight novels, including *The Manikin* (2002), *Tourmaline* (2003), *Arrogance* (2004), and *Follow Me* (2010), and two collections of short fiction. Her stories and essays have appeared in *The Nation, Harpers, Esquire, Conjunctions, Black Clock, Subtropics,* and other journals. She is the Roswell Smith Burrows Professor of English at the University of Rochester.

Cole Swensen is the author of a collection of critical essays, *Noise That Stays Noise* (2011), and fourteen volumes of poetry, most recently *Gravensend* (2012). Much of her work focuses on ekphrasis, exploring new ways that the written and visual arts can interact. She is also the coeditor of the 2009 Norton anthology *American Hybrid* and the founding editor of the translation press La Presse. A 2007 Guggenheim Fellow, she is a professor of literature and chair of the Literary Arts Department at Brown University.

Marianna Torgovnick is Professor of English and Professor of Arts of the Moving Image at Duke University and Director of Duke in New York Arts and Media. Her books include *Gone Primitive: Savage Intellects, Modern Lives* (1991), *Crossing Ocean Parkway* (1997), *Primitive Passions* (1998), *The War Complex* (2008), and a forthcoming sequel to *Crossing Ocean Parkway* called *Picnic in the Dark: Classic Books, Family Recipes*. She works as a literary and cultural critic in print and also on her website and on Twitter as Marianna_tor.

Caroline Vout is Senior Lecturer in Classics at the University of Cambridge and a Fellow of Christ's College. In 2008 she was awarded a Philip Leverhulme Prize and in 2010 was the Hugh Last Fellow at the British School at Rome. Her publications include *Antinous: the Face of the Antique* (2006), *Power and Eroticism in Imperial Rome* (2007), "Laocoon's Children and the Limits of Representation," in *Art History* 33 (2010), and *The Hills of Rome: Signature of an Eternal City* (2012). She has published widely on Greek and Roman art, and is currently working on her forthcoming book, *Sex on Show: Seeing the Erotic in Greece and Rome.*

Marina Warner is professor in the Department of Literature, Film, and Theatre Studies at the University of Essex and visiting professor at NYU Abu Dhabi. Her publications include *Alone of All Her Sex: Cult of the Virgin Mary* (1983, 2012), *Fantastic Metamorphoses, Other Worlds: Ways of Telling the Self* (2002), *Phantasmagoria: Spirit Visions, Metaphors, and Media* (2006), *Stranger Magic: Charmed States and The Arabian Nights* (2011), and *The Symbol Gives Rise to Thought: Writings on Art* (2012). She was elected a fellow of the British Academy in 2005 and has served as President of the British Comparative Literature Association since 2010.

Photography Credits

Permission to reproduce illustrations is provided by courtesy of the owners listed in the captions. Unless otherwise noted, photos of works belonging to the Sterling and Francine Clark Art Institute are by Michael Agee.

Additional photography credits are as follows:

Albright-Knox Art Gallery/Art Resource, NY (p. 30); Alinari/Art Resource, NY (pp. 20, 80, 94, 131 bottom left and center); © Marco Anelli and © 2010 The Museum of Modern Art, New York, NY (pp. 191, 192 top); © Trustees of the British Museum. All rights reserved (p. 74); © Country Life (p. 126 right); © Gregory Crewdsen (p. xi); © Gianni Dagli Orti / The Art Archive at Art Resource, NY (p. 77); © Gianni Dagli Orti/CORBIS (p. 130); Deutsches Archäologisches Institut–Rom, Neg. D-DAI-ROM 67.1587, Rom, Neg. D-DAI-ROM 67.1582, Rom, Neg. D-DAI-ROM 67.1606, Photographs by Singer (pp. 75, 76, 78); Photograph by Bill Engdahl and Bob Shimer for Hedrich Blessing: (p. 124 bottom); © The Fitzwilliam Museum, Cambridge (p. 96); Imaging Department, © President and Fellows of Harvard College (p. 135 bottom); Erich Lessing/Art Resource, NY (p. 87); Image © The Metropolitan Museum of Art. Image source: Art Resource, NY (p. 9); Courtesy David Zwirner, New York/London and Digital image © 2012 Museum Associates/LACMA. Licensed by Art Resource, NY (p. 81); Digital image © The Museum of Modern Art/Licensed by SCALA/Art Resource, NY (pp. 12, 199 top); NGS Image Collection/The Art Archive at Art Resource, NY (p. 126 left); © National Gallery, London/Art Resource, NY (pp. 38, 41); Image courtesy of Pennsylvania State University Libraries (pp. 143, 146, 156); Réunion des Musées Nationaux-Grand Palais/Art Resource, NY (p. 110); Scala/Art Resource, NY (p. 39, 40 top and bottom, 91 bottom, 119 bottom, 128 right); Studio Morra, Naples (p. 192); © Tate, London 2011 (p. 28); Photograph by George Tatge; Alinari/Art Resource, NY (p. 94); Photograph by Stephen White (p. 24)